100 *Best*

Spas

of the

BERNARD BURT &
PAMELA LECHTMAN

The
Globe
Pequot
Press

GUILFORD, CONNECTICUT

Cover and interior design: Nancy Freeborn
Cover photo credit: Linda Troeller

Photo credits: Many thanks to the following people and organizations for providing photos: p. i © Luca Tettoni, The Regent Resort Chiang Mai; p. iii © Jane Lidz, The Golden Door; p. v Sheila Donnelly & Associates, Rajvilas; p. viii Thalassa Spa at Anassa; p. xii Thalassa Spa at Anassa; p. 1 Las Ventanas Al Paraiso; pp. 2-3 Canyon Ranch; pp. 4-5 Marriott's Camelback Inn Resort; pp. 6-7 Mraval; p 8 Marlove; p 9 Cal-a-Vie; pp. 10-11 The Golden Door; pp. 12-13 The Oaks at Ojai; pp. 14-15 Ojai Valley Inn & Spa; pp. 16, 17, 19 The Palms at Palm Springs; p. 17 The Spa Hotel & Casino; pp. 20-22 Sonoma Mission Inn & Spa; pp. 23-24 Two Bunch Palms Resort & Spa; pp. 25-26 Wyndham Peaks Resort & Golden Door Spa; pp. 27-28 Diplomat Resort Country Club & Spa; pp. 29-30 PGA National Resort & Spa; pp. 31-32 Grand Wailea Resort Hotel & Spa; pp. 33-34 Kohala Spa at Hilton Waikoloa Village; pp. 35-38 Canyon Ranch; pp. 39-40 Regent Las Vegas; pp. 41-42 Grove Park Inn Resort; pp. 43-44 Nemacolin Woodlands Resort & Spa; pp. 45-47 Green Valley Spa & Tennis Resort; pp. 48-49 The Greenbrier; pp. 50-51 Banff Springs Hotel; pp. 52-54 Centre de Sante d'Eastman; pp. 55-57 Echo Valley Ranch Resort; pp. 59-60 © Don Weixi, The Hills Health Ranch; pp. 61-62 © Roberto Lissia, Ste. Anne's Country Inn & Spa; pp. 63-64 Four Seasons Resort Punta Mita; pp. 65-66 Las Ventanas Al Paraiso; pp. 67-68 Rancho La Puerta; p. 69 Thalassa Spa at Anassa; pp. 70- 72 © 1997 Maxum, © by Rogner-Dorint, © Hundertwasser, Rogner-Bad Blumau; pp. 73-75 Le Meridien Limassol Spa & Resort; pp. 76-77 Thalassa Spa at Anassa; pp. 78-79 Grand Hotel Pupp; pp. 80-81 Naantali Spa Hotel & Resort; pp. 82-83 Alice Marshall Public Relations, Victoria King Public Relations, Domaine du Royal Club Evian; pp. 84-85 Institut de Thalassotherapie Louison Bobet at Hotel Miramar; pp. 86-88 Les Fermes de Marie; pp. 89-90 Guy Hervais, Les Pres d'Eugenie; pp. 91-92 Les Sources de Caudalie; pp. 93-94 Thalgo La Baule; pp. 95-97 Bad Woerishofen; pp. 98-100 © Rolf Gotwald Fotodesign, Brenner's Park-Hotel & Spa; pp. 101-102 Schlosshotel Lerbach; pp. 103-105 Toskana Therme; pp. 106-107 Thermae Sylla Grand Hotel & Spa; p. 108 Gellert Spa; p. 109 Kiraly Baths, Gellert Spa, Angelo Cavalli; p. 110 Brian A. Gauvin; pp. 111-112 The Lodge & Spa at Inchydoney Island; pp. 113-114 Capri Beauty Farm at the Palace Hotel; pp. 115-116 Grand Hotel Terme Abano; pp. 117-118 Grotta Giusti Terme; pp. 119-120 Hawkins & Widness Public Relations International, Plazzo Arzaga Hotel—Saturnia Spa; pp. 121-122 Spa 'Deus; pp. 123-124 Hotel Terme di Saturnia Resort; pp. 125-126 © Moreno Maggi, Villa D'Este; pp. 127-128 San Lawrenz Resort; pp. 129-130 Les Thermes Marins de Monte-Carlo; pp. 131-132 Vilalara Thallasso; pp. 133-134 Sturebadet; pp. 135-136 Grand Hotels Bad Ragaz; pp. 137-138 Hotel Les Sources des Alpes; pp. 139-140 Victoria-Jungfrau Grand Hotel; pp. 141-142 Klassis Resort Hotel & Country Club; pp. 143-145 Champneys Health Resort & Spa; pp. 146-147 C. Evans, CCM, The Pavillion at Cliveden; pp. 148-149 Alice Marshall Public Relations, The Dorchester; pp. 150-151 Forest Mere Health Farm; pp. 152-153 C. Evans, CCM, The Royal Crescent Hotel—The Bath House; pp. 154-155 Turnberry Hotel, Golf Courses, and Spa; pp. 156-157 The Celtic Manor Resort; pp. 159-162 Rajvilas; pp. 163-164 Serenite Wellness Center; pp. 165-166 Hotel Hasdrubal Thalassa; pp. 167-168 The Residence; p. 169 Movenpick Resort and Spa; pp. 170-171 The Ritz-Carlton Sharm El Sheikh; pp. 172-173 Carmel Forest Spa Resort; pp. 176-177 Herods Vitalis; pp. 178-179 Movenpick Resort & Spa; pp. 180-182 Burj Al Arab; p. 183 Four Seasons Resort Bali at Jimbaran Bay; pp. 184-185 Begawan Giri Estate; pp. 186-187 Four Seasons Resort Bali at Jimbaran Bay; pp. 188-190 Le Meridien Nirwana Golf & Spa Resort; pp. 191-192 Inn Seiryuso; pp. 193-195 Sheila Donnelly & Associates, The Datai-Mandara Spa; pp. 196-198 Banyan Tree Phuket; pp. 199-Chiva-Som International; pp. 201-202 Lou Hammond & Associates, The Oriental Hotel Bangkok; © Luca Tettoni, The Regent Resort Chiang Mai; p. 205-207 Hawkins & Widness Public Relations, CuisinArt Resort & Spa; pp. 208-209 Sandals Royal Bahamian Resort & Spa; pp. 210-211 © Len Kaufman, Spring O'Brien & Co., Inc., Grand Lido Sans Souci Resort; pp. 212-213 The Ritz-Carlton San Juan Hotel & Spa; pp. 214-215 Marilyn Marx Public Relations, Le Sport; pp. 218-219 Kurotel; pp. 220-221 Tara Resort Hotel; p. 222 Windstar Cruises; p. 223 Radisson Seven Seas Cruises; p. 224 Seabourn Cruise Line; p. 225 Cunard Line; p. 226 Len Kaufman, Windstar Cruises. Spot art throughout: PhotoDisc.

Library of Congress Cataloging-in-Publication Data

Burt, Bernard.
    100 best spas of the world / Bernard Burt & Pamela Lechtman.
        p. cm. — (100 best resorts series)
    ISBN 0-7627-0807-7
    1. Health resorts—Guidebooks. I. Lechtman, Pamela. II. Title. III. Title: One hundred best spas of the world. IV. Series.
    RA794.B88 2001
    613'.122'025—dc21   00-052811

Printed in Canada
First Edition/First Printing

WITH APPRECIATION TO
THE CAREGIVERS,
UNITING BODY AND SOUL
WITH ENERGY FROM THE HEART
—Bernard Burt

TO MY AGELESS, BEAUTIFUL MOTHER,
LEONA EFFRESS
—Pamela Lechtman

CONTENTS

The prices and rates listed in this guidebook were confirmed at press time but under no circumstances are they guaranteed. We recommend that you call establishments before traveling to obtain current information.

INTRODUCTION

Defining the Spa Experience

he mystique of spas is as ancient as Roman baths, and yet spas are on the cutting edge of the way we vacation in the 21st century. Still, the spa experience is a very personal one. Whether you want to be pampered on an exotic island, learn the latest techniques for stress management, or simply seek a relaxing retreat, you have more choices than ever.

Each spa visit becomes an adventure, sensory and physical, that helps you learn how to cope with the stress of your personal and professional life. But expectations don't always match the experience. Increasingly there is confusion about terminology—what's a "full-service" spa?—and professional standards for staffing and operating. Throughout this book you will learn not only the best places to spa, but also how to get the best values in services, treatments, and accommodations.

The New Spa

During our journeys (which span 35 years) as travel and spa journalists, we have seen the evolution of a new breed of health resort. One that provides a variety of options in wellness and well-being along with spa services. Ancient traditions of natural healing such as Ayurvedic medicine and yoga are meeting high-tech methods for the prevention of illness. Indeed, spas these days must do more than offer massages or trendy treatments to be ranked as world class. The most basic ingredients of the spa experience are being redefined. You can expect cutting-edge developments in:

Design: As old distinctions make way for new approaches to total wellness, spa designers are creating environments where you feel comfortable, safe, and well cared for. For example in the beautiful Laurel Highlands of western Pennsylvania, the distinguished interior design consultant Clodagh used natural elements of water and light, wood and stone to create spaces that

inspire a surge of energy along with your workout at Nemacolin Woodlands Resort & Spa. At her New York design studio, Clodagh speaks of her inspirations, from Zen Buddhism to Feng Shui, the Chinese art of placement, as well as astrology and channeling: "I just channel some kind of energy." Blending Asian and Western sensibilities, she adds, is not a logical process, but the result is a total design that creates an experience.

The Seven Kinds of Spas

Not all spas are created equal. The seven categories described by the International Spa Association (ISPA) can help you choose the best experience for you:

1. **Club spa: Primarily a fitness facility, with services offered on a day-use basis.**

2. **Cruise ship spa: Aboard a cruise ship, professional treatments, personal training, and salon services are offered on an a la carte basis.**

3. **Day spa: Professionally administered services offered on a day-use basis.**

4. **Destination spa: Focused on lifestyle improvement and health enhancement through professionally administered services, physical fitness, educational programs, and on-site accommodations.**

5. **Medispa: Individuals, solo practices, groups, and institutions comprised of medical and spa professionals whose primary purpose is to provide comprehensive medical and wellness care in an environment that integrates spa services with conventional and complementary therapies and treatments.**

6. **Mineral springs spa: Hydrotherapy treatments that use natural mineral or thermal waters, or seawater, from an on-site source.**

7. **Resort hotel spa: Located within a resort or hotel, professionally administered spa services, fitness and wellness components, and spa cuisine menu choices are available on a daily or mutliday basis.**

Fitness and exercise: Whether it's aerobics, walking, or jogging, on a treadmill or a mountain trail, fitness and exercise are the basics of a wellness program. Each workout at a spa gives you new perspectives on your personal progress—and nowadays there may be new equipment with lots of bells and whistles to try. At Canyon Ranch, Champneys in Britain, and Rancho La Puerto in Mexico, as many as five classes each hour (all rated according to fitness level) are yours to choose from. The camaraderie of group exercise and sessions with a personal trainer will help you learn what works and add value to your daily regime at home.

Cuisines: Eating healthy is another part of the spa experience that's getting a new look. Tofu and veggie burgers, once staples of spa cuisine, now share the menu with meat, fish, and pasta. According to trends forecaster David Pursglove, some spas are now serving wine as well as waters.

The Spa Criteria

From London to Singapore, Malaysia, Thailand, Italy, and the American southwest, at the pioneering Canyon Ranch in Arizona and its sibling SpaClub at the Venetian Resort in Las Vegas, the new health resorts offer something for everybody. Still, some of our favorite places to relax and be pampered are at hot springs in

historic towns that haven't changed much since our first visits. Bringing all of these experiences together for the first time into this book has been a voyage of discovery that encompasses some of the oldest and newest places to rejuvenate. Ultimately, all of these 100 spas are the best of their type, be it a destination spa or resort spa, day spa, or mineral springs spa. What distinguishes them might be the program, the location, the design—or that indefinable look of happiness on people's faces as they leave.

Packing for Your Spa Vacation

Visiting a spa presents a packing dilemma: What to bring? You'll be changing clothes often for hiking, exercise classes, evening programs, and special events. Should you bring hiking boots, socks, warm-ups, comfortable jeans, a bathing suit, all-weather jackets? Assembling your wardrobe and compressing it into one easy, compact suitcase can be a challenge. But a little planning can solve the problem. Take easy-care but rugged fabrics woven from microfiber; you can wad them up in your suitcase and just shake them out later. They are entirely presentable. *TravelSmith*, a company that specializes in travel clothing and accessories, suggests that travelers pack such items as Supplex shirts, Coolmax T-shirts, explorer's shorts, Coolmax socks, trekking boots, a hat that offers sun protection, a travel twill shirt, a Great Escape shirt, a warm-up suit, and a bathing suit. To prevent spills, pack a leak-proof bottle set (with screw-on tops for each container). You can consult with a TravelSmith outfitter who can send you free packing lists and reports on your destination. Call TravelSmith for a catalog (800) 950–1600 or check out their Web site at www.travelsmith.com. Readers of *100 Best Spas of the World* are entitled to a 10 percent discount on all orders if they mention the following code: PR66000.

Here's what we looked for:

1. *The design:* Does the physical setting have trend-setting infrastructure?
2. *The experience:* Does it live up to reputation, advertisements, and hype?
3. *The treatments:* Is the range of treatments indicative of current advances?
4. *The products:* Are product lines tested and reputable?
5. *The sense of place:* How does the program complement the location?
6. *The staffing:* Do therapists and aestheticians enjoy thorough education and in-service training?
7. *The cuisine:* Rather than spa cuisine, think healthy cuisine. Does the food hav eye appeal and taste as well as low-fat nutritional value?
8. *The cleanliness:* How are housekeeping standards maintained?
9. *The facilities:* Regardless of size, does the combination of treatment areas, outdoor recreation, fitness equipment, and staff provide complete satisfaction?
10. *The journey:* Would you go out of your way to experience this spa?

Price guidelines used in this book are based on a typical package or one-week program:

$$$ Ultraluxurious . . . $5,000 and up per person.
$$ Superior . . . . $3,500 and up per person.
$ Value . . . . Under $3,500 per person.

The Spa Journey

What you need from your own spa experience can't always be measured. Each experience is unique—there's really no such thing as "the best." With this book you will discover multiple subtle and not-so-subtle variables that can make each spa visit an experience that enhances your life. The choices are yours to enjoy.

The merger of traditional medicine with the spirit of spa therapy defines our selection of the 100 Best Spas of the World. The union will bring life to our years and years to our lives.

Global Well-Being Sets the Standard for Spa Travelers at Health-Conscious British Airways

Getting to those super spas in Dubai, Amman, Tunis, or Paris is a cinch when you fly British Airways. Check into their schedule, which serves more than 180 destinations around the world. You'll find their approach to 21st-century air travel innovative.

New to the company are Well-Being Ambassadors—cabin crew members who have received special training in alertness management. Their job is to pass information on to passengers during their flight to take the travail out of travel. They provide advice covering everything: when and what to eat, when to nap, when to exercise, and when to change clocks to local time.

Special in-flight videos and magazine columns enhance this personal health service and provide tips on how to prevent jet lag. At the arrivals lounge at Heathrow Terminal Four, you'll find a gym, masseurs, rest areas, and a vitamin-packed breakfast bar. The lounge features the fresh scent of cut grass and ocean air, which rises from the floor. Passengers can even have their clothes pressed while showering. And the health spa offers mini facials, aromatherapy massages, and beauty services. There is even a sanctuary, designated a "no-mobile-phone" zone, reserved for resting, with comfortable recliners, daybeds with footstools, and tables designed to aid relaxation.

The British Airways program was designed by David Flower, a British Airways physician, and Alertness Solutions, a California company headed by former NASA scientist Dr. Mark Rosekind. Here is a sample of their advice for a flight between Los Angeles and London, returning a week later:

- Adapt to local time.
- Upon arrival, eat a light meal and if necessary take a nap no longer than forty-five minutes.
- In the afternoon take some gentle exercise and expose yourself to daylight.
- Eat an early dinner and go to bed in the early evening.
- During your spa vacation stay in bed until your normal wake-up time and dine as usual.
- Try to avoid daytime naps; get light exposure in the afternoon.
- Move your bedtime closer to normal as the days progress.
- Sleep as much as possible on the return flight.

For reservations on British Airways,
call **1–800–AIRWAYS (1–800–247–9297)** or visit www.britishairways.com.

Knowing what to expect before you go will enhance both the spa experience and the value of your vacation. Talk to the spa director by telephone or e-mail to learn about services and treatments offered. If you've never been to a spa, discuss your goals with a qualified professional, and consult your personal physician to set guidelines. Study the daily routine of scheduled group exercise and personal time to select a balanced program that suits your needs and fitness level. Hard-line, fixed programs are a thing of the past; today the key word is *revitalize*. Become an empowered spa-goer with these ten questions:

What's included in my spa package?
Ask about seasonal specials, as well as the best combinations of services and treatments offered in daily and multiday programs. Get a description of each treatment and its therapeutic value.

How much does it cost?
All-inclusive programs are typical at destination spas, which offer a fixed packages that include accommodations, meals, treatments, and exercise/fitness training. Seasonal specials include mother-daugther weeks and bring-a-friend-for-free weeks. Resort and cruise ship spas offer more options and flexible pricing. At historic spa towns, such as Palm Springs, California, and Budapest, Hungary, you will find a wide range of accommodations at all price levels.

Are tips included?
Although some resorts include gratuities for therapists as well as staff in the restaurant and hotel, the policy varies, especially in Asia and Europe. Ask at the reception desk. Spa tipping is actually similar to salon and restaurant tipping: 15 to 20 percent, depending on how satisfied you are with the service. Take small envelopes to reward special people with extra cash.

What do I wear?
Modesty is never compromised. Most often robes are supplied. Under the robe? It's up to you. If water therapy is involved, a swimsuit may be appropriate. Bring exercise clothing and shoes, but ask what the spa provides, like jogging suits, slippers, and rain gear. Basics may be fine for dinner, or you might enjoy changing into something more dressy.

Are there special health considerations?
Prior to strenuous exercise or thermal treatments, a physical evaluation or fitness screening is recommended. European spa doctors require a checkup (usually a separate fee) as the basis for scheduling services. If you have a particular injury or physical condition, explain it to the therapists and instructors. They can suggest appropriate adjustments or enhancements.

Can I request a male or female therapist?
Usually, yes, but some spas have only female therapists. And most spas are coed but offer separate facilities for men and women.

What is the size of the group during a typical week?
Get a profile of the typical guest as well as typical activities. You may prefer destination spas with fixed programs and a small band of fellow spa-goers. Sharing experiences builds camaraderie.

Can I bring my family?
Resort spas cater to all ages, and some have special programs for children. Destination spas usually have a minimum age limit of 16 or 18.

What else should I bring?
Sunscreen, alarm clock, gym bag or fanny pack, lots of socks, well-worn aerobics shoes, and hiking hear. Don't forget business cards—spas have become networking hot spots.

And leave behind?
Don't bring jewelry, alcohol, office work, or food. Distance yourself from the people, problems, and responsibilities of your real life.

ACKNOWLEDGMENTS

Countless experiences and conversations with spa professionals went into the preparation of this book. We were inspired by Deborah Szekely, cofounder of The Golden Door and Rancho La Puerta, as well as her son Alex. The leadership of Canyon Ranch cofounder Mel Zuckerman and his associates can be found at three resorts, and we'll probably have to add their spa cruise ship in the next edition. Sharing insights from world travels, Jenni Lipa of Spa Trek Travel in New York opened doors for us. And then there's Sheila Cluff, who shared Pamela's vision of spas from the beginning.

Special thanks to Mary Tabacchi, Ph.D, School of Hotel Administration at Cornell University, who is a dedicated educator in spa management. The archival collection of spa materials covering two decades (1976–1996) contributed by Pamela Lechtman is now housed at Cornell. We are also indebted to the publisher of *Spa Management Journal*, Guy Jonkman, and to Vincenzo Marra, CEO of Italian Beauty Innovations, for continuing support of industrywide education programs. For technical advice, Dr. Reinhard R. Bergel of H.E.A.T., Inc., in California, and Dr. Jonathan de Vierville at the Alamo Plaza Spa in San Antonio, Texas, were invaluable. European colleagues guided our selection of new destinations: Josef Bartholemy, former Kurhouse director in Baden-Baden, Germany, who now writes and lectures on spas worlwide; Dr. Susan Horsewood-Lee in London; and Jane Crebbin-Bailey of HCB Associates, vice president of the ISPA European Chapter. In Asia we had input from longtime residents Kim and Cary Collier, founders of Jamu; Darryll Leiman and Donna Wells at Mandara Spas; and Sylvia Sepielli, design and management consultant. Thanks to Ezzadine Hammedi in Washington, D.C., and Lufti Bourguiba in Tunis, Tunisia, both from the Tunisian Tourist Board, for their assistance coordinating information on Tunisian spas.

Family support was indispensable. Tony Lechtman, in New York with the Cyprus Tourism Organization, and Arthur Lechtman, Washington, D.C.-based attorney, shared their mother's enthusiasm for spas. Jeffrey A. Burt keeps tabs on his uncle. And our extended family includes the founders of ISPA who have made this book possible. Thanks also to Bernard M. Bubman, Kathy Strong, and Cindy Corman for the editorial assistant they provided.

To our editors at The Globe Pequot Press, Laura Strom and Mimi Egan, and to Sara Davis, Publicity Director, deep appreciation for believing in this book.

Bernard Burt
Washington, D.C.

Pamela Lechtman
Palm Springs, California

NORTH AMERICA

CANYON RANCH
Tucson, Arizona

Established in 1979, this year-round, award-winning spa accommodates up to 240 guests in single-story, adobe-style cottages on seventy acres in the foothills of the Santa Catalina Mountains. Canyon Ranch was voted "Best Spa" by *Condé Nast Traveler* magazine in 1990, 1992, and 1997 and is an internationally recognized pioneer in preventive health programs for every stage of life and every fitness level.

The staff at Canyon Ranch is composed of physicians, nurses, psychologists, fitness instructors, body-work therapists, art and music therapists, hiking guides, and a support staff. The staff-to-guest ratio is nearly three to one. It requires a seventy-page guide to describe the activities and services, and it will take you at least a week to benefit from the range of offerings, from classes focused on spiritual awareness to behavioral health.

The resort's ambience is created by lush landscaping highlighted by tropical trees, streams, pools, fountains, original sculpture, and cactus gardens. It takes about a day to become oriented with the comprehensive facilities, including the 62,000-square-foot spa complex honeycombed with treatment rooms for massages and facials, whirlpools, sunbathing areas, herbal and hydromassage rooms. There are seven gyms, seven lighted tennis courts, a yoga/meditation dome, and men's and women's locker rooms complete with sauna, steam, and inhalation rooms. New at the spa is the aquatic center with three watsu pools, an exercise pool, two aqua-therapy pools, and a whirlpool. The golf school, staffed by professionals, is another impressive addition.

The daily program is exciting, with guided walks starting as early as 6:30 A.M., and there are lots of choices. For example, at 10:00 A.M. you may select from seven classes, such as H_2O Power Hour in the pool or a cardio circuit. After lunch, there are lectures, such as "Is It My Hormones?" or "The Skinny on Fat." The upbeat attitude of the staff and guests is motivating, and the ambience is casual and unpretentious. In the evening, there are musical concerts, watercolor classes, and a variety of presentations, from travelogues to health lectures.

Leading the way to quality aging, the Life Enhancement Program has its own spa and health center

Canyon Ranch
8600 East Rockcliff Road
Tucson, AZ 85750
Phone: (520) 749–9000
Fax: (520) 749–0662
Web site: www.canyonranch.com
Season: Year-round
General Manager: Jona Liebrecht
Spa Director: Sharon Stricker
Fitness Director: Jane Roberts
Reservations: (520) 749–9000 or (800) 742–9000
Accommodations: 165 rooms; variety of room styles and sizes, accommodating 240 guests.
Meals: The Spanish-Colonial clubhouse hosts the spacious dining room and demonstration kitchen. Canyon Ranch offers healthy menus that include gourmet favorites.
Facilities: The grounds include cactus gardens, tropical trees, streams, pools and fountains; the clubhouse holds the dining room, registration, guest services, meeting rooms, and boutique. The demonstration kitchen and creative arts center are adjacent to the clubhouse. The spa has skin care and beauty salons, as well as massage and hydrotherapy rooms. Medical clinic. Coed gym with full cardio and strength training equipment; aquatic center.
Services & Special Programs: Lunch & Learn cooking classes; Life Enhancement Program; medical assessments; golf school; daily guided biking and hiking; men's fitness program daily.
Rates: $$$
Best Spa Package: Between September and June, seven nights in a standard accommodation, double occupancy, is $4,199 per person, which includes tax and service charges. The week's stay covers three meals daily, use of spa facilities, fitness classes, hiking, biking, a health and fitness assessment, some spa services, sports services, and health and healing services. Also offers fifteen minutes with an exercise physiologist and group presentations. Service charges cover round-trip transfers from the airport, gratuities, and unlimited local phone calls.
Credit Cards: Most major
Getting There: Airport transfers are provided for guests from Tucson International Airport, 21 miles from the ranch.
What's Nearby: Sabino Canyon Recreation Area; all Tucson area shops, restaurants and attractions; Nogales, Mexico; the Desert Museum.

designed to serve small groups in a supportive environment. Group memebers share common life-improvement goals, ranging from controlling cardio-vascular disease, diabetes, stress, or weight to smoking cessation and healthy aging issues. Group members participate in a structured week-long program.

Everything at Canyon Ranch is touched by the spirit of health, including Lunch & Learn. This special cafe is devoted to those who want to learn how to prepare Canyon Ranch cuisine at home. There is a demonstration kitchen, and guests are seated at tables for four to watch as a full lunch is prepared from scratch. The

"show" might include such healthy choices as tomato soup, ahi tuna with salsa, and dessert, which could be chocolate chip cookies, peach oatmeal crumble, or fudge brownies—all calorie controlled, of course.

Canyon Ranch is definitely the vacation you take home with you!

MARRIOTT'S CAMELBACK INN RESORT, GOLF CLUB & SPA

Scottsdale, Arizona

This classic resort, nestled in Paradise Valley, opened in 1936 and has changed gracefully with the times. In 1989 Marriott's Camelback added a spa, and today the 27,000-square-foot facility has a list of services long enough to warrant a full-week spa program stay. The resort is also an ideal family vacation destination, with three outdoor pools, a children's playground, seasonal children's programs, six tennis courts, and two 18-hole golf courses.

Accommodations are in 453 pueblo-style casitas, including twenty-seven suites; all rooms have private patios, and seven suites boast private pools. Camelback's loyal clientele (some guests span three generations) still watch the sun set from Mummy Mountain and enjoy the charm that has characterized this landmark since its opening. There are family reunions, and you'll hear guests talking about the good times shared since the 1930s, but time has not stood still here. Camelback has been enhanced by a serious spa offering more than just pampering treatments.

This friendly resort with a history of Southwestern hospitality attracts health-seekers with a blend of all the major spa components, from a fitness and exercise center to a lifestyle-enhancing wellness program. The facilities include sixteen massage rooms, two rooms each for bindi, loofah, herbal wrap, and natural sunbathing, and separate Turkish steam rooms and Finnish saunas. Water-lovers appreciate the heated outdoor lap pool, coed Jacuzzi, the two hot tubs, and the two cold plunge pools. Dr. Kenneth Cooper, founder and president of the Institute for Aerobic Research in Dallas, Texas, designed the wellness programs, so expect the best. The wellness center has a serious program with computerized body composition analysis, nutritional counseling, and personal training. The spa offers

Pilates, a method of physical and mental conditioning, in programs of one, five, or ten sessions. Exercise begins at 7:00 A.M.; among the many classes scheduled are power walks, tai chi, aeroboxing, body sculpture, yoga, healthy back stretching, and water aerobics.

The body care menu is extensive, with twenty-eight different services from a full body mud mask to a paraffin-jojoba body conditioner. Staying on the cutting

edge, the spa has added three new services: Hot Stone Massage, Desert Nectar Honey Wrap, and Southwest Botanical Facial. The highly efficient personal planning service enables guests to schedule a program in advance by selecting from spa packages, such as the Ultimate Day, which includes a massage, European facial, beauty salon services, and breakfast or lunch.

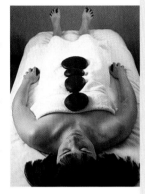

Marriott's Camelback Inn lives up to its reputation for over five decades as a diamond in the desert, but now it now shines even brighter with a dynamic spa and fitness program.

Native American-Inspired Spa Treatment

Using pure red adobe clay and herbs indigenous to the Arizona desert, such as sage, juniper, and sandalwood, Camelback Spa offers a unique treatment inspired by the ancient healing rituals of the Native American culture. Native American holistic health rituals included the use of red clay because of its healing and rejuvenating properties. The adobe clay purification process begins with a total body exfoliation using a special cloth woven with fiber from the cactus plant. A mineral-rich clay is then applied to the body and face. As the clay soothes muscles and nourishes the skin, it also draws impurities from the system. During a warm shower, a special aromatherapy soap containing Southwestern herbs is lathered to remove the clay. The ritual ends with a soothing application of warm juniper and sage oil, followed by a cup of peppermint-sage tea. Red adobe clay continues to work its restoring wonders at Camelback.

Diamond in the Desert for Generations of Families

Marriott's Camelback Inn Resort, Golf Club & Spa
5402 East Lincoln Drive
Scottsdale, AZ 85253
Phone: (480) 948–1700
Fax: (480) 951–8469
E-mail: cbibizctr@aol.com
Web site: www.camelbackinn.com
Season: Year-round
General Manager: Wynn Tyner
Fitness Director: Joe Romero
Reservations: (480) 948–1700 or (800) 24–CAMEL
Spa Appointments: (480) 596–7040
Accommodations: 453 pueblo-style casitas, including twenty-seven suites; all with private patio; seven suites with pools. In-room refrigerators, coffeemakers, safe, fax/computer data port, and voice mail.
Meals: Among several choices: the Chaparall offers American cuisine for dinner; the Navajo, with Southwestern decor, serves breakfast, lunch, and dinner, as well as a poolside buffet; Sprouts at the spa offers healthy spa cuisine for breakfast and lunch.
Facilities: Two 18-hole golf courses, golf shop, driving range; six tennis courts (five lighted); three outdoor pools, whirlpools; children's playground; 9-hole pitch-and-putt course; mountain biking trail; bicycle rentals; gift shop.
Services & Special Programs: Seasonal children's programs; personal planning service for designing spa packages and arranging for golf, reservations, and sightseeing.
Rates: $$$
Best Spa Package: Spa Renewal Week includes six nights/seven days in deluxe accommodations, three meals a day, and choice of any twelve one-hour a la carte spa services, salon treatments, or fitness services. $3,220 single occupancy; $4,480 double occupancy; tax additional.
Credit Cards: Most major
Getting There: Located 10 miles northeast of Phoenix Sky Harbor Airport in Paradise Valley and minutes from downtown Scottsdale.
What's Nearby: Shopping in Old Town Scottsdale; Phoenix Zoo; McCormick Railroad Park; horseback riding; ballooning; Scottsdale Center for the Arts.

MIRAVAL

Catalina, Arizona

A recent guest appropriately nicknamed this spa "Miracle." At Miraval guests discover a carefully planned strategy of treatment focused on a "single belief that each of us has the innate capacity to live a more fulfilling life." It is no wonder that Miraval has been cited as the number one spa in the world by *Condé Nast Traveler* Readers' Choice Awards and was rated in the top one-third of all travel destinations in the world by the same publication.

When experts gathered to create a new educational vacation alternative at Miraval, the bottom line became "balance of life." And that goal is embraced in every aspect of the program, from the self-discovery and stress management workshops to the spa's Conscious Cuisine (the use of foods that are appealing, satisfying, and healthy) developed by Chef Cary E. Neff. The experts also made another precise decision to categorize Miraval as a "health leisure resort" rather than as a spa.

Miraval literally means "view of the valley," which it indeed grants in its setting on 135 acres at the foot of the Santa Catalina Mountains. Resembling a dude ranch with adobe-style buildings, Miraval is worthy of four-star resort status.

One glance through the fifteen-page Personal Services Guide will give you an understanding of the structure and depth of this program, which covers every aspect of body care, from a self-heating mud and massage treatment to nine kinds of facials. If your goal is to jump-start your life, this the place to make it happen. Miraval has expanded on the usual spa offerings to include such unique programs as the Equine Experience. Self awareness is increased through greater "communication" with your horse, including increased awareness while cleaning the horse's shoes and hooves. Other self-challenging activities include mountain biking, meditation, yoga, and specialized body work ranging from craniosacral to ayurvedic body treatments. For the intrepid there are extra-challenging activities, such as wall climbing, night climbing, and desert and mountain hiking. For the imaginative there are classes in the sacred art of sand painting and an introduction to journal writing. In fact, there is almost everything under the Arizona sun to stimulate your creativity. You may do as little or as much as you choose, but, if you want to do it all, plan to stay about a week.

At Miraval there are no required classes or rules against drinking alcohol or wine, which are available in the dining room and bar. Abstinence and deprivation are not part of the well-planned agenda. This fact sets Miraval apart from the many spas that eschew alcohol, sweets, and other decadences. If ever there was a feel-good resort, this is it! The key here is to make

Miraval
5000 East Via Estancia Miraval
Catalina, AZ 85739
Phone: (520) 825–4000
Fax: (520) 825–5163
E-mail: miravalaz@aol.com
Web site: www.miravalresort.com
Season: Year-round
General Manager: Joseph A. DeNucci
Spa Director: Beth Kelley
Fitness Director: Nordine Zouareg
Reservations: (800) 232–3969
Spa Appointments: (800) 363–0819
Accommodations: 106 casita-style rooms (most with private patios), two luxury suites, four king rooms with fireplaces. All have cotton velour bathrobes, minibar, two-line telephones, morning newspaper.
Meals: The Cactus Flower (breakfast, lunch, and dinner); the Palm Court (continental breakfasts, gourmet sandwiches, snacks); the Brave Bill (4:00–10:00 P.M.; wine, alcoholic drinks, light snacks).
Facilities: Three swimming pool areas; fitness center; conference rooms; horseback riding; tennis courts; volleyball; croquet; hiking and mountain biking trails; Zen and desert gardens; nearby golf; personalized spa treatments; facials and salon services.
Services & Special Programs: Flexible, personalized programs, classes, and services, including self-discovery, lifestyle management, recreation/fitness.
Rates: $$–$$$
Best Spa Package: Miraval's Life in Balance Deluxe Package is the only option. It includes casita-style accommodations; three gourmet meals daily; all nonalcoholic beverages; access to group programs and activities; one personal spa service or one one-on-one consultation or round of golf per night of stay; use of facility; round-trip Tucson International Airport transfers. Low Season (June–September): $420 per person per night, double occupancy; High Season (October–mid-June): $445; with 7.5% tax and 17.5% service charge.
Credit Cards: Most major
Getting There: Miraval is located 20 miles outside of Tucson, between Tucson and Phoenix, near the small community of Catalina. Guests most conveniently fly into Tucson International Airport.
What's Nearby: Biosphere; two golf courses; a multitude of attractions in Phoenix and Tucson.

choices that work for you, based on "mindfulness." Mindfulness simply means that there is something for everyone at Miraval. The positive environment that surrounds the guest at this spa nurtures sensible choices—from fitness to food—that lead to a life in balance.

Weight Control Through Mindfulness

Weight loss without dieting is possible according to Lisa MacDonald, registered dietitian at Miraval. She recommends you get in touch with your own body by paying attention to how food affects your energy level and your general health (for example, noting if eating dairy products causes stomach aches). She also suggests you notice how emotions affect your food choices. The idea is to slow down and focus your attention on eating: Scrutinize the junk food in your diet and take a look at your family's medical history. MacDonald advises her clients to always eat breakfast and to include protein in it (a few almonds, natural peanut butter, or cottage cheese will do), to eat frequently to keep blood sugar stabilized, and to balance carbohydrates and proteins. MacDonald also suggests you take at least twenty minutes a day away from your workplace for lunch and also plan a healthy afternoon snack. "There is no such thing as a good or bad food," stresses MacDonald. "It's a matter of how much you eat and how often."

CAL-A-VIE
Vista, California

Leave the city stress behind once you arrive at Cal-a-Vie, a destination spa in a garden setting 40 miles north of San Diego. Opened in 1986, this oasis of serenity has attracted considerable media attention thanks to dozens of celebrities who have "spa-ed" here. No more than twenty-four guests at a time attend this posh, camplike spa sequestered on 150 acres. Cal-a-Vie demands that you invest 100 percent of yourself; chores are left to an attentive staff of seventy. During the year, there are coed weeks as well as exclusive women's weeks. The standard program runs Sunday to Sunday.

Guests stay in European-inspired cottages furnished with a country French decor. The huge armoire

could go empty because fitness attire is provided—right down to jacket and sweatpants, provided fresh daily. The ambience is egalitarian; you can even wear your sweats to dinner and feel comfortable. The king-size bed is turned down each evening, but don't expect a chocolate truffle on your pillow! The calorie count, presided over by Chef Steven Pernetti, is 1,200, but it can be adjusted to fit individual requirements.

The day begins at 6:15 A.M. with a before-breakfast hike that revs up the system for what is ahead. To soften the "boot camp" agenda, there is a break at 10:50 A.M. when a tray of beautifully arranged fruit and glass mugs filled with vegetable broth is delivered to the lounge. By 1:00 P.M. guests have challenged their heart rate with aerobic circuit training, sports training, and a killer abdominals class, as well as water volleyball when the sun is shining (about 320 days a year!). And before you can say "aromatherapy," the day has slipped away and it is time for dinner at 7:00 P.M.

Everyone starts their spa journey with a fitness assessment, so this is the time to set your goal, whether the focus is weight loss, inch loss, or—the best goal of all—to attain a healthier lifestyle. Cal-a-Vie offers a concentrated spa program designed to produce results. Fitness is enhanced by daily spa treatments ranging from two-hour European hydrotherapy treatments and body scrubs to daily massages and a series of three facials. The beauty salon offers the finishing touches, from hand and foot treatments to scalp treatments. Special women's weeks (around sixteen a year) have a sorority-house feel, but without the agonizing over finals!

Three evenings a week feature lectures on nutrition, stress, and current health topics. On Friday nights Chef Pernetti shares spa secrets on how to prepare the recipes used throughout the week. A typical menu might include vine-ripened tomato salad with fresh mozzarella and basil, asparagus-stuffed chicken breast,

roasted red peppers, grilled zucchini, and potatoes with roasted garlic sauce. Desserts are consistently beguiling—the chocolate mousse made with tofu and maple syrup is a perfect example.

If you can splurge on one spa experience this year, Cal-a-Vie would be the place to consider for a concentrated one-week program.

Breathe to De-stress

Yvonne Nienstadt, director of nutrition at Cal-a-Vie, discusses stress management with guests one evening during the weeklong program. "Stress is considered the disease of our time," she says. **Her recommendation for coping with stress is through proper breathing. She tells guests to breathe deeply. "When under stress, oxygen requirements increase," Nienstadt explains. "Breathing abdominally is energizing, yet will calm the mind and body." She advises guests to breathe to a comfortable count, such as six or twelve, and hold for the same length if possible or to a natural point. Then exhale to the same count. This method of "cycle breathing" is effective in maximizing oxygen intake and carbon waste removal. She maintains that this psycho-physio therapy is one way of dealing with stress.**

Cal-a-Vie
2249 Somerset Road
Vista, CA 92084
Phone: (760) 945–2055
Fax: (760) 630–0074
E-mail: calavie@adnc.com
Web site: www.cal-a-vie.com
Season: Year-round
Owners: John and Terri Havens
General Manager: Deborah Zie
Spa Director: Deborah Zie
Fitness Director: Judy Wood
Reservations: (760) 945–2055
Spa Appointments: (760) 945–2055
Accommodations: Twenty-four guest cottages, individually decorated in the style of a European country villa with hand-carved furniture and pastel floral chintz fabrics; private terraces.
Meals: Carefully prepared spa cuisine with low calorie count built around herbs, fruits and vegetables from the spa's own gardens; flavors are Provençal and Mediterranean style.
Facilities: Gym with state-of-the-art equipment; tennis courts; adjacent private golf club; swimming pool; hydrotherapy pool.
Services & Special Programs: Cooking classes; individualized fitness courses; morning and afternoon hikes; massages; aromatherapy; seaweed wraps; skin, hair, hand and foot treatments; evening lectures on various healthy living topics; hydrotherapy; reflexology.
Rates: $$$
Best Spa Package: There is only one available: $4,850–$5,150 per person/per week, but better rates can be found during the summer (mid-June to early September) and during some holiday periods. Program starts and ends on Sunday.
Credit Cards: American Express, MasterCard, Visa
Getting There: The spa is 40 miles from San Diego International Airport; complimentary transfers provided on Sunday.
What's Nearby: This 150-acre site is in a secluded valley north of San Diego, yet close to all the San Diego area attractions, shopping, and beach.

THE GOLDEN DOOR
Escondido, California

he Golden Door, the stellar spa that set the stage for the others, has retained its crown by keeping pace with the times, from the personalized spa day to cuisine that thwarts pounds while satisfying even the fussiest guest. Awards are too numerous to list. The highest accolades range from its being rated the number one spa in the *Robb Report*'s 1998 "Best of the Best" to its coveted rating as the number one spa in America by *Zagat's U.S. Hotel, Resort and Spa Guide* every year since that survey began in 1988.

The Golden Door opened in 1958 and, from the beginning, added programs reflecting the changing needs of men and women, with fitness classes, cre-

ative spa cuisine for specific dietary requirements, and perfectly maintained accommodations. The spa accepts only thirty-nine guests on a seven-day program that begins each Sunday. There are over four staff members per guest, including twenty-two instructors in the fitness department, each with a university degree. You'll get a perfect night's rest after putting yourself through a plethora of classes, ranging from sunrise hiking to tap or jazz dancing, from weight training and water volleyball to strength and flexibility classes. The day is a harmonious schedule of upbeat fitness in the morning tempered by a generous array of passive activities later in the day.

In addition to a conventional daily massage, you can choose from aromatherapy, seaweed thalassotherapy, moortherapy, and deep-cleansing facials that combine mineral masques with chamomile. A personal exercise therapist is assigned to each guest for the entire week with the goal of overseeing the schedule and charting daily progress.

The weather is year-round perfect in this 377-acre rural corner of San Diego County, 30 miles north of San Diego and 8 miles north of Escondido. Sunny days here number 341, making it one of the most geographically desirable spots in the United States. In this utopian setting, the Golden Door unfolds its serene Japanese theme, reflected in the bell courtyard, sand garden, and architecture. Each guest is given a Japanese yukata (cotton robe) along with warm-up clothing, T-shirts, and shorts. The "uniform" is a great equalizer and takes the competitive edge off of dressing up (or down, as the case may be).

The spa's inclusive gourmet menus, prepared by noted spa cuisine chef and author Michel Stroot, feature healthful, natural foods—many from on-site organic vegetable gardens and fruit orchards. The evenings are reserved for guest lecturers. The informa-

tive topics range from cooking demonstrations and lifestyle programs to stress management and dried flower arranging.

Deborah Szekely, founder of Rancho La Puerta in 1940, created the Golden Door's fitness spa, the first destination spa recognized for lavish personalized service in a stunning Asian ambience. With dedication and ability to change with the times, the Golden Door legend continues to flourish and recharge the lives of those who participate in its time-tested program.

Tips to Improve Your Body Image

You don't have to change your appearance to improve the way you feel about your body. Find ways to regularly give your self-esteem a boost: Stop reinforcing the negative. Every time you say to yourself, "I hate my flabby thighs," you reinforce exactly what you don't want. Focus on your attributes. Make a list of the things about your appearance that you like. If you don't like something about your body that you can't change, make peace with it. Replace judgments about your body with real knowledge and understanding of how your body works. Focus more on health and energy than on appearance. Increase your awareness of your physical self. Monitor your body for areas of stress or tension (relax your shoulders, etc., at least once an hour). Before you eat, calm yourself and check in with your body to see if food is really what you need at that time.

The Golden Door
PO Box 463077
Escondido, CA 92046-3077
Phone: (760) 744–5777
Fax: (760) 471–2393
Web site: www.goldendoor.com

Season: Year-round

General Manager: Rachel Caldwell

Spa Director: Judy Bird

Fitness Director: Judy Bird

Reservations: (760) 744–5777 or (800) 424–0777

Accommodations: Thirty-nine private guest rooms, with shoji screens, black jalousie windows, CD players, outdoor decks, and private gardens.

Meals: All meals and snacks are included in the stay. Pre-hike, midmorning, and late afternoon snacks are provided. Hors d'oeuvres are served in the early evening; dinner is in the dining room.

Facilities: This is a self-contained destination spa whose 377 acres are filled with hiking trails, gardens, groves, a lake, and a swimming pool. The 45,000-square-foot facility contains a boutique, beauty court, three lounges, dining room, two gyms, and a bathhouse.

Services & Special Programs: Private lessons and consultations; archery and fencing; evening lectures and demonstrations; all clothing provided; special dietary needs; weekly cooking class; library; personal laundry service; safety deposit boxes. Men's weeks are scheduled five times yearly in March, June, September, November, and December. Coed weeks are four times yearly in March, June, September, and December. Otherwise all women.

Rates: $$$

Best Spa Package: There are summer and special rates, such as a four-day coed special and a New Year's ten-day program. The California Plan includes meals, accommodations, all fitness classes, and six body treatments for one weekly fee of $4,850, plus room tax.

Credit Cards: American Express, MasterCard, Visa

Getting There: Limousine pickup and return Sundays is complimentary from the San Diego International Airport (forty-five-minute drive). By car: from Orange County's John Wayne Airport (ninety minutes); and from Los Angeles International Airport (three hours).

What's Nearby: All San Diego area attractions: Old Globe Theatre, Old Town, Tijuana, SeaWorld, Wild Animal Park, La Jolla.

THE OAKS AT OJAI

Ojai, California

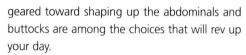

ust being in the lively art community of Ojai melts away stress. The Oaks opened in this small town in Ventura County—ninety minutes from Los Angeles—in 1977. It inhabited a former country inn that had held landmark status since the 1920s. Since its inception, the spa has hosted nearly 50,000 health seekers who have reveled in the Oaks program created by Sheila Cluff. Cluff, a former professional figure skater and physical education teacher, has devoted her energy over the last forty-plus years to spreading the fitness gospel.

The Oaks keeps the cost of this spa experience at an affordable level without sacrificing a quality fitness, nutrition, skin-care, and wellness program. From the moment you enter the intimate inn, you will be surrounded by a beehive of activity. Announcements remind guests of evening lectures, menu choices, and special events. There is hardly an idle moment.

The majority of the spa's guests are executive women who enjoy a nonstop schedule from 6:15 A.M. with a mountain hike to a stimulating evening program, covering anything from Ukrainian egg decorating to lectures by well-known authors.

Sixteen optional fitness classes daily provide ample opportunity for those who are serious about shaping up. Low impact aerobics, aqua-toning, yoga, and classes geared toward shaping up the abdominals and buttocks are among the choices that will rev up your day.

Three gourmet, low-calorie meals are served daily. There is a broth break at 10:45 A.M. and a happy hour, featuring juice cocktails, at 5:15 P.M. The basic 1,000-calories-a-day menu designed by Chef David Dal Nagro is imaginative and nutritious. Alternative menus, such as those for high-fiber, high-protein, athletic, or vegetarian diets, may be ordered.

The Spa Sanctuary has a eucalyptus steam room, redwood sauna, indoor whirlpool, and locker room. The adjacent Coral Gym hosts cycles, StairMasters, treadmills, and Paramount equipment. A facial and massage department features aromatherapy, body scrubs, reflexology, a full-service beauty salon, a nail salon, and a well-stocked boutique in case you lose so many pounds and inches you need to freshen up your wardrobe.

The staff-to-guest ratio is one to three, which means everyone receives ample personal attention in this casual and informal setting. Personal trainers are available for yoga, weight training, and even ballroom dancing.

The Oaks is situated in the heart of downtown Ojai, surrounded by boutiques, antiques shops, and a

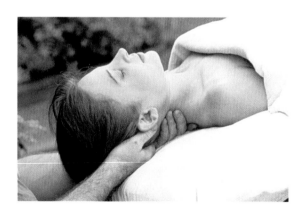

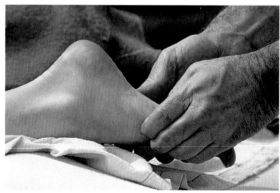

noticeable absence of fast-food outlets. Guests have ample opportunity to explore the area. Pack only the essentials—a warm-up suit, fitness wear, and hiking/biking shoes—to blend into this unpretentious environment.

Exercise "For the Road"

Sheila Cluff, founder of this popular health spa, was so sure that a mere five minutes of daily exercise could be beneficial she implemented a study on the concept at Cornell University. Ultimately, along with Toni McBride and Mary Tabacchi, she authored a book about her revolutionary findings. The book, *Take 5,* outlines an exercise program that even travels well, according to Cluff. Cluff recommends assembling an exercise kit that includes exercise clothing appropriate for your destination, proper footwear, a tape player and extra batteries, a variety of tapes that include some for unwinding following busy days on the road, a few exercise videos in case your hotel room has a VCR, and your favorite bath products (aromatherapy essential oils and lotions are a good choice) to help you relax before you retire for the night.

The Oaks at Ojai
122 East Ojai Avenue
Ojai, CA 93023
Phone: (805) 646–5573
Fax: (805) 640–1504
E-mail: info@oaksspa.com
Web site: www.oaksspa.com
Season: Year-round
Owners: Sheila and Don Cluff
General Manager: Dietrich Pahnke
Activities Director: Elizabeth Horton
Reservations: (800) 753–6257
Spa Appointments: (805) 646–5573 (for day use)
Accommodations: Forty-six guest rooms, including private rooms, double lodge rooms, double cottage rooms, and large triple cottages.
Meals: Three meals a day with menus based on 1,000 calories per day; alternative menus and additional dishes offered. Meals are served in the dining room and poolside.
Facilities: Swimming pool, whirlpools, saunas, cycles, StairMasters, treadmills; hiking and biking; special area for women includes a locker room, eucalyptus steam room, redwood sauna, indoor whirlpool, and washrooms/showers. Handicap accessible.
Services & Special Programs: Full range of fitness classes; treatments a la carte: reflexology, aromatherapy, massages, facials, body scrubs, paraffin treatments, manicures/pedicures; hair salon, makeup design, wardrobe planning consultation, body analysis, private fitness consultation. Special weekend and weekday programs on such topics as spa cuisine, yoga, and feng shui. Theme weeks (water aerobics, hiking and biking) with guest instructors.
Rates: $
Best Spa Package: Request the seven-night package, which includes accommodations in a standard double room, three meals daily, activities, and two complimentary treatments. The base price is $1,015 per person; with tax and service it is $1,196.09.
Credit cards: Most major
Getting There: The spa is located in northern Ventura County, two hours from the Los Angeles International Airport and forty-five minutes from Santa Barbara. Inquire about shuttle services when making your reservation. Rental cars are also an option.
What's Nearby: The Ojai Music Festival at the Libby Bowl, for four nights in May and June, is an annual event.

OJAI VALLEY INN & SPA
Ojai, California

ust getting to Ojai will raise your spirits. And by the time you reach the narrow country road that leads you to the historic Ojai Valley Inn & Spa, you'll understand why filmmaker Frank Capra chose this valley to depict Shangri-la in his 1937 classic movie, *Lost Horizon*. Surrounded by the Topa Topa Mountains, this 206-room inn, set on 220 scenic acres and designed in the Andalusian Spanish architectural style, conveys casual elegance.

The spa portion of the Mediterranean-style village creates a self-contained cocoon where guests leave the world of cellular phones, computers, deadlines, and stress behind. The spa consists of twenty-eight treatment rooms, the 1,600-square-foot mind/body center with a fully equipped exercise room, a cardiovascular workout area, and a studio for yoga, spinning, meditation, and tai chi.

The centerpiece of the spa experience is the Kuyam, a fifty-minute purifying session that in Native American Chumash culture means a "place to rest together." This communal experience starts with a self-application of cleansing moor mud, followed by guided meditation. Herb-infused steam softens the mud (and you!) before a walk through a Swiss shower. After the shower, lotion is gently applied, and you are rewrapped in warm linen and led to the outdoor loggia to rest. If the treatment sounds tempting, consider the Ojai honey body masque, the elderberry herbal wrap, and the orange blossom facial as well.

Enhancing the spa treatment program is a schedule of mind/body classes that begin daily at 7:00 A.M. with morning hikes, restorative yoga, and boxercise. The last classes of the day are scheduled at 5:00 P.M. and include yoga essentials and retro-dance aerobics. Since Ojai stands as an internationally known art community, the spa, not surprisingly, offers a comprehensive list of enrichment/art programs from basic watercolor to landscape painting.

The newest program at the spa is a health assessment developed by Florence Comite, M.D., which includes a complete physical examination, nutritional evaluation, lab studies, and a session on individual fitness needs with a trainer.

Pacific Provincial cuisine, created by Chef Brian Wuest, stresses the use of local ingredients, ranging from seafood to produce. Maravilla is the signature restaurant of the resort. Other dining spots offer casual outdoor dining and spa cuisine.

This is no ordinary spa, and neither is the inn's 3,500-square-foot ultraluxurious penthouse with private elevator, treatment room, sauna, indoor and outdoor fireplaces, and whirlpools. The terrace of the indulgent retreat provides an ideal spot to view Ojai's

legendary "pink moment"—when sunsets and the sky reveal a marvelous panoply of pink.

The resort's 6,235-yard, par 70 golf course has hosted seven Senior PGA Tour events and the EMC Golf Skills Challenge televised by NBC Sports. If golf isn't your game, visit the inn's 800-acre ranch and stables with horseback riding for all levels. The Ojai Valley Inn & Spa is one of those rare destinations offering something for everyone, including Camp Ojai—a children's program operating year-round.

Signature Blends for the Perfect Massage

The spa at Ojai Valley Inn has blended four specialty massage oils and a massage lotion that guests may choose from when experiencing their massages. The specialty blends are attributed to certain massage goals—you choose your goal and enjoy!

Creative Energies: **grapefruit, lemon, bergamot, and jasmine**

Ojai Elements: **French lavender, sage, and bitter orange**

Health Potential: **vanilla, sandalwood, sweet orange, and ylang-ylang**

Vital Energy: **lavender and rosemary**

Protection: **eucalyptus, rosemary, peppermint, and spearmint**

Ojai Valley Inn & Spa
Country Club Road
Ojai, CA 93023
Phone: (805) 640–2000
Fax: (805) 640–0305
Web Site: www.ojairesort.com or www.spaojai.com

Season: Year-round

General Manager: Thad Hyland

Spa Director: Christi Cano

Mind/Body Manager: Travis Anderson

Reservations: (805) 646–5511 or (800) 422–6524

Spa Appointments: (805) 640–2000 or (888) SPA–OJAI

Accommodations: 206 deluxe guest rooms and suites, many with private balconies or patios, all with king-size or double-queen beds, minibars, hair dryers, personal amenities.

Meals: Maravilla for Pacific Provincial cooking and panoramic mountain views; the Oak Grill & Terrace for casual lunches and dinners; the Club Bar for light fare, wine, and cocktails. Spa cuisine lunches, drinks, and snacks served poolside. Room service available.

Facilities: Championship golf course; weight room, workout area; horseback riding; spa with treatment rooms, whirlpools, steam rooms, sunbathing loggias, hair and nail salon, lap/exercise pool; mediation garden; eight tennis courts (four lighted); meeting center; two heated swimming pools; jogging and bicycling trails.

Services & Special Programs: Camp Ojai children's program; artist studio tours; bird-watching; wine tours; shopping; jeep tours; Outward Bound programs; health assessment program; gardening and art classes.

Rates: $$

Best Spa Package: The Spa Ojai Discovery Package includes a luxurious guest room, unlimited use of spa facilities, mind/body evaluation, and two spa treatments or spa activities per person; the double occupancy rate is $578 per person per night. This includes room tax.

Credit Cards: Most major

Getting There: The resort is 73 miles northwest of Los Angeles, 35 miles southeast of Santa Barbara, and 14 miles from the Pacific Ocean. Airport transfers can be arranged through the concierge desk.

What's Nearby: Lake Casitas, with boating and fishing; the town of Ojai, with art galleries, boutiques, cafes; Santa Barbara and Ventura attractions.

PALM SPRINGS DESERT RESORTS: SPA TOWN

Palm Springs, California

alm Springs has been blessed with more than enough spas to keep visitors rejuvenated—all year-round. Nestled between the San Jacinto and Santa Rosa Mountains, the area affords views of peaks glistening with snow in the desert sunshine. The Agua Caliente Indians flocked here in centuries past, and their sacred healing waters have evolved into the essence of the spa experience here today.

Discovered in the 1930s by the movie industry, Palm Spring's prominence accelerated during World War II when General George S. Patton chose the area to train over a million troops just east of Palm Springs. In addition, the U.S. Army established an air base and a general hospital.

The movie stars who flocked to the area left legendary marks and hideaway homes that still attract sightseers. Today many celebrities retire here, often tak-

ing up second careers. At the Fabulous Palm Springs Follies, long-legged lovelies (as producer Rif Markowitz refers to them) must be fifty years or older in order to kick up their heels in the chorus line! Is Palm Springs the Fountain of Youth? A lot of people who visit and live here think so.

Spa-lovers cherish this oasis, and day spas continue to proliferate along El Paseo, the resort area's legendary shopping avenue that features a tree-lined promenade accentuated by contemporary outdoor sculpture (www.palmsprings.com/elpaseo). The El Paseo Directory lists over 150 expert aestheticians, manicurists, and hairstylists, who staff over fifty spas and beauty salons along this chic avenue. It is obvious that the healthy, wealthy, and wise are serious about looking good for the charity events and the society pages. This social whirl monopolizes the season (November through

April) with nonstop golf and tennis tournaments and the endless array of parties for charitable causes.

This environment is paradise for spa-lovers. The Palm Springs Desert Resorts Convention and Visitors Bureau lists twenty-two spas in the immediate area, and there are dozens more in nearby Desert Hot Springs, where glamour diminishes, along with the cost of a spa vacation.

Here is our list of the best spa resorts offering a complete range of spa programs, from one-day packages to a full week of fitness, spa dining, and treatments.

Marriott's Desert Springs Resort & Spa

74–855 Country Club Drive
Palm Desert, CA 92260
Phone: (760) 341–1865 or (800) 255–0848
Fax: (760) 341–1846

Although the resort is a magnet for conferences, the full-service spa is off on its own, creating a more private feel within this immense resort property.

Rancho Las Palmas Marriott Resort & Spa

41–000 Bob Hope Drive
Rancho Mirage, CA 92270
Phone: (760) 568–2727
            (760) 836–3106 (spa reservations)
Fax: (760) 568–5845

This two-level spa boasts the best spa cuisine in the desert, found at Frescas.

The Palms at Palm Springs

572 North Indian Canyon Way
Palm Springs, CA 92262
Phone: (760) 325–1111
            (800) 753–7256 (spa reservations)
Fax: (760) 327–0867

This is a serious spa resort, housed in a historic structure; the ambience is hospitable and friendly. Under the guidance of Sheila Cluff, one of the world's leading health and fitness experts, the well-qualified staff shepherds guests through a comprehensive health and fitness experience. Marilu Rogers, general manager, directs hikes beginning at 6:00 A.M.; sixteen classes for all fitness levels, from walks to water classes, fill the remainder of the day. The all-inclusive rate is one of the desert's best spa values.

Merv Griffin's Resort Hotel and Givenchy Spa

4200 East Palm Canyon Drive
Palm Springs, CA 92264
Phone: (760) 770–5000
Fax: (760) 324–6104

This elite spa caters to the carriage crowd, with skin-care treatments housed in an exquisite structure sur-

rounded by a gorgeous garden. The most expensive spa week in the desert is yours for $5,500 (plus tax and gratuities) for the ultimate in personalized pampered luxury.

La Quinta Resort & Club
49–499 Eisenhower Drive
La Quinta, CA 92253
Phone: (760) 564–4111 or (800) 598–3828
Fax: (760) 564–5723

This resort marks the debut of the WellMax Clinic, which, under the supervision of Dan Cosgrove M.D., provides a detailed medical history and analysis of those seeking more than a routine physical. This evaluation may be linked to determining your spa services and exercise program at Spa La Quinta.

All About Massage
74121 Highway 111
Palm Desert, CA 92260
Phone: (760) 346–7949
            (888) 772–2442 (reservations)
Fax: (760) 346–4549

A mecca for those who appreciate serious massage in a quiet setting, despite its location at the end of a shopping mall. Peruse the retail section so that you can create your own home spa.

The Spa at the Ritz Carlton Rancho Mirage
69–900 Frank Sinatra Drive
Rancho Mirage, CA 92270
Phone: (760) 321–8282 or (800) 241–3333
Fax: (760) 321–6928

A compact yet chic spa awaits a well-dressed clientele who crave expensive European-inspired body treatments, such as massages and facials.

The Spa Hotel & Casino
100 North Indian Avenue
Palm Springs, CA 92262
Phone: (760) 325–1461
        (800) 854–1279 (reservations)
Fax: (760) 778–1519

The spa building is classic 1960s-style architecture. The spa's traditional treatments, such as massage and facials, feature the legendary mineral water that helped put Palm Springs on the map. The spa boasts two outdoor mineral pools. The Spa Experience is a forty-five-minute treatment that includes steam, sauna, eucalyptus inhalation, mineral bath, and a relaxation room. This is a popular choice for those casino-goers wanting a quick rejuvenation. The spa is best considered for day use.

Palm Desert Healing Arts Center
73–241 Highway 111, 3-B
Palm Desert, CA 92260
Phone: (760) 568–0094
Fax: (760) 340–0606

This well-known therapeutic massage center has been specializing in healing techniques for the past sixteen years, under the ownership of Irene A. Hall. The center's therapeutic massages are used to alleviate discomfort from sciatica, arthritis, and muscle soreness.

Desert Hot Springs Spa Hotel
10805 Palm Drive
Desert Hot Springs, CA
Phone: (760) 329–6000
        (800) 808–7727 (reservations)

Under the same ownership as its sister spa, Miracle Springs Hotel & Spa, this resort is one of the desert's originals. Treatment rooms surround several mineral spring pools of varying temperatures, offering a casual, value-priced spa getaway. Both resorts are suitable for families.

Ten Stellar Spas Shimmer in the Desert Sun

Palm Springs Desert Resorts

Getting There: The Palm Springs International Airport is three minutes from downtown Palm Springs and is served by the following airlines: Alaska Airlines, American Airlines, American Eagle, American West Express, United Airlines, USAir Express/Northwest Airlines, and Canadian Airlines.

What's Nearby: For information contact the Palm Springs Desert Resorts Convention and Visitors Bureau, 69–030 Highway 111, Suite 201, Rancho Mirage, CA 92277; Phone: (760) 770–9000; (800) 42–RELAX (reservations in the United States and Canada); Fax: (760) 770–9001; Web site: palm springsusa.com. The bureau covers the desert resort communities of Palm Springs, Palm Desert, Cathedral City, Indian Wells, Indio, Rancho Mirage, and Desert Hot Springs.

SONOMA MISSION INN & SPA

Sonoma, California

ou can stay at the re-created historic Sonoma Mission Inn & Spa without a romantic partner and have a memorable stay, but it is definitely a resort that has been designed for couple closeness. Its idyllic setting in the heart of Sonoma wine country—surrounded by bursting grapevines, rolling hills, sunshine, and three dozen wineries that invite intimate wine-and-cheese picnics—makes this a perfect place to begin a new life together or rekindle a tiring one. But the spa at the inn adds its own magic to the equation: natural hot mineral waters with sensual, almost mystical, rejuvenation powers.

The Sonoma Mission Inn was built in 1927 on the site of an earlier hotel that also operated as a spa. Native Americans had long ago discovered the hot underground springs at this location. The new inn was designed to replicate the California missions, with arcades and bell tower. And in 1993 a new source of the legendary, underground hot springs surfaced when 135-degree thermal mineral waters were discovered directly below the inn.

A recent $20 million expansion and renovation of the Sonoma Mission Inn & Spa is impressive, from the beautifully landscaped grounds to the elegant suites with all the appointments. But undoubtedly the highlight of this recent infusion of money and glamour is the 40,000-square-foot spa, which features an elaborate Roman bath ritual, treatment rooms, a watsu treatment mineral pool,

and a lounge with wood-burning fireplace and healthy snacks. The "king's bath" is a massive, bell-metal tub for couples filled with the inn's own mineral water and a selection of rejuvenating herbs.

Rather than the day-spa approach, consider three-to four-day treatment packages, called spa immersion programs. In these programs, guests begin slowly, first relaxing with the ultradecompressing, European-based bathing ritual and then progressing to their personal treatment rooms for deeper immersion. Tailored packages range from active wellness to a romantic retreat to golf immersion, which includes rounds of golf, lessons, and appropriate spa treatments.

The full menu of services available includes watsu mineral pool treatments, private couple rooms with bath, shiatsu, aromatherapy, reflexology, signature grapeseed body polishes, and herbal, seaweed, and mud wraps. The spa uses local herbs and products, such as grape seeds from local vineyards and an abundance of lavender for its many massage and hydrating treatments.

Guests can enjoy two fine restaurants at the Sonoma Mission Inn, both serving chef Toni Roberts's innovative healthy cuisine, and both using herbs and vegetables from the inn's own garden or the surrounding area. The Big 3 Diner with adjacent gift shop is a casual, enjoyable spot for all three meals. The inn's main dining room, The Restaurant, serves fresh Califor-

nia cuisine in its newly redone interiors off the main lobby. Its award-winning wine list offers more than 200 Sonoma and Napa County labels. Specialties from the tandoori ovens include flat breads and meat and fish skewers.

Healing Through Water

The spa at the Sonoma Mission Inn has incorporated the mineral waters that flow from the earth below with its own concept of a bathing ritual. Borrowed from the bathing practices of the ancients, this sixty-minute ritual is sure to slow down your perception of time and prepare you for treatments that follow. The setting for the bathing ritual is a European-inspired circular room with high, arched ceiling decorated with a soothing mural. At their own pace, guests begin the unwinding process with an exfoliating shower, followed by a warm bath, then a hot 102-degree mineral bath, on to a cool shower, then an herbal steam, a sauna, another cool shower, ending with rest in the peaceful, adjacent lounge. Rehydrating drinks are provided throughout the self-administered treatment.

Romance Amid Magical Waters

Sonoma Mission Inn & Spa
PO Box 1447
Sonoma, CA 95476-1447
Phone: (707) 938–9000
Fax: (707) 938–4250
E-mail: smi@smispa.com
Web site: www.sonomamissioninn.com
Season: Year-round
General Manager: Ulrich Krauer
Spa Director: Jeff Kohl
Fitness/Activity Director: Michele Kohl
Reservations: (800) 862–4945
Spa Appointments: (707) 938–9000 or (800) 862–4945
Accommodations: Guest rooms total 228, with sixty suites; many have fireplaces and terraces or patios. Accommodations include complimentary bottle of wine; private-label bath accessories; robes and slippers; hair dryers.
Meals: Breakfast, lunch and dinner available in the Big 3 Diner; dinners served in The Restaurant; snacks and light breakfasts and lunches offered poolside; beverages available all day.
Facilities: Full fitness center open to all Inn guests. Natural hot artesian mineral water swimming pools for families or adults-only; complimentary valet parking; meeting rooms; spa; fitness center with private counselors; guided hikes and bicycle outings. Golf nearby.
Services & Special Programs: Spa treatments and services designed to meet the guest's personal goals, from stress reduction to togetherness with a loved one to reviving your golf game. Packages may be designed for two, three, or four days with recommended add-on services.
Rates: $$–$$$
Best Spa Package: The Spa Sampler for couples to enjoy the spa experience together. Highlights include $400 in credits for spa treatments, the use of the Bath House, and unlimited use of the fitness center; room and tax, valet parking. $725 per couple per night.
Credit Cards: Most major
Getting There: From the San Francisco International Airport, 75 miles, it's a ninety-minute ride. From San Francisco by car, take the Golden Gate Bridge to Highway 101, then Highway 37 to Highway 12 (forty-five minutes). By van, Sonoma Airporter.
What's Nearby: Sonoma wineries and organic farms, Calistoga mud baths, Culinary Institute of America, Jack London State Park, Sears Point Raceway.

TWO BUNCH PALMS RESORT & SPA
Desert Hot Springs, California

his exclusive fifty-six acre desert hideaway is in a town renowned for its curative mineral water. The constant flow of geothermal springs from the northern slope of the Coachella Valley is cooled down at Two Bunch Palms, from an amazing 148 degrees. The steamy water splashes over a rock waterfall and envelops bathers who steep, like floating tea bags, in the grotto pool. This is a spa where you are apt to spot a celebrity with eyes shut, meditating in the water or slipping into a pool for a Watsu or Wassertanzen appointment. What guests cherish here is absolute privacy—the mantra of Two Bunch. Children under eighteen years of age are not permitted, nor are pets, and if you use a cell phone, keep your voice down. The serious staff at the gate-guarded entrance are vigilant: Nobody wanders into this sanctuary by accident.

The meticulously manicured grounds hold forty-four villas and suites, plus a spacious home on the hill for larger parties. Unlike most destination spas, there is no fixed schedule. Instead there are over forty treatments on the spa menu to choose from, some standard and others more inventive. It is advisable to schedule treatments in advance.

The spa therapists at Two Bunch are among the best in California, and their talented hands are capable of reducing your stress level significantly.

Just look at the blissful faces in the grotto for proof. Treatments include the Roman Tub Rejuvenator, an hour massage followed by a lavender Epsom salt bath by candlelight, and jin shin do, a meditative acupressure technique designed to balance energy flow through acupuncture—the result being deep relaxation. The mud treatments, which are legendary here, take place in a separate pavilion surrounded by trees and soft desert breezes. They can be enjoyed solo or side by side.

Breakfast, lunch, and dinner are served in the Casino Restaurant, and although the cuisine is not calorie- or carbohydrate-counted, it is healthy and eschews oils and preservatives. Choose from soups, salads, and a variety of entrees, which frequently find their way to the private villas via room service. Casual dining is nearby in Desert Hot Springs and in numerous restaurants and clubs in Palm Springs, but a car is necessary.

Two Bunch Palms holds status as one of the most unique resorts in Southern California and perhaps the world. Its history and legends are worthy of poolside reading while here. Al Capone may have been its original developer, but today it caters to the elite of the entertainment and corporate worlds, as well as those who just want to be treated to seclusion and privacy.

An Oasis of Tranquillity
in a World of Stress

Two Bunch Palms Resort & Spa
67–425 Two Bunch Palms Trail
Desert Hot Springs, CA 92240
Phone: (760) 329–8791
Fax: (760) 329–1317
E-mail: whiteowl@twobunchpalms.com
Web site: www.twobunchpalms.com

Season: Year-round

Operations Manager: Jay Ramsted

Spa Director: Lorna Schmuckle

Fitness Director: None

Reservations: (800) 472–4334

Spa Appointments: (760) 329–8791 or (800) 472–4334

Accommodations: Forty-five guest units of varying styles, all with private patios and queen- or king-size beds, some with stained-glass windows, television, VCR, kitchenette, Jacuzzi.

Meals: The Casino Restaurant features healthful fare and a good selection of wines; menu varies according to seasonal availability of fresh ingredients. A continental breakfast is served buffet-style; lunch is served from noon to 2:00 P.M. (picnic baskets available); dinner by reservation.

Facilities: Spa; hot mineral-water pools; man-made lake; two lighted tennis courts; swimming pool; grotto; watsu pool; mud bath complex; nude sun-bathing bins.

Services & Special Programs: Over forty spa treatments, including massages, skin and body care, specialty treatments, and water therapy.

Rates: $$

Best Spa Package: The midweek Roadrunner Package (Sunday through Thursday, June through September) includes a guest room spa suite or villa, continental breakfast, lunch, one or two one-hour spa treatments, robe, use of facilities, and all taxes and gratuities. Price ranges from $95 to $410 daily, double occupancy.

Credit Cards: Most major

Getting There: From nearby Palm Springs International Airport, or by car, take I–10; the resort is located less than 5 miles from the interstate.

What's Nearby: Desert Hot Springs restaurants and shopping; nearby desert communities, including Palm Springs, with restaurants, theater, art galleries, boutiques.

"Miracle" Clay Used at Spa

Adjacent to the site of the artesian well at Miracle Hill that produces the magical waters for Two Bunch Palms is a vein of unusual green clay found to contain unique qualities that help restore the skin's natural tone and balance, absorb toxins, and leave the skin feeling fresh and smooth. This clay, now known as "hydroterra," may also contain the ability to store energy and catalyze reactions, explaining why the clay at Two Bunch Palms, which has soaked for millennia in the miraculous waters, can rejuvenate the skin so thoroughly when continuously activated by mineral water refresher. The clay mud treatments at the spa are intended to cleanse you physically, emotionally, and spiritually and leave your skin glowing.

WYNDHAM PEAKS RESORT &
GOLDEN DOOR SPA
Telluride, Colorado

p, up, and away if you choose to take the 9,500-foot uphill trek to this spa hideaway in the San Juan Mountain Range, about a ten-minute car trip from Telluride Mountain Village. Within the handsome 174-room Wyndham Hotel is a full-service, 42,000-square-foot spa spread over four levels and honeycombed with forty-four treatment rooms. Many of Golden Door's signature massage techniques and body treatments are offered here. The Southwestern motif throughout the hotel reflects Telluride's colorful history. Not only is this town the site of one of America's most complete spas, it was also the site of Butch Cassidy's first bank robbery in the late nineteenth century.

Considered one of the nation's best ski mountains and rated by readers of *Snow Country* magazine as the most scenic resort in America, the mountain is known for vertical drops of over 3,000 feet and for some of the most challenging ski trails on the continent. And

what better place is there to relax after a day on the slopes than at the Golden Door, ranked second among the Top Five Spa Resorts in the world by the *Condé Nast Traveler* magazine? And during the summer, hiking and biking opportunities test fitness levels with a challenging terrain.

Here, under one roof, is a spa that has it all, including a Cybex weight room, cardiovascular deck, squash and racquetball courts, an indoor climbing wall, saunas, steam rooms, Jacuzzi, and a water slide that invites swimmers to plunge from an indoor lap pool to a lower-level indoor/outdoor pool. Exercise classes are scheduled throughout the day and can be combined with the latest spa therapy. Reflexology, bindi balancing, reiki, shiatsu, targeted massage with fango, and facials for any skin type are among the offerings from which to choose. It is essential to speak with a spa concierge first to personalize your program.

Accommodations at the resort are spacious, with luxury-sized rooms (400 square feet) overlooking Telluride village. Rooms are equipped with either a king-size bed or two full-size beds, and children sixteen and under are free. The KidSpa offers day care and scheduled adventure-oriented activities, making this a family destination. A separate enclave of thirteen guest rooms offer twenty-four-hour spa access with one-on-one attention provided by a spa concierge. This spa-within-a-spa is the first of its kind in the United States.

Golden Door cuisine, which is light and healthy, is served in both the Legends and Appaloosa restaurants. Colorado ingredients are used and incorporated into flavors from all over the world.

Cradled on three sides by the majestic peaks of the San Juan Mountain Range, this first-class resort and spa has become the standard by which other North American mountain resorts are measured.

Golden Door Spa at Wyndham Peaks Resort
136 Country Club Drive
PO Box 2702
Telluride, CO 81435
Phone: (970) 728–6800
Fax: (970) 728–6175 (resort); (970) 728–2525 (spa)
Web site: www.wyndham.com

Season: Year-round

General Manager: John Paul Olivier

Spa Director: Suzanne Livermore

Fitness Director: John Bennett

Reservations: (800) 789–2220

Spa Appointments: (970) 728–6800 or (888) 772–4584

Accommodations: The 174 guest rooms, including twenty-eight suites, one- to four-bedroom condominiums, and penthouses; minibars, cable television, VCRs, CD players.

Meals: Legends and Appaloosa restaurants offer healthy cuisine with an emphasis on local ingredients and flavors of the world, as well as Golden Door spa cuisine.

Facilities: Forty-four treatment rooms, saunas, steam rooms, Jacuzzis, Cybex weight room, cardiovascular deck, squash and racquetball courts, indoor climbing wall; full-service salon, men's and women's kivas; ski rental and retail shops; adjacent Telluride Ski and Golf Company with 18-hole championship course; five outdoor tennis courts; conference and banquet facilities.

Services & Special Programs: Customized spa programs; ski-in/ski-out access to ski area; complimentary ski valet; group and private tennis instruction; jeep tours; hiking and mountain sports available; KidSpa program.

Rates: $$$

Best Spa Package: The Ski & Spa Five-Night Package offers upgraded accommodations, four lift tickets per person, four fifty-minute spa treatments per person, breakfast daily, purification ritual in the kiva spa. Rates are seasonal and range from $2,164 to $3,094 per person double occupancy.

Credit Cards: Most major

Getting There: The resort is a ten-minute drive from the Telluride Regional Airport and a one-and-a-quarter-hour drive from Montrose Airport. It is two-and-one-half hours to airports in Grand Junction, Durango, and Gunnison.

What's Nearby: The historic town of Telluride; ski and all mountain sports; Durango and Grand Junction.

Spa 101

For those of you who are new to spa-going, Wyndham Peak's Golden Door publishes a handy "guide for the uninitiated" entitled "How to Spa Like a Pro." The pamphlet includes information on types of spas, the spa experience, planning a spa vacation, and spa etiquette. And it lists a glossary of spa terms. Have you wondered if you should wear makeup? What should you avoid if you are claustrophobic? And how to tip. Their glossary clears up the meaning of *phytotherapy, fango,* and *lomi lomi.* Even if this is your first spa experience, a quick brush-up with this brochure will make you a spa scholar. Best yet, study time won't exceed fifteen minutes; you'll have plenty left over for a Vichy shower!

THE DIPLOMAT RESORT COUNTY CLUB & SPA
Hollywood, Florida

reated at a cost of $600 million, this South Florida resort straddles the Intracoastal Waterway and offers championship golf, a European style spa, and tennis facilities for true enthusiasts of all levels.

Designed in the style of an Italian villa, the spa building, guest rooms, and clubhouse are linked by covered walkways. Overlooking the golf course, the spa has a separate floor for fitness classes and strength training, so noise does not intrude on the calm of spa services rooms. Its interior courtyards and gardens make for a relaxing ambience, set apart from resort's fun and games, where wellness and fitness become meaningful.

All the elements of a destination spa experience can be integrated with your personal program. Led by a highly credentialed staff (personal trainers as well as a nutritionist), programs address issues like weight management, stress, and aging. With a full range of face and body care, and seventeen private treatment rooms, the spa's core philosophy is holistic: health in body, mind, and spirit.

Beyond serious pampering, the country club's 155-acre golf course is a soothing setting for the spa. Morning runs along a network of lakes are shaded by palm trees. Tennis buffs can book ten clay courts, as well as workouts with nationally recognized tennis pro Fred Stolle. Dining at the country club features spa cuisine. The newly designed menu concentrates on high-energy food that is low in fat, salt, and sugar.

The Diplomat Resort Country Club & Spa
501 Diplomat Parkway
Hallandale, FL 33009
Phone: (954) 457–2000
Fax: (954) 457–2045
E-mail: info@diplomatresort.com
Web site: www.diplomatresort.com

Season: Year-round

Managing Director: Michael Hall

Spa Director: Chuck McElligott

Reservations: (800) 327–1212

Accommodations: 1,000 beachfront rooms in the dual-tower main building, including one hundred suites and the top-floor concierge rooms, plus sixty rooms at the country club. Elegantly appointed, the rooms have hair dryer, ironing board and iron, coffeemaker, and dual phone lines.

Meals: Seventeen restaurants, plus poolside bar and grill. A signature restaurant at the Country Club offers spa cuisine selections.

Facilities: The spa has state-of-the-art exercise equipment, private rooms for bodywork, skin care, and physical therapy. Separate locker rooms for men and women have sauna/steam rooms and whirlpools. In addition to tropical swimming pools, there is an ocean beach with equipment for water sports. The Country Club offers ten clay tennis courts, 18 holes of golf, and yacht slips.

Services & Special Programs: Massage, reflexology, shiatsu, facials, wraps; lifestyle and nutritional management; scheduled aerobics and group exercise.

Rates: $$

Best Spa Package: The Ultimate Escape, a $270 day-spa package; includes four treatments, lunch, use of spa facilities. Services include an exfoliating body polish, seaweed massage, manicure and pedicure.

Credit Cards: Most major

Getting There: Located ten minutes from Fort Lauderdale/Hollywood International Airport, and thirty minutes from Miami International Airport, the resort's main building is on Highway A1A; the country club entrance is just off Hallandale Beach Boulevard. From I–95, take exit 21 or 22, and proceed 4½ miles east on the beach boulevard.

What's Nearby: Fort Lauderdale, Broward Center for the Performing Arts, the Galleria shopping mall, Sawgrass Mills outlet shops, Museum of Contemporary Art, Everglades National Park, Miami Beach, Gulfstream Park (Thoroughbred horse races), Biscayne dog racing track, jai alai fronton.

Getting to the beach is simple; hail a free water taxi at the marina. The hotel towers frame a view of the ocean and swimming pool. From the Intracoastal Waterway, a series of pools and fountains lead to open-air terraces where alfresco dining is available year-round. Water-sports equipment adds to a constant whirl of activity.

Fresh from the Garden

Built around four courtyards planted with tropical gardens, the spa features in its signature treatments freshly picked herbs and flowers. Starting with fragrant chamomile swirled over your body in a gentle scrub that cleanses and polishes the skin, you are ready for total immersion in a chamomile bath. This potent herbal remedy soothes skin exposed to sun, and dryness. Following the bath, you're ready for a full-body massage with gentle floral essences. Plan on eighty minutes for this tropical treat, then relax in the garden.

PGA NATIONAL RESORT & SPA
Palm Beach Gardens, Florida

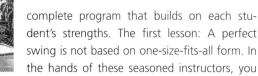

et into championship shape at the home of the Professional Golfers Association of America. From five golf courses to a nineteen-court tennis club, racquetball, and croquet, the PGA resort offers a winning combination of sports and spa.

Like a cool oasis, the spa at PGA provides a refreshing change of pace. Here you are in the hands of professionals who know how to make you look and feel your best. Set up a personalized regimen to include workouts with a trainer at the fitness center, salon services for hair and nails, and nutrition-balanced meals in the resort's theme restaurants.

Drenched with light, the Mediterranean-style spa building is surrounded by subtropical gardens and bubbling fountains. Soak in Waters of the World, pools infused with mineral salts from springs in Europe and Israel, or try Watsu, a water-borne massage therapy for total relaxation. The spa has a full complement of hydrotherapy tubs, mud and algae wraps, and Swiss showers to relieve muscular aches and pains.

Sports massage, neuromuscular and craniosacral therapy, and skin care to repair sun damage help keep you in shape. The spa aestheticians are schooled in the latest European face and body treatments. Aromatherapy, detoxifying seaweed body masque, remineralizing gel, and oxygenating facial are among one hundred services offered. Available a la carte, spa services and treatments come in several packages, from half-day getaway to four-night escape.

From reception in the spacious, glass-walled lobby overlooking palm-lined fairways, to guest rooms furnished in tropical tones, this is a country club with world-class credentials. Day-spa packages come with workout clothing and poolside lunch at the signature Waters of the World garden. Sport-specific exercise gets you in shape for the main game. The Academy of Golf, directed by PGA professional Mike Adams, combines physical and mental aspects of the game into a

complete program that builds on each student's strengths. The first lesson: A perfect swing is not based on one-size-fits-all form. In the hands of these seasoned instructors, you learn how to maximize your body type to deliver the club on the most direct route to the ball. The three-day golf school, as well as the three-times-daily clinics, are for acers and duffers of all ages.

Dining at the resort's eight restaurants includes everything from Italian cuisine at Arezzo to spa cuisine. A fusion of Floridian and Asian flavors, the spa cuisine

PGA National Resort & Spa
400 Avenue of the Champions
Palm Beach Gardens, FL 33418
Phone: (561) 627–2000
Fax: (561) 622–0261
E-mail: marketing@pga-resorts.com
Web site: www.pga-resorts.com
Season: Year-round
General Manager: Michael Metcalf
Spa Director: Margaret Byrnes
Fitness Director: Randy Myers
Reservations: (800) 633–9150
Spa Appointments: (800) 843–7725
Accommodations: 339 rooms and suites in main hotel; sixty-five golf course cottage villas with two-bedroom suites.
Meals: Spa Plan breakfast and lunch includes spa cuisine of the world. Dinner a la carte at eight restaurants, including Shula's Steak House, and Italian-themed Arezzo.
Facilities: Full-service menu of massages, skin care, hydrotherapy rooms equipped with tubs, Vichy shower, nine swimming pools, lap pool; salon for hair/nails and makeup consultation; golf on five 18-hole courses; Health & Racquet Club with cardiovascular/strength building equipment by Cybex, Trotter, Nautilus; nineteen tennis courts (twelve lighted), two racquetball courts (air-conditioned); croquet complex.
Services & Special Programs: Fitness evaluation, personal trainers, golf clinics, golf school, tennis clinics, tennis camp, croquet instruction, concierge, laundry, dry cleaning, Budget Rent-A-Car.
Rates: $$
Best Spa Package: Two-night Ultimate Getaway with daily golf, spa treatments, breakfast and lunch. Single, $550–$1,120; double, $450–$815.
Credit Cards: American Express, Diners, Discover, Master-Card, Visa
Getting There: From Palm Beach International Airport, transfers by limousine, van. By car from West Palm Beach: 1–95 to exit 57, PGA Boulevard west to resort entrance; Florida Turnpike to exit 44.
What's Nearby: Palm Beach has Worth Avenue shops, Flagler Museum; West Palm Beach for Clematis Street arts district, CityPlace, Kravis Center for the Performing Arts, Norton Museum of Art, the Gardens Mall, Palm Beach Polo Club. Day trips to Kennedy Space Center, Walt Disney World, Orlando, Delray Beach: Morikami Museum & Japanese Gardens, the Everglades.

menu is available for breakfast and lunch at The Citrus Tree, an informal cafe and outdoor terrace, as well as poolside at the spa. Dinner menus highlight heart-healthy versions of classic dishes created by executive chef Michael Vlasich. Selections from the sports nutrition plan provide a diet high in complex carbohydrates, low in fat calories.

Designed to complement an active lifestyle, the resort is a two-hour drive from Disney World's sports complex and theme parks, twenty minutes from West Palm Beach's CityPlace nightlife and art galleries. Making you feel like a champion is what PGA does best.

One Side at a Time

Isolateral conditioning strengthens muscles by focusing on each side of the body independently of the other. At the PGA health club, fitness director Randy Myers recommends using light dumbbells and free weights for optimal benefits. This strengthens each side of the body equally. Stretching between sets assists development of muscles that retain endurance and are functionally strong. After age thirty-five, adults lose approximately 2 percent of their muscle per year. Weight training offsets this loss.

GRAND WAILEA RESORT HOTEL & SPA

Wailea, Maui, Hawaii

hat would Hawaii be without volcanoes, beaches, hula skirts, and a world-class spa? Welcome to the Grand Wailea Resort Hotel & Spa. This 780-room hotel, on the southwestern shore of Maui, opened its 50,000-square-foot Spa Grande in 1989. The spa has become known for its blending of Hawaiian and ancient Eastern healing and relaxation techniques with European rejuvenation therapies. The signature Terme Wailea Hydrotherapy Circuit—a selection of international water therapies—forms the basis of all the treatments here. The circuit begins with a brief shower, followed by a soak in the Roman tub. Then guests are invited to use the steam, sauna, and cold plunge pool. The loofah scrub is next, followed by a cas-

cading waterfall shower. Then come the specialty baths, with a choice of moor mud, aromatherapy, tropical enzyme, limu (seaweed), or mineral salt. The final step is the Swiss jet shower. If you arrived feeling jet-lagged, this water treatment is a perfect antidote.

The spa facilities are divided into the wet and dry areas, and both are accentuated with inlaid Italian marble, original artwork, Venetian chandeliers, and mahogany millwork. The spa's interiors harmonize beautifully with the resort's $30 million art collection, which includes original works by Pablo Picasso and Andy Warhol.

Thirteen types of massage are offered, so if you don't want to try the Lomi Pohaku (a thermal massage using smooth steamed lava stones to massage avocado and olive oil into your skin), there is always the Hawaiian Lomi Lomi Wela Pohaku, a total body massage that incorporates heated lava pebbles in a small denim bag. The less adventurous can choose from ten varieties of Swedish massage and aromatherapy facials.

For those who overdose on the irresistible Maui sun, the spa offers a sunburn/aloe mud wrap, utilizing a blend of natural aloe vera gel and herbal mud to cool the skin. The spa's color light therapy is a combination of colored light, warmth, music, and natural aromatherapy to soothe the body and mind. Couples will enjoy the Abhyanga-pizichili, a two-step treatment that includes a massage by two therapists and a moisturizing warm oil treatment. It is advisable to make spa appointments in advance.

Pampering aside, there are squash and racquetball courts, and cardiovascular and strength-training facilities. Fitness services include one-on-one instruction. And if you aren't interested in a conventional stretch class or boxercise, try the hula class for an overall workout!

Grand Wailea Resort Hotel & Spa
3850 Wailea Alanui Drive
Wailea, Maui, Hawaii 96753
Phone: (808) 875–1234
Fax: (808) 874–2411
E-mail: spa@grandwailea.com or info@grandwailea.com
Web site: www.grandwailea.com
Season: Year-round
General Manager: Stephen J. Ast
Spa Director: David Erlich
Fitness Director: David Erlich
Reservations: (808) 875–1234 or (800) 888–6100
Spa Appointments: (800) SPA–1933
Accommodations: 780 guest rooms, including fifty-two suites. Napua Tower is a one-hundred-room exclusive small hotel within the resort. Accommodations are spacious, surrounded by six gardens with sculptures and tropical flowers.
Meals: At the Humu Humu restaurant, a cluster of thatched-roof Polynesian huts, guests are able to "catch" their own seafood dinner; Kincha is a creative Japanese restaurant; the Grand Dining Room serves a breakfast buffet and a la carte; Bistro Molokini is an open-air cafe with an exhibition kitchen; Cafe Kula offers casual terrace dining.
Facilities: Tsunami, a high tech nightclub; Camp Grande for children; seaside chapel for weddings; the Canyon Activity Pool (nine separate pools, a baby beach, waterslides, waterfalls, caves, rapids, and grottoes); three 18-hole golf courses; an eleven-court tennis complex; meeting facilities; shops.
Services & Special Programs: Scuba diving lessons; business center; wedding services and packages; cruises on the resort's 60-foot catamaran for picnics, snorkeling. Winter whale-watching cruises.
Rates: $$$
Best Spa Package: The Grand Pampering Package, based on a daily rate of $554 per night, double occupancy, includes accommodations, two massage treatments or facials, loofah scrub, and the hydrotherapy circuit.
Credit Cards: Most major
Getting There: Twenty-minute drive from Kahului Airport; Maui is a twenty-minute flight from Honolulu.
What's Nearby: Wailea Beach; Lahaina; all island attractions.

The spa's juice bar offers smoothies and energy drinks. Spa cuisine is served in the Bistro Molokini, an open-air cafe.

This resort attracts major conferences and is a popular venue for weddings and romantic getaways. Guests can also stay at the Napua Tower, a small hotel within the resort that offers exclusive access to a private lounge serving complimentary continental breakfasts and evening hors d'oeuvres and cocktails. Children aged five to twelve can enjoy the resort's Camp Grande.

A Tropical Bath To Go

The tropical enzyme bath, which accompanies the Terme Wailea Hydrotherapy Circuit, uses a secret recipe mixed right on the property. Key ingredients include Japanese bath crystals and dried papaya enzyme. In addition to enjoying the special blend at the spa, guests may take home or mail order the private-label product.

KOHALA SPA AT HILTON WAIKOLOA VILLAGE

The Big Island, Hawaii

standout among Hawaii's spectacular resorts, the Hilton Waikoloa Village sprawls across sixty-two acres of lush, tropical gardens and lava-rock cliffs dotted with swimming pools and cascading waterfalls. Set amid lush green golf courses, the resort has monorail trams and boats for transport between six restaurants and guest rooms in three towers. Family-oriented fun, serious golf, some of Hawaii's most creative chefs, and the holistic Kohala Spa complete the experience.

Hidden away in one of the hotel towers, the Kohala Spa and Fitness Center provides Pacific pleasures alongside European-style pampering. Healing rituals on the Big Island of Hawaii originated with Polynesian settlers who worshiped Pele, goddess of fire, on the volcanic slopes. Hilton's mega resort updates island traditions for vacationers. If you have never tried Hawaiian Lomi Lomi massage or Ti-leaf Wrap, this is an opportunity to experience an authentic treatment in the hands of trained Hawaiian bodyworkers. Island sources provide sea salts for an invigorating body scrub, native red clay for skin care, ki tree leaves for wraps, and honey-mango gel for showers. A body wrap begins with coco-mango oil massaged into your skin, followed by acupressure facial and foot reflexology massage. Calming aloe and lavender are applied in a cooling wrap of ti-leaf (ki) plant, to pull excess heat from skin overexposed to sun.

The range of tropical treatments is extensive. Papaya from local farms supplies an enzyme (papain) for body exfoliation, encouraging renewal of skin cells. Macadamia nut oil, rich in

skin softeners, enhances a hydrotherapy soak, as hibiscus flowers float amid fragrant milky water. Bathing with island limu (seaweed) and blue-green algae is said to promote elimination of toxins and improve circulation. Most relaxing: Lomi Lomi massage on the beach.

Practicing tai chi and chi gong is one way to feel the benefits of a moving meditation. Developed over hundreds of years in China, the movements enhance muscle tone and release tensions. Practitioners of these movements teach groups to breathe deeply in the sea air while working out.

Exploring the Big Island by jeep or on horseback, the prime attraction is Hawaii Volcanoes National Park. There is probably nowhere else on this planet where you can see, hear, and smell the process of the earth's creation as vividly. Hikes through the park's rain forest and lava tubes are included in all-day nature tours

operated from the Hilton by Hawaii Forest & Trail. If you are interested in birding, there is a naturalist-guided trek to Mauna Kea, an ancient coned volcano.

The Kohala Spa approach to well-being and treatment of the mind, body, and spirit lays its foundation in the Hawaiian word *ho'oponopono*, which translates as a feeling that inspires healing. Five elements are necessary: wind, water, earth, air, and fire. Only on the Big Island do these essential elements come together for health and wellness.

Getting Stoned

On this volcanic island, lava stones are a reminder of creation. Hawaiian kahuna healers use lava stones in treatments, wrapping a ki (or ti) leaf around the stone for healing and protection. The introduction of LaStone Therapy by Arizona-based massage therapist Mary Hannigan inspired the Kohala Spa to use polished lava stones found in nearby rivers. Puhaku (the Hawaiian word for stones) are heated and placed on your body for muscular relief. Smooth and potato-size, the stones make ideal implements for a massage therapist to work on aching muscles. The experience focuses physical and spiritual energies, creating emotional and mental balance.

The Healing Island

Kohala Spa at Hilton Waikoloa Village
425 Waikoloa Beach Drive
Waikoloa, HI 96738
Phone: (808) 886–1234
Fax: (808) 886–2903
E-mail: info@kohalaspa.com
Web site: www.kohalaspa.com
Season: Year-round
General Manager: Dieter Seeger
Reservations: (800) 445–8667
Spa Appointments: (808) 886–2828
Accommodations: 1,241 rooms in three low-rise towers. Contemporary furnishings: king-size or two queen-size beds, marble-floored bathroom; lanai balcony, 75 percent have ocean view.
Meals: Lunch included in spa packages can be taken in the tennis garden cafe or at an oceanfront restaurant, Kamuela Provision Company. Choices include salmon salad, Hilo-grown greens, charred spiced ahi with three-bean salad, filet of beef, fruit carousel. Other options: five restaurants, luau, nearby mall.
Facilities: Gym with CardioTheater, StairMasters, Gravitron, PTS Tubo recline bikes, StarTrac treadmills, Lifesteps, Bodymaster strength-training system with free weights. Separate sections for men's and women's treatments, with steam room, sauna, outdoor Jacuzzi, hydrotherapy tub, showers, locker rooms, robes. Beauty salon, spa cafe, lap pool, and tennis complex.
Services & Special Programs: Massage, loofah body scrub, facials, body wraps; hair care, manicure/pedicure. Personal trainers and group exercise sessions, health evaluation.
Rates: $$–$$$
Best Spa Package: Pleasure in Paradise, a four night spa vacation package that includes oceanview accommodations, two spa cuisine meals daily, unlimited exercise classes, personal training session, medical and nutritional evaluation, snorkel trip, and daily spa treatment program. Also included are taxes, airport transfers, tote bag, and water bottle. Single, $2,265; double, $3,025.
Credit Cards: Most major
Getting There: From Honolulu or California, direct flights to Kona International Airport. Transfer by taxi or rental car (twenty minutes).
What's Nearby: Hawaii Volcanoes National Park, Kona coffee plantations, Captain Cook (fishing port), Hilo (shopping), Puukohola Heiau (temple).

CANYON RANCH IN THE BERKSHIRES
Lenox, Massachusetts

f improving your lifestyle is your objective, the New England version of Tucson's Canyon Ranch has the solution. This state-of-the-art destination spa is a beautiful sprawling complex, and one of the main buildings here is an 1897 mansion, known as Bellefontaine, designed to echo Louis XV's Petit Trianon at Versailles. Today guests wearing warm-up suits and leotards walk briskly through the lobby, symbolizing a new life for this vintage landmark.

Opened in 1989, Canyon Ranch offers an ambitious program of fitness, skin care, lifestyle management, sports activities, wellness consultations, and nutrition that has set the standard for the spa industry. This spa holds the distinction of being a four-time winner in the Best Spa award given by *Condé Nast Traveler* magazine.

The daily program is similar to camp for adults on a grand scale. The 100,000-square-foot spa is connected to the rooms by a glass-enclosed walkway. Women predominate during the week, and men arriving for the weekend balance out the gender ratio.

The approach to wellness spans mind, body, and spirit. You will learn new ways to walk, breathe, exercise, and eat. You won't want to skip exercise class or anything else on your schedule, because it is fun to be here and participate without having to worry about being graded. There are three indoor tennis courts, three outdoor courts, an indoor track, and two racquetball courts. Other outdoor options include canoeing, biking, and kayaking. Forget television and videos; excellent evening programs cover a multitude of topics, from time management to tarot cards.

Fitness, the nerve center of Canyon Ranch, is considered a reward here, not a punishment. And you do see a lot of happy faces. As the week progresses, those who once led a sedentary lifestyle acquire a glow. The goal is to keep the glow going once you check out.

Chefs produce healthy, great-tasting cuisine. Fitness takes the lead over weight loss, and it is the guests who decide how much to eat. There is no incentive to smuggle in pizza and soda because the

Canyon Ranch in the Berkshires
165 Kemble Street
Lenox, MA 01240
Phone: (413) 637–4100
Fax: (413) 637–0057
Web site: www.canyonranch.com

Season: Year-round

General Manager: Carl Pratt

Spa Director: Jennifer Gigliotti

Fitness Director: Jennifer Gigliotti

Reservations: (413) 637–4100 or (800) 726–9900

Spa Appointments: (413) 637–4100 or (800) 726–9900

Accommodations: The 120 guest rooms are located in a modern New England–style inn that connects via glass-enclosed walkway to either the spa or the mansion.

Meals: Healthy, imaginative cuisine with a high degree of customer service and satisfaction served in the mansion. Salad and pasta buffet.

Facilities: 120 woodland acres, with the turn-of-the-century mansion as its centerpiece, containing the dining room, restored library, and Health & Healing Center. The two other structures are the spa complex and the inn. All three buildings are connected by climate-controlled, glass-enclosed walkways. Indoor and outdoor tennis courts; racquetball; squash; indoor and outdoor pools; indoor running track; salon facilities.

Services & Special Programs: Hiking, bicycling, canoeing, kayaking, cross-country skiing, snowshoeing, downhill skiing. Wellness consultations, workshops, and cooking demonstrations are offered year-round.

Rates: $$$

Best Spa Package: During the winter (December through March), the seven-night package, double occupancy, in deluxe accommodations is $3,185.87. The all-inclusive package covers accommodations, meals, hiking and biking programs, five spa services per person , and a $210 health and healing allowance that can be used for consultations with nutritionists, exercise physiologists, and other experts.

Credit Cards: Most major

Getting There: Arrive via Albany International Airport (New York) with a one-and-one-quarter-hour drive to the resort or via Bradley International Airport (Hartford, CT/Springfield, MA), a one-and-one-half-hour drive away.

What's Nearby: Skiing; fall colors; Williamstown Theater Festival; Jacob's Pillow Dance Festival; Tanglewood Festival.

menu is diverse, with entrees ranging from ahi tuna dressed with fresh salsa and risotto to Santa Fe–style chicken. Cooking demonstrations show you how to prepare it all at home. The salad and pasta bar are popular with buffet enthusiasts, and there is always plenty of iced tea and water to keep you properly hydrated.

Stress and tension get attention here, with information and ideas that can transform your life. Fending off heart disease is taken seriously at the Ranch, and, if you want to confront this issue, this is the spa where you can make it happen. Canyon Ranch helps you acquire the skills to make health choices that will add years to your life and life to your years!

Healthy Hearts

Dr. Joseph S. Alpert has several recommendations on the subject of healthy hearts. He advises us to eat garlic and onions, since both discourage blood clots. He says to substitute soy protein for animal protein and consider taking 500 to 1,000 milligrams twice daily of vitamin C. An intensely colored vegetable or fruit (carrots, spinach, sweet potatoes, oranges, mangoes, or cantaloupe) will provide ample beta carotene. Dr. Gordon Ewy recommends a can of sardines daily. He advises, "It's better than any medicine I know. And send the butter dish back before it even hits the table!"

CANYON RANCH SPACLUB AT THE VENETIAN
Las Vegas, Nevada

ou can spend your time exercising at a one-armed bandit or you can make a more sensible choice and check into the Venetian's 63,000-square-foot Canyon Ranch SpaClub and really be a winner.

Just being at this $1.2 billion, 3,036-room megaresort is a trip in itself. Imagine yourself in Venice, recreated in all its charm right down to a gondola ride through an elaborate Disney-esque Grand Canal, and a Rialto Bridge. Everything is on a grand scale here, from stunning 700-square-foot guest rooms replete with private bed chambers draped in canopies to a

500,000-square-foot themed indoor retail mall with its own St. Mark's Square.

Those who choose to bypass the immense casino and seek refuge at the spa will find a world of health opportunities. The spa's two levels are honeycombed with fifty treatment rooms, offering 120 spa services. Spa-goers enjoy dozens of treatment options with enticing names, such as Men's Metamorphosis and Beautiful Backs. Thirteen different facials await.

Fitness reaches a new level with fifty pieces of cardio equipment, thirty spinning bikes, and classes such as boxercise, chi gong, yoga, and strength training. A staff of physicians, nutritionists, exercise physiologists, aqua therapists, health educators, and physical therapists use an integrated approach that combines Western and alternative health practices. There is a daily fee ($25) for hotel guests to use the facilities.

If you have decided to trim down and quit smoking (a healthy anti-casino move), the SpaClub has the cure with smoking cessation and weight-loss programs. The Spa Cafe (note the absence of burgers and fries) presents a selection of salads, bran muffins, and other nutritionally balanced food choices.

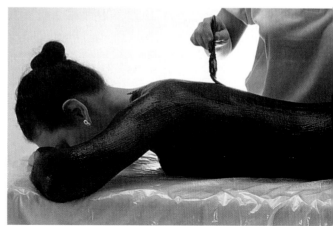

The goal of the SpaClub is to provide sanctuary from the nonstop, frenetic ambience of the Strip with its smoke-filled casinos, rich food, and surging traffic. And, amazingly, it does.

Eyes, Thighs, and Sighs!

Health food stores hold a world of remedies for spa-goers. Here are three products you should consider adding to your home spa. Herbal chamomile is available as an eye stick that soothes while firming and can reduce the appearance of puffiness and dark circles under the eyes. Thigh cream has been getting a lot of press. Results have been noticed by those who report it helps smooth out the appearance of spongy tissue (cellulite) from the thighs and buttocks. And finally, consider skin formulas containing alpha hydroxy acids. These are natural biological substances found in fruits. They have several beneficial effects on the outer and deeper layers of the skin. Similar to Retin-A, they slow down the aging process, which is accelerated by stress and UV exposure. Unlike Retin-A, they are safe and gentle and do not cause photo-sensitivity, excess redness, or excessive skin peeling. When these products are used in conjunction with a sensible nutrition and fitness program, you may see results.

A Winning Spa on the Vegas Strip

Canyon Ranch SpaClub at The Venetian
3355 Las Vegas Boulevard South
Las Vegas, Nevada 89109
Phone: (702) 414–3600 or (877) 220–2688
Fax: (702) 414–1100
Web site: www.venetian.com

Season: Year-round

General Manager: Michael D. French

Spa Director: Michael Leboeuf

Fitness Director: Samantha Radcliff

Reservations: (702) 733–5000 or (800) 494–3556

Spa Appointments: (800) 975–8880, ext. 201

Accommodations: The resort, the world's largest all-suite hotel/resort, shopping, casino, and convention complex, offers 3,036 suites featuring 130-square-foot bathrooms finished in Italian marble, a sunken living room, minibar, fax machine/copier; telephones with dual lines and dataport, color televisions, and a living room entertainment center.

Meals: Upscale dining in a dozen restaurants, including Wolfgang Puck's Postrio and the Canyon Ranch Cafe, serving world-famous spa cuisine.

Facilities: 63,000-square-foot SpaClub with beauty salon, fitness center, fifty treatment rooms, three aerobics studios; five acres of pool area with cabanas, and 40-foot indoor rock climbing wall.

Services & Special Programs: Several spa packages, including hiking, massage, fitness, men's treatments, and sport; medical, behavioral, and beauty consultations; area tours; creative arts center; complete guest concierge services.

Rates: $$$

Best Spa Package: The Personal Creation II enables you to design your own package. Selecting three services from twelve possibilities is an exciting prospect. Some of the services included in the $300 fee are a fifty-minute Swedish massage, a European Edge facial, a fifty-minute rock-climbing session, an Essential Signature Pedicure, or a Canyon Ranch Body Cocoon. For couples the four-hour Beautiful Beginnings ($1,075 per couple) unfolds in the luxurious 1,000-square-foot Spa Suite and includes a Satin Smooth Body Cocoon, Aromatherapy Massage, and the European Edge Facial. There are no spa packages combinable with room rates at this time.

Credit Cards: Most major

Getting There: The resort is a short drive from the McCarran International Airport.

What's Nearby: All Las Vegas Strip attractions. Valley of Fire National Park, Red Rock Canyon, Lake Mead.

THE REGENT LAS VEGAS—AQUAE SULIS SPA

Las Vegas, Nevada

he Regent Las Vegas is just far enough from the Strip to provide for a relaxing spa vacation. At the heart of the resort, with its 541-room twin hotel complex, is the Aquae Sulis Spa, a 40,000-square-foot facility nestled within the hotel. There are 286 rooms and suites in the Spa Tower, with the remaining accommodations in the Palms Tower, anchored at the south and west ends of the property. Views to the west are of the Red Rock Canyon National Conservation Area; to the east, the lights of Las Vegas.

Located twenty-five minutes northwest of McCarran International Airport, this chic hotel complex dressed down in soft colors bears little resemblance to the neon and glitz usually associated with Las Vegas. Don't look for faux Eiffel Towers or dancing waters here. This is casual elegance. The architecture is Spanish, with an eye-stopping swimming pool complete with waterfall and exquisite gardens. The casino is down a long corridor, away from the lobby; the Aquae Sulis Spa adjoins the casino in a surprisingly quiet environment.

The spacious gym, under an impressive dome, has strength-training and cardiovascular equipment; next door is the aerobics studio. Beyond here is the outdoor pool where underwater jets massage you, each focused on a specific part of the body. (The pool has twelve chambers, so two can use the treatment at a time.) There are over sixty water treatments available. It is advisable to meet with a spa host to decide on which of fitness classes, outdoor activities, and treatments you will schedule.

The Aquae Sulis brochure gives an overview of spa therapy, from the time of the Roman baths to the present, then explains each treatment offered at the resort, from siddha vaidya (herbal medicine) to thalassotherapy (sea water minerals) to moor mud therapy, color therapy, and phytotherapy. Massage therapies include eighteen varieties, with many unusual ones such as Aquae Sulis swe-atsu (based on the Asian concept of a unified

mind, body, and spirit) and reflexology with renform, another Asian technique using warm, self-heating mud for the feet to stimulate reflex points. Aura imaging begins with an aura photograph to determine blocked energy areas; then a colored bath designed to restore balance and a sense of well-being. Several treatments, such as the aqua-flow shiatsu, are especially recommended for golfers and outdoor athletes.

Guest rooms are luxurious. Rooms in the Spa Tower feature an oversized bathtub with mirrors on two sides. Adjacent showers are equipped with cascading showerheads.

Although there is not a spa restaurant at the resort, healthy choices are available in the Ceres Restaurant. And it is easy to select a healthy breakfast from the options at the Upstairs Market, a typical behemoth Las Vegas–style buffet. The sophisticated Parian Restaurant features a dramatic spin on dining, with china and silver from around the world on the tables and also framed as art on the walls.

Cold Water Cure

A burst of cold water can alleviate problems with unsightly veins. This efficient antiaging treatment is both easy and inexpensive. After you shower, finish with a cold water rinse. The heat of the shower dilates blood vessels, and blood can pool in the veins. A burst of cold water following the shower will constrict the veins and help pump blood back to the heart.

No Gambling on Your Health

The Regent Las Vegas—Aquae Sulis Spa
221 North Rampart Boulevard
Las Vegas, Nevada 89128
Phone: (702) 869–7777
Fax: (702) 869–7771
Web site: www.regentlasvegas.com
Season: Year-round
President and CEO: Paul Hanley
Spa Director: Keri Printy
Fitness Director: Jane Dudley
Reservations: (702) 869–7777 or (877) 857–1691
Spa Appointments: (702) 869–7777 or (877) 857–1691
Accommodations: 541 guest rooms and suites; luxurious decor with oversized bathtubs and cascading showerheads. Guest rooms are located in two towers, The Spa Tower and The Palms Tower.
Meals: Dining in twelve restaurants, including the sophisticated Parian Restaurant, the Ceres Restaurant; and the Upstairs Market with buffet fare.
Facilities: Spa with several hydrotherapy pools, a salon, boutique, workout area, aerobics studio, thirty-six treatment rooms. Casino; garden with pools and waterfalls; shops; putting greens; conference and banquet center.
Services & Special Programs: Adventure tours/activities of Red Rock Canyon National Conservation Area; preferred golf tee times arranged at ten nearby golf courses; wedding planning and arrangements.
Rates: $$$
Best Spa Package: There is a one night Regent Spa Package at $400 plus tax, double occupancy, which includes accommodations in the Spa Tower, breakfast at the Upstairs Market, and two spa treatments—a fifty-minute massage and a fifty-minute facial. Price includes the gratuity on the spa treatments.
Credit Cards: Most major
Getting There: The resort is located twenty-five minutes from McCarran International Airport.
What's Nearby: The resort is twenty-five minutes from the Las Vegas Strip attractions; Lake Mead; Grand Canyon.

THE GROVE PARK INN RESORT
Asheville, North Carolina

onstruction of The Spa at The Grove Park Inn Resort capped the hotel's transformation from southern inn to world-class resort. When owner Elaine D. Sammons committed to building the finest spa in North America on this historic property, she chose the design team responsible for Solace Spa at Banff Springs.

With the goal of bringing the Blue Ridge Mountains indoors, the designers have forged earth, water, and light into a synthesis of the new American spa. Ancient granite boulders arch over the pools and reception area, creating the feeling that you are deep inside a grotto devoted to health and fitness. Waterfalls and soaring glass skylights frame indoor and outdoor swimming pools. Designed by award-winning Canadian architect Robert LeBlond, of Calgary, Alberta, and Florida-based Michael McCaffrey of MCM International, the 40,000 square foot spa is spread out among hillside gardens. With an expanded sports complex and outdoor pool terrace, the new complex integrates with the U-shaped hotel, yet retains a sense of refuge and sanctuary.

Beyond the reception desk, the spa is divided into men's and women's lounges, each with locker rooms, showers, and shaving/makeup areas. Fireplaces warm the lounges, and there is a view of the pools below. Skylit steps lead to the indoor swimming pool, sauna, inhalation room, hot tubs, and cool plunge pool. A lap pool and two therapeutic waterfall pools face window walls with stunning views of the city and valley below.

Staying here is like returning to another era. The hotel was first opened in 1913 to offer sophisticated travelers an exclusive retreat in the Blue Ridge

Mountains of North Carolina. The Resort is on the National Register of Historic Places. It currently houses the world's largest collection of Arts and Crafts antiques and lighting fixtures. Just across town is the Biltmore Estate, George Vanderbilt's 250-room mansion, which awes visitors with its French chateau grandeur and 250-acre gardens designed by Frederick Law Olmsted in 1895. For col-

lectors of Americana, the area remains a source of inspiration and discovery.

Emerging from a $36-million makeover in 2000, The Grove Park Inn preserves its period grandeur with touches of modern comfort. In the Great Hall lobby, guests encounter twin massive fireplaces flanking a hall full of antique furnishings, while a stenciled ceiling with hand-hammered copper chandeliers reflects warm light. Original guest rooms at the main inn have new wall, window, and floor treatments, new armoires and stereos, and updated bathrooms. Two wings of contemporary rooms boast mountain and garden views.

Downtown Asheville, only five minutes away, has become a thriving center for the arts. Situated at an elevation of 2,500 feet in the spectacular Blue Ridge Mountains of western North Carolina, the area is blessed with four distinct seasons. Yet the mild climate permits golf year-round on the resort's par-70 Donald Ross–designed golf course. Tennis fans can choose from three hard-surface outdoor courts and three indoor courts. The spa's all-weather attractions include racquetball, aerobics classes, strength-training and cardiovascular exercise equipment, and some real down-home massage.

Sanctuary of the Senses

The signature treatment at Grove Park is much more than a facial. Using sounds, smells, and sensations associated with the Blue Ridge Mountains, the facial transports you to a place of complete relaxation. A massage therapist choreographs moves to the gentle sounds of water and ends by applying a skin-rejuvenating refining cream scented with mountain herbs. A final touch: a CD of the natural, soothing sounds used in the treatment is provided for you to use in your room during a relaxing bath, and to take home.

Going to the Mountain, Southern Style

The Grove Park Inn Resort
290 Macon Avenue
Asheville, NC 28804
Phone: (828) 252–2711
Fax: (800) 374–7432
E-mail: dtomsky@groveparkinn.com
Web site: www.groveparkinn.com
Season: Year-round
General Manager: Craig Madison
Spa Director: Ellen McGinnis
Reservations: (800) 438–5800
Spa Appointments: (800) 438–0050 (Call five days in advance)
Accommodations: 510 rooms, including suites, featuring Arts & Crafts movement furniture and decorative objects from the early 1900s. Newly renovated and updated rooms and bathrooms. Completely air-conditioned, all with TV. Deluxe rooms enjoy best views; value rooms in main inn are small, have one bed, and no view. The Club Floor has twenty-eight oversized guest rooms with Jacuzzi tub, robes, and private lounge for complimentary continental breakfast and beverages. The Grove Park Inn Resort is on the National Register of Historic Places.
Meals: A la carte menus in two restaurants: Sunset Terrace, newly covered and heated, features broiled steak, lamb, and pork chops, grilled tuna, pan-seared salmon. Horizons has classic cuisine; no spa menu available. The Spa has a juice bar and light snacks.
Facilities: Hydrotherapy underwater massage tubs, couples treatment room, waterfall pools, swimming pool, lap pool. Fitness center with exercise equipment. Sports include golf, tennis, racquetball. Rocking chairs on the terrace and in Great Hall are traditional.
Services & Special programs: Massage, aromatherapy bath, body polish, scrub, herbal wrap, moor mud bath, lymphatic drainage, facials.
Rates: $$
Best Spa Package: Two-night sports/spa package with choice of golf or tennis, use of indoor sports complex.
Credit cards: Most major
Getting There: From Atlanta, by car I–40 (204 miles). By air, Midway Express and USAir commuter flights to Asheville Regional Airport.
What's Nearby: Biltmore Estate, Blue Ridge Parkway, Charlotte, Southern Highlands Folk Art Center, Mount Pisgah, Chimney Rock Park (hiking trails)

NEMACOLIN WOODLANDS RESORT & SPA
Farmington, Pennsylvania

prawling over 1,500 acres of the Laurel Highlands mountains in southwestern Pennsylvania, this is one of the most original resorts in America. Nemacolin's two PGA-rated championship golf courses wrap around a French Renaissance–style chateau and English lodge. The resort's centerpiece is the Woodlands Spa. Energized by natural light, water, wood, and native stone, and designed according to feng shui principles, it is a place that sends spirits soaring.

Framed by trees, boulders, and a reflecting pool, the Woodlands Spa harmonizes natural elements inside with the mountains and meadows surrounding the resort. Designed by environmental architect Clodagh, the three-story spa building was transformed in 1999 by Nemacolin's owners to serve the diverse interests of families and fitness buffs, as well as sophisticated spa-goers. Spaces for aerobics and swimming enjoy woodland views, while treatment rooms are secluded, with nature-inspired furnishings, crystals, and wall coverings in soothing tones. And the menu at Seasons, the Woodland Spa's restaurant, satisfies hearty appetites while meeting the nutritional needs of active or weight-conscious guests.

Scents of the forest, and a cascading waterfall, set the scene as you enter from an arched bridge over the reflecting pool. The garden-terrace restaurant is open to all guests, breakfast through dinner. Group activities include fitness walks, water aerobics, and hikes, plus trail rides, ski lessons, and golf instruction. Or simply relax at the outdoor pool, complete with swim-up bar.

Services range from eight types of massage and nine body therapies to a variety of facials and hydrotherapy baths. Special treatments include a vitamin facial by Dermalogica, to repair skin elasticity and tone by combining vitamin-infused cream cleansing and hydroxy acid exfoliation. Body kurs by Kerstin Florian utilize European moor mud, marine algae, and thermal water salts. Treatments can be reserved individually or as part of a value-added package. The daily facility fee of $20 is waived when you book treatments.

Family-oriented programs let parents share spa experiences with kids. In the beauty salon, teenagers can have a manicure or facial. The Kidz Klub has supervised activity for children ages four to twelve, full or half-day. Saddle up for a trail ride at the Equestrian Center, which has ponies for youngsters; practice target shooting with an instructor (minimum age sixteen) at the Shooting Academy; go to golf school or schedule private lessons at the Golf Academy for adults and juniors (sixteen and under). There are two golf courses, which are open to the public, and Nemacolin guests get reduced greens fees of $125 at the top-rated Mystic Rock course; the fee for eighteen holes at the Links course is

$79 for guests. (Fees are lower after 3:30 P.M.) Winter adds a different outdoor dimension to the activities: downhill and cross-country skiing at Mystic Mountain. Kids' programs, tubing, snowboarding on a half-pipe, and lessons are available.

Accommodations are equally varied. Families can occupy an entire townhouse, or get additional bedrooms in the main lodges for 50 percent off the applicable rate. Rooms at both Chateau Lafayette and the mountain lodge are spacious, tastefully furnished, and have all the usual amenities. Some come with whirlpool bathtub, balcony, and suites.

Whether taking tea, gourmet dining, or luxury pampering, you are king of the mountain.

Water Walk Stimulates Circulation

Adapting a European thermal therapy, the Woodlands Spa has the first American water path. Designed to stimulate circulation and improve immune functions, the experience consists of a guided walk through shallow pools of water, alternately warm and cold, followed by relaxing in a soaking pool infused with salts from European hot springs. Similar to treatments in Baden-Baden and Kneipp spas in Bad Woerishofen, the water path is a sure way to enhance energy and a feeling of well-being. Available by reservation; $65 per session.

Nemacolin Woodlands Resort & Spa
1001 Lafayette Drive
Farmington, Pennsylvania 15437-9901
Phone: (724) 329–8555
Fax: (724) 329–6385
E-mail: colon@nwir.com
Web site: www.nemacolin.com
Season: Year-round
General Manager: Ron Cadrette
Spa Director: Patricia Schneider
Reservations: (800) 422–2736
Spa Appointments: (800) 422–2736
Accommodations: Chateau Lafayette has 124 oversize rooms, including twenty-five suites. The Lodge offers ninety-eight inn-style rooms. Both buildings are linked to the Woodlands Spa via walkway. Townhouses also available.
Meals: Seasons restaurant serves organic food. The Caddy Shack, country club fare; the Golden Trout, regional specialties; Lautrec for contemporary French cuisine.
Facilities: The spa offers hydrotherapy, bodywork, Krauter baths, massage, wraps, facials, hair and nail care; glass-walled fitness center with full line of equipment; indoor swimming pool, therapy pool, and whirlpools for men and women. Swimming pools, fly-fishing, volleyball, croquet, bocce ball, skiing, polo field, sleigh and surrey rides.
Services & Special Programs: Twenty-eight private treatment rooms for massage, body scrubs and wraps, reflexology, shiatsu, and ayurveda. Fitness instruction. Full salon services. Registered dietitian available.
Rates: $$–$$$
Best Spa Package: The Laurel Relaxer half-day package for $190 includes a facial or Swedish massage, body scrub or reflexology, and spa cuisine lunch. Full use of the Woodlands Spa swimming pools, fitness equipment, scheduled group exercise and walks, plus a spa gift.
Credit Cards: Most major
Getting There: Located 61 miles southeast of Pittsburgh International Airport, the resort offers transfers (fee) by limousine. By car, on scenic I–70 west to I–68, exit 14 to Route 40 west; from I–70 east, Route 43 south to Route 40 east.
What's Nearby: Frank Lloyd Wright's Fallingwater and Kentuck Knob; Youghiogheny River whitewater rafting; kayaking; Fort Necessity (French and Indian War)

GREEN VALLEY SPA & TENNIS RESORT

St. George, Utah

rom the decor to the lay of the land to the services, Green Valley Spa & Tennis Resort is an authentic slice of the Southwest. Set amid red rock canyons of Utah, the spa draws inspiration and products from the desert. Combined with an active hiking program, this is one of the best destination spa programs in America.

Rugged terrain changes to rolling high desert hills as you approach St. George. Following trails of Mormon pioneers, hikers head into wilderness areas and the breathtaking heights of Zion National Park. Each day is a new challenge, guided by knowledgeable staffers who encourage you to go the extra mile.

Vistas of mountains against blue sky and multihued desert surround the resort complex. Located within an affluent community of ranch-style homes set on immaculate lawns, Green Valley is an upscale version of the Old West. Spa guests are housed in deluxe suites at Coyote Inn. Spread among cactus gardens and tennis courts, the Coyote suites are the best of the west. A sunny swimming pool is steps from your private patio, and a communal pantry is stocked with refreshments. These secluded suites perfectly complement an active, outdoor-oriented program, pampering the inner person with freshly ground Starbucks coffee beans (regular and decaf), feather bed in front of a real fireplace, two TVs, and microwave oven for food cravings.

Hiking is the main event; groups often depart prior to sunup, avoiding midday heat. Winter schedules allow more time for breakfast, although the weather in southern Utah can be surprisingly warm in January and February. Tourist brochures compare the area to Dixie (there is a Dixie College campus in town, and the Dixie convention center), but St. George's quiet western lifestyle is an attractive alternative to Las Vegas, 120 miles to the south. Gateway to the largest concentration of national parks and monuments in America, the town also hosts the World Senior Games every year in mid-October.

Scampering over rocks and ravines, hikers are awed by contrasting hues and textures of the red sandstone rocks. Bathed in the warm, hazy light of morning sun, Snow Canyon State Park is a place of stunning views. Indian pictographs invite exploration. Longer hikes in Bryce Canyon National Park, as well as Zion, include transportation to trailheads. Water canteens and lunch packs are supplied, and there are warm-up stretches before and after the hike.

Tennis camp is an alternative to hikes. With indoor and outdoor courts, and a team of teaching professionals at the Vic Braden Tennis College, the spa offers choices between pampering and playing. Also available are an indoor golf learning center, and two racquetball courts. A fully equipped gymnasium is open day and night for shape-ups.

Rewarded by deep-tissue massage and soothing soaks scented by desert sage and lavender, your days take on a pleasant balance. Treatments can be scheduled outdoors in warm weather; baths are color-coded

for energy and relaxation, featuring Green Valley's personalized Good Medicine products. Join scheduled sessions of aquacise, step class, stretch, or meditation. Evening programs in the spa's new auditorium include an introduction to Native American healing. And there is line dancing in the gym. Bring your boots and jeans for a vacation that combines New Age holistic healing with New West fun and adventure.

The Body Code

How does your body shape affect your weight and well-being? Green Valley teamed up with Jay Cooper, author of *The Body Code*, to develop a weight management program. After a physical evaluation, you are typed and counseled on everything from diet to exercise. Spa staff coordinate with the counselors on a personalized program that you can continue at home.

Along with workouts, try baths matched to your mood. Processed in the spa lab, mineral salts deposited in desert cliffs by an ancient inland sea are mixed with powdered pearls, pure essential oils, and traces of Vitamin C. Each bath is a sensory experience, color-coded to invigorate or relax your spirits, enhanced by matching flowers and candles. The spa's line of skin care products is called Good Medicine, symbolizing purity honoring the sacred ways of Indian cultures.

Red Rock Renewal, Southwestern Style

Green Valley Spa & Tennis Resort
1871 West Canyon View Drive
St. George, UT 84770
Phone: (435) 628–8060
Fax: (435) 673–4084
E-mail: Request@infowest.com
Web site: www.greenvalleyspa.com
Season: Year-round
General Manager: Alan Coombs
Spa Director: Carole Coombs
Reservations: (800) 237–1068
Spa Appointments: (800) 237–1068
Accommodations: Thirty-five single suites and ten two-bedroom suites at Coyote Inn. Oversize suites have four-poster bed or two queen-size beds with feather mattress, goose down comforters, down pillows. Modern bathroom with 6-foot whirlpool tub. Amenities include robes and leisure suit, fax machine, CD and tape player, TV sets, daily complimentary laundry service. Hospitality lounge with pool table, fireplace, snack bar.
Meals: Three meals daily included in rates. Special diets accommodated with advance request, but choices are limited.
Facilities: Hydrotherapy suite, two aerobics studios, six swimming pools, two saunas, nineteen tennis courts, indoor golf learning center, two racquetball courts, cardiovascular and strength-training equipment.
Services & Special Programs: Massage, reflexology, reiki, mud and herbal wraps, facials, powdered pearl body scrub, mineral bath. Weight management program, tennis/spa package.
Rates: $$
Best Spa Package: Seven-night program includes all meals, daily spa service (fifty minutes), golf and tennis instruction, guided morning hikes, fitness classes, full use of facilities.$3,150–$3,500 single; $2,800–$3,150 double.
Credit Cards: American Express, Discover, MasterCard, Visa
Getting There: From Las Vegas McCarran International Airport, scheduled shuttle van (800–933–8320), ninety minutes; car rental; commuter flights to St. George.
What's Nearby: Zion National Park, Bryce Canyon National Park, Pah Tempe Hot Springs, St. George Mormon Tabernacle, pioneer homes.

THE GREENBRIER

White Sulphur Springs, West Virginia

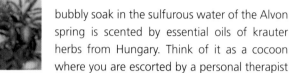

et in the Allegheny Mountains, this monumental Georgian-style hotel is a world unto itself. Founded more than 200 years ago, it is the grande dame of American spa resorts.

Surrounded by 6,500 acres of forest and golf courses, the white-columned hotel is a National Historic Landmark. With its international academy of culinary arts, a private health clinic, tennis academy, and three championship golf courses, a constant stream of activity crosses the marble lobby. The spa will emerge in 2001 with a new look and expanded treatment facilities. In addition, a meditation garden is planned; it will include native plants and herbs designed to soothe the mind and spirit.

The resort's impressive indoor swimming pool is one of the few parts of the 1913 Greenbrier hotel still in use. Lavishly tiled, the 140-foot pool is filled with spring water and the pool area has a juice bar and lounge with garden wicker furniture. All guests can use the pool without charge.

But the famous Greenbrier mineral spring waters flow only in the spa's hydrotherapy baths, where a bubbly soak in the sulfurous water of the Alvon spring is scented by essential oils of krauter herbs from Hungary. Think of it as a cocoon where you are escorted by a personal therapist and treated with cordial Southern care. Select from an extensive menu of services, from body exfoliation to hydrotherapy, facials, and massage. New is a makeup consultation shop, the Perfect Image, which adjoins the spa salon for hair and nail care. Use of exercise equipment and an aerobics studio are charged on an a la carte basis, or as part of packages to be introduced when the new spa opens.

More than fifty recreational activities are offered to guests. In addition to the Sam Snead Golf Academy, there is indoor and outdoor tennis, Land Rover Driving School, croquet, horseback riding, carriage rides, Falconry Academy, skeet- and trapshooting, fishing. Jogging and biking trails take you into the quiet forest, or downtown where a small business center services needs of the community. Scattered around the hotel are thirty shops offering sportswear, gifts, kitchen accessories, and books.

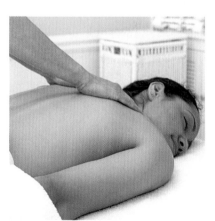

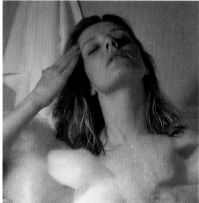

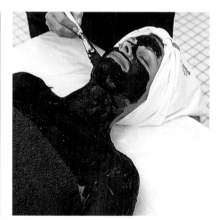

The traditional Greenbrier spa experience starts with a private hydrotherapy bath. Next comes a steam inhalation room enhanced by aromatherapy oils to clear congested sinuses. More hydrotherapy in a Swiss shower or the Scotch hose treatment, to enhance circulation, followed by a body scrub or soothing buff. The finishing touch is a full-body massage with herbal potions.

Medical checkups can be coordinated with a spa program. The fully staffed, privately operated Greenbrier Clinic located on the resort grounds has diagnostic, nutritional, and executive health programs.

Ideal for families, the resort has a movie theater, bowling alley, instruction in shooting and falconry as well as golf and tennis. Staying in one of the seventy-one deluxe cottages and guest houses scattered about the grounds adds privacy and extra space for the kids. Perhaps the most unusual attraction is a once-secret underground bunker built during World War II to be used by the Congress in case of an emergency. Still fully outfitted, the bunker can be toured with a historian leading you through its fascinating history.

A New Look

Treat yourself to a new look while at The Greenbrier Spa. The Perfect Image cosmetic shop is staffed with consultants who can analyze your skin type and suggest the latest shades of eye coloring, lipstick, and sun protection. A signature line of Greenbrier products is available at the spa shop.

When the Greenbrier's first sister spa opened in Savannah, Georgia, at the new Westin Resort, the mineral content of the West Virginia spring water was duplicated for use in the traditional baths, and you can replicate this experience in your bath at home.

Taking the Waters with History

The Greenbrier
300 West Main Street
White Sulphur Springs, WV 24986
Phone: (304) 356–1110
Fax: (304) 536–7854
E-mail: kathryn_tuckwiller@greenbrier.com
Web site: www.greenbrier.com
Season: Year-round
General Manager: Jack Damioli
Spa Director: Kathryn Tuckwiller
Reservations: (800) 624–6070
Spa Appointments: (800) 624–6070
Accommodations: 637 guest rooms, including forty-six suites and seventy-one estate houses. Traditional furniture and draperies, large walk-in closets in the older rooms, TV, the usual amenities, large tiled bathrooms, air-conditioned. (Greenbrier green is used in carpets and window shades.)
Meals: Two meals are included in daily packages. From morning doughnuts and coffee in the lobby to dress-up dinners with a string quartet in the vast dining room, American cuisine shines. Spa selections are low-calorie, with reduced salt and sugar. Alternatives include a cafe called Drapers, and Sam Snead's for pub-style food.
Facilities: Full-service spa with hydrotherapy, salon for hair and nail care. Aerobics studio and cardiovascular/strength-training equipment. Indoor and outdoor swimming pools, saunas, steam rooms, whirlpools. Tennis on five covered courts, fifteen all-weather outdoor courts.
Services & Special Programs: Executive health checkup, massage, skin care, bodywork. Personal trainers and scheduled group exercise. La Verenne cooking weeks; Land Rover driving academy; falconry academy.
Rates: $$$
Best Spa Package: Two-night Spa Escape with hotel room, three meals daily, unlimited use of exercise equipment, Alvon krauter bath and aromatherapy massage, facial, women's hairstyling or men's scalp massage. Cost includes gratuity, tax: $1,433 (available January–March, some weeks in November).
Credit Cards: MasterCard, Visa, American Express
Getting There: From Washington, D.C., by car on I–66 west to I–81 south, I–64 to White Sulphur Springs exit (six hours). By train, Amtrak scheduled service, "The Cardinal" (six hours). The closest airport is in Lewisburg, which has scheduled van service to The Greenbrier.
What's Nearby: New River Gorge National River, Lewisburg (Civil War history), Beckley (coal mine museum).

BANFF SPRINGS HOTEL—SOLACE SPA

Banff, Alberta, Canada

rom the moment you enter this well-established icon in the Canadian Rockies, the sheer size of Banff Springs will awe you. Built in 1888 and modeled on a Scottish baronial castle, the resort, surrounded by mountains and wildlife, is a statement of grandeur. Canadian hospitality reaches its zenith here, where all is done on a grand scale—from the monumental lobby to the indoor saltwater pool. Hospitable touches include fresh fruit, coffee, tea, and water available in the lounges throughout the day.

The resort's 32,000-square-foot, two-level Solace Spa seeks to create a relaxing, stress-free environment. You enter via a spiral staircase and arrive in the reception area where there is a boutique, well-stocked with Kerstin Florian spa products, and a full-service beauty salon.

Check in and begin your tour of the premises. First you'll visit the extensive pool areas, where you should plan to spend a part of the day. The dome-covered mineral pool with its view of the surrounding natural beauty is a masterpiece of architecture, combining the best of both worlds—spa and wilderness. During the

ski season, the idyllic mineral pools of the resort attract even the hardcore skiers.

The Solace Spa is a sanctuary amidst the finest displays of nature, the setting one of most impressive in the world. There are separate areas for men and women, but the gyms are coed. Sixteen treatment rooms offer an excellent repertoire of treatments, such as the Hungarian moor mud wrap, a chamomile body scrub that produces soft, smooth-looking skin. There are also more esoteric treatments, such as the organic black mud facial, the therapeutic thermal mineral bath, and the spirulina body wrap. The spa brochure describes the facilities and details spa treatments and spa etiquette. The spa alerts guests that "arriving late is a breach of etiquette and will shorten the spa treatment."

Although you might not want to tear yourself away from the slopes or the invigorating mountain hikes, there is an excellent schedule of fitness classes throughout the day, starting around 9:00 A.M. Class offerings fluctuate with the seasons, but examples include sessions focusing on the abdominals, stretch-

ing, water aerobics, weight training for women, and full-body workout.

There are no evening programs or speakers, but many recreational options are available at the resort's seventeen restaurants and lounges. Banff Springs with its Solace Spa lives up to its reputation as one of the world's finest resorts. The uncompromising attention to quality and service provides a sky-high experience.

Alpine Acclimatization

An alpine environment, while phenomenally beautiful, can provide distinct health challenges. Although some individuals will not experience symptoms, getting acclimated to high elevations can take days to weeks, during which time the body may experience dehydration, sleeplessness, and even swelling of the hands and feet. The problem can be aggravated if visitors unused to the mountains overexert themselves—they may suffer headaches, extremely sore muscles, severe sunburn, shortness of breath, and even nosebleeds. To enjoy the beauty of the mountains and become acclimated gradually, Banff Springs recommends taking it easy for a little while, increasing water intake, using high SPF sunscreen and lip balm, and limiting caffeine and alcohol consumption.

A Regal Spa with Canadian Charm

Banff Springs Hotel—Solace Spa
405 Spray Avenue
PO Box 960
Banff, Alberta T0L 0C0
Canada
Phone: (403) 762–2211
Fax: (403) 762–5755 (hotel); (403) 762–1766 (spa)
E-mail: bsshres@cphotels.ca
Web site: www.cphotels.com

Season: Year-round

General Manager: Ted Kissane

Spa Director: Gordon Tareta

Reservations: (403) 762–2211 or (800) 404–1772

Spa Appointments: (403) 762–2211 or (800) 404–1772

Accommodations: 770 guest rooms and suites, offering river or mountain views. Chateau deluxe rooms are suitable for up to four guests; Heritage Premier rooms have chandeliers, mock fireplaces, and traditional decor. Junior and one-bedroom suites are also available.

Meals: There are seventeen restaurants in the resort; spa cuisine is served in the Solace Light Restaurant.

Facilities: Solace Spa mineral pool; full-service spa; fitness evaluation; saltwater outdoor pool (heated in winter); outdoor whirlpool; indoor whirlpool; cascading waterfall pool; inhalation and sauna rooms; salon for hair and nails; fitness/cardio room; 27-hole golf course; 76,000 square feet of meeting and conference facilities.

Services & Special Programs: Interpretative hiking and guided mountaineering program; horseback riding; guided snowshoeing expeditions; ski trips to Norquay, Sunshine, and Lake Louise ski areas; tours of Banff National Park.

Rates: $$

Best Spa Package: The Ultimate Retreat includes accommodations for three nights in a deluxe chateau room; breakfast, lunch, and dinner daily; choice of one of four therapeutic spa programs: thalassotherapy, thermal mineral, aromatic, or fitness. The aromatic program, for example, might include a full-body scrub, herbal wrap, massage, facial, manicure, and pedicure. From $1,883 to $2,211 per person, double occupancy, depending on the season.

Credit Cards: Most major

Getting There: From Calgary International Airport, transfer by limo, bus, or van. By car, Banff Springs is 80 miles west of Calgary on the TransCanada Highway.

What's Nearby: The Columbia Icefield, Banff National Park, three major ski areas, Banff Center for the Arts.

CENTRE DE SANTÉ D'EASTMAN

Eastman, Quebec, Canada

Let among farming villages in the eastern townships an hour southeast of Montreal, the town of Eastman is a cluster of Victorian homes and New England–style churches, antiques shops, and crafts studios. A crossroad for skiers heading to nearby slopes, and summer cottagers, Eastman is on the old stage coach road between New York and Montreal, chemin des Diligences. Amid this bucolic charm is one of the best country spas in North America.

Turning off chemin des Diligences, you discover a 315-acre nature preserve that harbors the Centre de Santé d'Eastman, also known as the Eastman Health Center. There is an old barn that no longer stables horses and a new therapy building that looks more like a ski chalet than a spa. Totally secluded among spruce and pine trees, rustic wooden lodges offer modern comforts in forty-five guest rooms on ten acres. The natural beauty and quiet are an instant tranquilizer.

Founded in 1977 as a center for naturopathy, Eastman evolved gradually as a full-service destination spa. Under the direction of founder/owner Jocelyna Dubuc, the center's growth climaxed in 1999 with the opening of a two-story pavilion that houses all of the treatment and relaxation rooms, a Watsu pool, swimming pool, hammam steam room and hydrotherapy baths. In addition to thirteen guest rooms, the building has a restaurant and lounge, which also serve as the social center for the town.

When selecting treatments (called *soins* in bilingual Quebec), you can opt for European hydrotherapy or California massage. Among unique experiences is an invigorating oxygen and steam bath, in which your head pokes out of a covered tub while showers of carbon dioxide, oxygen, and water promote blood circulation and oxygenation. Another way to perk up your skin during the seasonal dryness of winter is to have a body peeling done with sea salts and loofah, followed by an algae wrap, stimulating algae bath, and rub-down with moisturizing cream to finish.

With a naturopathic doctor on staff, the center offers programs that combine fitness and well-being. Shape-ups can start with something as simple as walking mindfully. "It's important to vary the rhythm," explains a trainer. "The heart is a muscle. Keeping one constant rate, as you often do when jogging, isn't very effective." So the morning walks become a test of skills as well as stamina.

The new dining room has the informality of a country inn, and a chef who creates spa cuisine with French flair. Menus tend toward vegetarian, but include fish, chicken, even rabbit. Between buffets of home-baked breads and muffins, farm-fresh yogurt and vegetables, fruit and herbal teas, you will not go hungry here.

The serious side of Eastman Health Center includes chiropractic and homeopathy sessions, applied kinesiology for rehabilitation after surgery or accidents, and workshops on a range of lifestyle issues. Dubuc and her staff (most of whom are English-speaking) present a caring, low-key approach, without a hint of dogmatic preaching on healthy living.

Enjoying the great outdoors is part of the program. Surrounded by gentle hills and woods crisscrossed by trails, with the majestic peak of Mount Orford lording over it all, you can don snowshoes or cross-country skis to explore the winter landscape. There are 8 kilometers of groomed ski trails, and 15 kilometers for hikes, on the center's property. In fact, walks through the frosty forest are a popular option on long winter nights. If you haven't brought gear, an outfitter named O'Kataventures rents snowshoes and skis (and mountain bikes in summer).

When it's time for a tune-up or self-indulgence, this is a hideaway with a big heart and affordable prices.

Naturopathic Shape-up Taps Energy Naturally

Getting into shape doesn't require strenuous exercise at the Eastman Center. A simple walking technique can be just as effective than many performance sports. Guided by physical fitness professionals, the walking program is part of a fifteen-day package that includes workshops on nutrition and group exercise classes. Supervised by a naturopathic specialist, participants learn healthy food combinations, how to select food rich in nutrients to boost energy. Stretching, posture, and balance are improved through workouts with free weights, FitBalls, and in the pool. Hikes along country roads and on the slopes of Mount Orford are designed to burn fat while increasing cardiovascular capacity. The bucolic charm of Quebec can work wonders.

Centre de Santé d'Eastman
895, chemin des Diligences
Eastman, Quebec J0E 1P0
Canada
Phone: (450) 297–3009
Fax: (450) 297–3370
E-mail: courrier@spa-eastman-com
Web site: www.spa-eastman.com

Season: Year-round

General Manager: Jocelyna Dubuc

Reservations: (800) 665–5272

Spa Appointments: (800) 655–5272

Accommodations: Forty-five rooms, including thirteen junior suites with fireplaces in the main building. Guests are housed in nine two-story lodges (pavilions) furnished in simple, modern style; the older units are rustic, reminiscent of summer camp. All rooms have private bathroom with shower or tub, air-conditioning.

Meals: Three meals daily, plus afternoon break, included in spa package. Breakfast buffet includes cereal, eggs, toast, French toast, coffee, herbal teas, and fruit juices. Lunch menu offers wheat soup with two beans, salad buffet, Norwegian-style cucumber salad, leek quiche. Supper features fettucini or baked chicken with vegetables, roast duckling, or poached salmon.

Facilities: The main building houses twenty-four treatment rooms, indoor swimming pool, Watsu pool, steam room, hydrotherapy tubs.

Services & Special Programs: Hydrotherapy, Watsu (shiatsu in pool), massage, lymphatic drainage, reflexology, shiatsu, shower massage, oxygen bath, aromatherapy, body wraps and peel, pressotherapy leggings, aesthetic care of nails and face. Cure programs for stress, weight loss, body cleansing.

Rates: $$

Best Spa Package: Seven-day Back-in-Shape fitness program with personal trainer and naturopathic services to develop a personal shape-up and home regimen. Includes walks, relaxation classes, and fitness assessment. $1,150 single, $895 per person double, plus tax; includes $225 credit for treatments.

Credit Cards: American Express, MasterCard, Visa

Getting There: From Montreal by car, Autoroute 10, exit 106 to Route 245 toward Eastman, then Route 112 toward chemin du Lac d'Argent, chemin des Diligences (one hour).

What's Nearby: Vermont, New Hampshire, New York

ECHO VALLEY RANCH: RESORT
Clinton, British Columbia, Canada

addle up for a unique adventure at Echo Valley Ranch. Amid the scenic splendor of the Canadian Rockies, a traditional Thai pavilion shimmers in a stand of pine and maple trees. A bit of the East has come west.

Combining a working ranch with an exotic spa is the kind of trans-Pacific experience that British Columbia seems to inspire. When the ranch owners, Norm and Nan Dove, met the architect who designed a summer palace for the king of Thailand, they conceived a structure that brings both worlds together. Completed in the summer of 2000, the Baan Thai pavilion has two houses equipped for spa treatments. Facing a tiled open-air courtyard, the pavilion is a peaceful place that enhances balance in body and mind.

On the top deck of the Baan Thai you can practice yoga or simply enjoy the scenery. Downstairs, exercise equipment is arranged to take advantage of natural light. There is an open space for workshops and group workouts. Crafted of teak wood, the entire two-story structure seems to have been transported from Thailand, yet houses the latest in hydrotherapy and skin care.

Vast wilderness explored by prospectors during the Gold Rush era is now the home of a golden pavilion staffed by Thai aestheticians. Coexisting comfortably with the spa, the ranch's horseback riding program features trail rides and training with forty Tennessee Walker thoroughbreds. Acres of meadows, 185 head of cattle, falconry flights, and an herb garden add to the feeling that you have entered a realm of nature where all things are in harmony.

Unwinding after a day on the trail, you can enjoy an indoor swimming pool, sauna, and gym. Three deluxe log lodges and cabins accommodate twenty-four guests most of the time, up to thirty-six as a group.

Forget roughing it; guest rooms feature huge beds with fluffy duvets, modern toilet and shower. Some rooms have lofts where teenagers (minimum age thirteen) can bring sleeping bags. Cabins are ideal for families; one has romantic furnishings for honeymooners.

Meals are served in the main lodge, a brawny three-story structure of one-hundred-year-old spruce logs that resembles a ranch house designed for corporate getaways. Ranch host Norm Dove can pilot one of the planes stabled on the landing strip, discuss wines of western Canada, and talk international business. On request, ranch hands take you fly-fishing, white-water

rafting, and hiking. Dove leads wildlife expeditions to Fraser River Canyon. In winter showshoeing, skiing, ice skating, ice fishing, and sleigh rides add to the spa and riding options.

Born in Bangkok, Nan Dove brought back Thai silks as well as specialists in Thai massage for the new spa. This is about as authentic as it gets. Think of the experience as a first-class spa hotel with horses, plus a taste of Thailand.

A Lifestyle Match

The focus of the fitness and nutrition programs at the ranch comes from a book entitled _Eat Right for Your Type_ by R. D. Adamo, M.D. The concept: Your correct diet is a function of your blood group. Chef Kim Madsen, a native of Denmark, brings world-class culinary talent to the ranch kitchen. Honored in New York at James Beard House, Madsen demonstrates heart-healthy cooking in his big, open-counter kitchen. Understanding your body type helps Madsen match food for maximum energy. Bring medical records with your blood type to set up a special diet.

East Meets West in Canadian Cowboy Country

Echo Valley Ranch Resort
Clinton, British Columbia V0K 1K0
Canada
Phone: (250) 459–2386
Fax: (250) 459–0086
Web site: www.evranch.com

Season: Year-round
General Manager: Norm Dove
Spa Director: Nan Dove
Reservations: (800) 253–8831
Spa Appointments: (800) 253–8831
Accommodations: Deluxe log lodges with private bedrooms for up to thirty-six guests. Choice rooms have private balcony, bathroom with shower or tub, twin or king-size beds with down-filled duvet. Main lodge has large lounge, leather furniture, large-screen TV, billiards, board games, outdoor hot tub.

Meals: Buffet breakfast, lunch, and seated dinner family-style included in daily room tariff. Fresh vegetables and herbs from organic farms, ranch-bred beef, pork, and poultry, prized salmon from nearby rivers.

Facilities: Spa complex has hydrotherapy tub, wet table, jet shower, steam room, massage room, fitness center with exercise equipment. Indoor swimming pool with spring water in separate building.

Services & Special Programs: Trail rides included in daily program price. Available a la carte: massage, facials, body wrap, aromatherapy bath. Cooking class and workshop on herbal gardening, falconry demonstration, roping and horse training demonstration are part of all-inclusive package. Wildlife safari, white-water rafting, fly-fishing by float plane (fee) on request.

Rates: $$

Best Spa Package: Ranch Revitalizer three-night program with spa treatments, available June through September. $894 per person double occupancy, $979 single, plus tax.

Credit Cards: American Express, MasterCard, Visa

Getting There: From Vancouver by car, scenic route via Fraser River valley to Highway 97; at Clinton pick up Kelly Lake Road (10 kilometers) to Jesmond Road (seven hours). By air, scheduled flights Sundays to/from the ranch (one hour) by North Vancouver Air; private plane landing strip. By train, British Canadian Rail to Clinton, free transfer (seven hours).

What's Nearby: Whistler ski area, Cariboo Trail, Fraser River, High Bar Indian Band teepee village, Barkerville Gold Rush ghost town.

THE HILLS HEALTH RANCH

British Columbia, Canada

destination spa within a wilderness ranch, The Hills has pioneered wellness vacations since 1985. Surrounded by 20,000 acres of western high country, the resort boasts the largest staff of health and wellness professionals in all of Canada.

Housed in one of the ranch's woodsy chalets, you join an informal group for daily hikes and rides, as well as workshops on health and fitness. While discussion topics range from the latest research results on obesity to the benefits of aromatherapy, the emphasis is on learning how to balance stress in your life. Programs focus on athletes and the mature person, including maintaining a healthy heart through exercise and nutrition. You can saddle up for the "horse whisperer" experience, or go for weight loss weeks. Also offered are short retreats devoted to hiking, beauty, and executive renewal.

Helping you achieve balance, the spa has an extensive menu of more than fifty healing body and beauty treatments. Earthy, natural products such as organically processed wild rosehip and chamomile oil are used in bodywork and facials. In the hands of licensed professional aestheticians, you gain an immediate sense of relaxation. For longer-lasting results, a take-home program and products are recommended.

All of these activities take place in the main lodge, where sixteen treatment rooms, an indoor swimming pool, exercise studio, and restaurant are located. Run like a guest ranch, the family-oriented resort also has stables with thirty riding horses and a resident wrangler, and a ski lodge for winter recreation. You can join morning and afternoon horseback rides most of the year, and explore over 130 miles of trails. Snow-making equipment assures downhill skiing, snowboarding, and tubing in the night-lit winter play park.

Far from rustic, this is more dude ranch than luxury resort. Bring jeans, boots, and sweaters along with workout clothing, or plan a shopping spree in the nearby town of Williams Lake. In addition to cattle ranches, the area's main industry is logging. Stacks of timber await processing at plants near Williams Lake, which also hosts a major rodeo. Evening entertainment can be line dancing, a hayride, and campfire at a teepee.

Heart-healthy fare is featured in the main dining room, and a cafe in the ski lodge takes care of

winter crowds. An extensive menu allows choices of calorie-counted food or typical ranch specialties, from barbecue to steaks and salmon. If you're trying to lose weight, there's a thirty-day package that includes all meals.

Having created the first Canadian wellness center, the ranch's resident owners devote a lot of personal attention to guests' well-being. In the homey dining room, staff are always on hand to discuss the day's activities, what's on the menu, and things to see in the area. Offering an all-inclusive program of indoor aerobics and fitness workouts, healthy meals, trail rides and guided treks over rolling ranch land around lakes and forests, The Hills turns "howdy" into a cheerful affirmation of health.

Healthy Hip Rose Harvest

Wild rose bushes grow in abundance on the ranch's Cariboo meadows. July is best time to enjoy full-bloom, but rose hip harvest in fall is when spa guests get the advantage of some of the world's best and richest creams to enhance body and skin conditions. Many gallons of Cariboo rose hips are handpicked, dried, then crushed into powder in a unique grinding process that preserves the vitamin and mineral content of the flowers. Taken as an infusion, rose hips are a ranch remedy for bladder and kidney problems, and prevention of colds. The Cariboo rose hip cream made locally is used in facials to heal broken capillaries, and helps with varicose or spider veins on the face and legs. The Hills' special formula adds rose hip powder to cold-pressed grapeseed oil, which is high in vitamin E and niacin—great for skin health and healing.

The Hills Health Ranch
Box 26, 108 Mile Ranch
British Columbia V0K 2Z0
Canada
Phone: (250) 791–5225
Fax: (250) 791–6384
E-mail: thehills@bcinternet.net
Web site: www.spabc.com
Season: Year-round
General Manager: Patrick Corbett
Spa Director: Juanita Corbett
Reservations: (250) 791–5225
Accommodations: Ranch House with ten deluxe junior suites, sixteen large rooms in two-story manor house, all with balcony, air-conditioning, private bathroom. Pine furniture, country comforters on beds. Families and small groups are housed in twenty private chalets.
Meals: Calorie-counted spa cuisine included in vacation packages, with options for ranch-style food. Lunch can be chicken fajita with sour cream and salsa; dinner choices include baked salmon with asparagus, venison in peppercorn-maple sauce, seasonal vegetables.
Facilities: Indoor swimming pool, aerobics studio, fitness center with free weights, cadiovascular and strength-training equipment. Spa suite with sixteen treatment rooms in main lodge. Full-time riding program on premises; ski lodge open to day guests.
Services & Special Programs: Scheduled group exercise, guided hikes, trail rides. Spa services include massage, reflexology, full-body mud pack, herbal wrap, aromatherapy facial, loofah scrub. Thirty-day weight loss program includes supervised diet, personal training with exercise physiologist. Children's programs for riding and skiing.
Rates: $
Best Spa Package: Six-night Executive Renewal program includes all ranch activity plus daily stress-management sessions and massage. $1,355 single, $1,155 double, plus tax and gratuity.
Credit Cards: American Express, MasterCard, Visa
Getting There: By car through the Canadian Rockies from Vancouver, or points along the U.S. border, Highway 97 to 108 Mile Ranch (5 hours). By air, scheduled flights to Williams Lake on Air Canada (1 hour). By train from Vancouver, British Canadian Rail's Cariboo Dayliner (7½ hours).
What's Nearby: Cariboo Trail historic sites, Williams Lake western art gallery.

STE. ANNE'S COUNTRY INN & SPA

Lake Ontario, Canada

baronial stone mansion overlooking Lake Ontario is the centerpiece of Ste. Anne's Country Inn & Spa. Operated like a destination spa, it's also popular with young Toronto professionals as a day spa excursion. But the laid-back ambience is conducive to long weekends, with sybaritic soaks in the hot tub and sunset walks.

Emerging from hectic traffic on Highway 401, you are suddenly surrounded by the farms and open meadows of Northumberland Hills. Toronto is less than an hour's drive, yet the air here feels soft, touched by breezes from the lake. And it is quiet, almost hushed, as couples stroll the grounds. In the main lounge, guests fix tea in the pantry, read, and get oriented with other guests. There is nothing high-tech in sight.

Downstairs is a rabbit warren of treatment rooms, locker rooms for men and women, steam room, and the mud bath—the only one of its kind in the eastern part of Canada and the United States. Two specially designed ceramic-tile vats heat moor mud, an organic skin cleanser that soothes muscular pains. Mud baths aren't for everybody. You get either a sense of being connected to nature or claustrophobia.

The Aveda spa menu here follows traditional lines: facials and skin care, bodywork, hairstyling, and nail treatments. Using pure essences of flowers and herbs, Aveda products complement the inn's nature-oriented ambience—not too rustic or too sophisticated, but a comforting place where body and mind are in balance.

One of the unique features is a "twinning" hydrotherapy room, where wet treatments get an added dimension. As you relax on the table, two therapists synchronize moves to scrub your body with sea salts, followed by application of moisturizer. And there are built-in showers, with piles of fluffy towels stacked in antique wooden cupboards.

Mornings start with guided stretches and meditation in an aerobics studio with wide windows over-looking lawns that slope toward Lake Ontario. On a clear day, the lake is more than visible; the horizon seems to expand, uniting water and sky. Brilliant sunlight reflects off the lake, giving the air an invigorating quality that's just right for bike trips to nearby villages, hikes, and walks on the estate's trails.

Meals are a combination of country and spa cuisine, featuring local produce and venison, and herbs from the inn's organic garden. Bread is baked daily (and can be wrapped to take home). Calories are not discussed, but the chef accommodates special diet requests. And you can bring your own wine.

Rooms at the inn come in many sizes and shapes. Several suites are in small tower wings connected to the manor house. Native stone and slate, topped by copper turrets, give the buildings an Old World look. Recent additions were skillfully blended with the original structure, allowing expansion of the dining room. Some bathrooms have cast-iron soaking tubs.

There are a few pieces of exercise equipment—treadmill, bike, rower, ski simulator—but most of the time guests lounge in spa robe and slippers, or soak in the outdoor hot tubs. Swimming pools are heated for year-round use (one has an underwater current). A bottling plant taps into the inn's natural aquifer, which supplies pure drinking water and fills the pools. Three clay-surface tennis courts are available, free of charge, and racquets are on loan. Borrow a bike or drive to nearby vineyards and antiques shops. Hiking the woodland trail, you're likely to encounter a herd of deer raised by a commercial rancher. Innkeeper Jim Corcoran may even take you sailing.

Mud Matters

Thousands of years ago, when the last glaciers melted, the land in what is now the St. Lawrence and Ottawa Valleys was so depressed by the weight of glacial meltwater that salt water flowed in from the Atlantic Ocean, forming an inland sea. Millennia passed as vast deposits of Leda clay were ground into rocky flour and deposited as sediment on the floor of this inland sea. Naturally rich in minerals and organic trace elements, the mud is processed and sterilized by an Ontario firm, Golden Moor, for bath use. It is mixed with a thickener, sodium betonite clay from Saskatchewan. Maintained at high temperature, and sterilized between treatments, the moore mud feels really neat on sore and tired muscles.

Romantic Escape for Sybarites

Ste. Anne's Country Inn & Spa
RR1, Grafton, Ontario K0K 2G0
Canada
Phone: (905) 349–2493
Fax: (905) 349–3531
E-mail: info@steannes.com
Web site: www.steannes.com
Season: Year-round
General Manager: Jim Corcoran
Reservations: (888) 346–6772
Spa Appointments: (888) 346–6772
Accommodations: Manor house with ten bedrooms, eight house suites, all air-conditioned, with private bathroom. All with fireplace, carved wooden beds, or a queen-size four-poster. Completely nonsmoking. Amenities include robes and slippers, TV.
Meals: Three meals included in daily tariff. Breakfast includes eggs or egg white omelette, homemade muesli, country breads. Dinner can be baked Chilean sea bass, wild mushroom and tomato risotto, venison steak, Atlantic salmon or char.
Facilities: Mud baths, aerobics studio, hydrotherapy tubs, steam room and sauna, outdoor lap pools, cold plunge pool, current pool, hot tubs, Vichy shower, Scotch hose.
Services & Special Programs: Scheduled group exercise and hikes. Spa services a la carte: massage, Swedish or Thai, shiatsu and reflexology, aromatherapy facial, sea salt body scrub, herbal wrap, mud bath, manicure/pedicure.
Rates: $
Best Spa Package: Stress Maintenance two-night program with all meals, accommodation, mud wrap, acupressure massage, flower essence scalp massage, customized facial for men and women, pedicure, evening relaxation sessions. Cost is $459 per person, based on double occupancy, plus tax and 12 percent service charge.
Credit Cards: American Express, MasterCard, Visa
Getting There: From Toronto, by car on Highway 401 to exit 487 (Grafton/Centreton), north on Aird Street to Academy Hill Road, left onto Massey Road (ninety minutes); by train, VIA Rail to Cobourg, complimentary limousine transfer.
What's Nearby: Presqui'le Provincial Park (bird-watching, beaches, marsh walk), Victorian Cobourg (Marie Dressler memorabilia museum), marina, Port Hope (antiques), golf courses, wineries, Niagara-on-the-Lake (Shaw Theatre Festival).

FOUR SEASONS RESORT PUNTA MITA—
APUANE SPA

Punta Mita, Mexico

his veritable Garden of Eden is located on the northern tip of the Bahia de Banderas, one of the world's largest natural bays. The Four Seasons Resort, with its stunning Apuane Spa, is a part of a new 2,716-acre development. Punta Mita means "tip of the arrow," and for centuries this deserted stretch of coastline was virtually tourist free. Until construction began at the resort, there was no electricity, running water, or phone lines. Today, the luxury resort coexists beautifully with the surrounding tropical environment.

Offering chic tropical decor in accommodations secreted away in thirteen thatched and red-tiled casitas, Punta Mita is the site of the best surfing beaches along the coast and irresistible spa treatments.

In this lush seaside setting overlooking the Pacific Ocean, the stress of the high-tech world slips away.

What better place to erect a world-class spa offering variations on traditional massage, such as the Punta Mita, a fifty- or eighty-minute treatment that incorporates tequila, indigenous sage oil, and Mexican healing techniques. The fruit scrub and the Punta Mita refresher facial will further convince you that you are in paradise. The full-service Apuane Spa offers massage and skin-care treatments, separate men's and women's steam rooms and dressing rooms, as well as a beauty salon and health club.

The guest rooms and suites are furnished in a style befitting a luxurious Mexican home, all with modern conveniences, including computer modems, color television, and two-line speaker phones. The secluded accommodations range from casita rooms with private terraces to one- to three-bedroom suites.

The distinctive flavors of nuevo latino cuisine, as

Four Seasons Resort Punta Mita—Apuane Spa
Punta Mita, Bahia de Banderas
Nyarit, Mexico 63734
Phone: 523–291–6000
Fax: 523–291–6060
Web site: www.fourseasons.com

Season: Year-round

General Manager: Ricardo Acevedo

Spa Director: Jeremy McCarthy

Fitness Director: Nora Orozco

Reservations: 523–291–6000 or (800) 332–3442

Accommodations: 140 guest rooms and suites housed in clay-tile roofed casitas, most with private plunge pools. In-room amenities include fax, terry bathrobes, private bar, television, telephones, in-room safe, pay-per-view movies.

Meals: Ketsi Pool Restaurant and Bar serves all meals; the Aramara is open for breakfast and dinner; the terrace bar is open from 5:00 P.M. to 1:00 A.M.

Facilities: A private 18-hole Jack Nicklaus–designed golf course; four night-lit tennis courts; large free-form pool with whirlpool; white-sand beach. Apuane Spa: eight massage rooms, two wet-treatment rooms, skin-care treatments, beauty salon, separate men's and women's sauna and steam rooms and locker/dressing rooms; health club with equipment.

Services & Special Programs: Airport transportation; complimentary children's services; nonsmoking rooms; twenty-four hour concierge; sailboat and powerboat charters, deep-sea fishing trips, surfing trips; seasonal whale watching and sea turtle hatching tours.

Rates: $$$

Best Spa Package: El Dia de Belleza (Day of Beauty) starts with a Swedish massage, followed by a deep cleansing facial. The three-and-one-half-hour package ends with a manicure and pedicure. Cost is $311. Accommodations during the high season, October 1–June 30, start at $590 single or double occupancy; during the low season, July 1–September 30, the rates start at $390.

Credit Cards: American Express, MasterCard, Visa

Getting There: The resort is a thirty-minute ride northwest of the Puerto Vallarta International Airport. The concierge can arrange transportation.

What's Nearby: Deep-sea fishing and other water sports; Los Veneros Beach Club with ecological park and artisan center; a horseback tour of Mismalya jungle.

well as a range of seafood and international dishes, dominate the menus at Punta Mita. Spa-goers will delight in the Four Seasons's own alternative cuisine menu choices, which limit cholesterol, sodium, and calories. The Ketsi Pool Restaurant and Bar, located in the pool area, offers spectacular ocean views. The Aramara Restaurant, with outdoor bar/terrace, has live music beginning each night at sunset.

The Four Seasonss' deluxe touches are found everywhere. If you yearn to indulge your senses in a quiet corner of Mexico, this is the place to make it happen.

More Than One Way to Sip Your Tequila

While some men are reluctant to experience the more esoteric spa treatments, those offered here in an ultraprivate ambience are too tantalizing to resist. The Man for All Seasons Facial, a cleansing and nutritive facial designed to neutralize the impact of stress, sun, and sports, as well as the harsh abrasives the male skin endures, will leave the skin feeling younger than springtime. El Dia del Guapo (The Handsome Man) package starts with a salt scrub followed by a relaxing Punta Mita massage. Men, if you think most lotions and potions don't pack a punch, this massage is your answer—the secret massage ingredient is tequila! The Volcanic Mud Wrap is another serious step for men on the verge of loving spas; the black mud stimulates metabolic functions and rejuvenates skin and body. Olé!

LAS VENTANAS AL PARAISO

Cabo San Lucas, Mexico

s you enter this stunning golf and spa resort, passing through the gates, your senses are confronted by "The Windows of Paradise," the translation of this aptly named enclave. Located at the southern tip of Mexico's 1,000-mile-long Baja Peninsula, where the desert meets the Sea of Cortez, this flower-filled retreat offers a distinct personality. Forget cookie-cutter, high-rise hotels, because once you experience the sheer drama of this Mexican Mediterranean-style getaway, you will never think about resorts in quite the same way. Original works of art are showcased throughout Las Ventanas. Woodcarvings, raised pebble walkways, and hand-painted accents, adorning furnishings and fireplaces, add charm and beauty.

The heart of this stunning resort is its spa, where out-of-the-ordinary treatments are the norm—such as the nopal anti-cellulite and detox wrap (featuring the special powers of Mexico's nopal cactus), the volcanic clay purification treatment, and the Tepezcohuite healing wrap. There are ample choices in facials, a half-dozen massage therapies, and eight exfoliation treatments. Hippocrates himself, the father of medicine, reputedly said, "The way to health is to have an aromatic bath and scented massage every day." Taking that seriously, the healing waters include a milk whey bath (said to be Cleopatra's secret weapon), which is prescribed for healing and restoring dry, sensitive skin. Then there are also an old-fashioned mustard bath, an antioxidant green tea bath, and a milk and honey wrap. Lovers are often seduced by the massage for two. New Agers are inclined toward the holistic crystal healing massage, which uses ancient Shamanistic purifi-

cation techniques to induce relaxation and generate healing memory patterns.

Adjacent to Las Ventanas is Cabo Real Golf Course, designed by Robert Trent Jones II, which winds down from the desert hills to the white-sand beaches of the Sea of Cortez, offering eighteen holes of dramatic natural beauty.

The restaurant provides bounty from the sea, with a wide variety of fish and seafood entrees, such as grilled snapper, Baja shellfish, and seared rare tuna. Light fare is included on the menu as well, with spa-compatible salads, low-fat yogurt soup, and a tomato-coriander glazed chicken breast. Room service is available twenty-four hours a day.

Spacious guest rooms and suites all open to the ocean, the coastline, or the golf course. The decor is handcrafted and features raised bed platforms, dressing areas, and glass doors to private terraces. Suite terraces host combination splash pools/Jacuzzis.

Las Ventanas al Paraiso
KM 19.5 Carretera Transpeninsular
Cabo San Lucas, San Jose del Cabo
Baja California Sur, Mexico 23400
Phone: 52–114–40300
Fax: 52–114–40301 or 214–880–4301
E-mail: pgworld@aol.com
Web site: www.rosewood-hotels.com

Season: Year-round (warm, arid climate; about 350 days of sunshine)

General Manager: Edward Steiner

Spa Director: Angel Stewart

Reservations: 888–525–0483

Spa Appointments: 888–525–0483

Accommodations: The sixty-one guest accommodations include fifty-six suites, four one-bedroom superior suites, and a three-bedroom suite with three baths, private pool, and roof-top terrace.

Meals: The Sea Grill offers open-air patio dining, indoor dining, and dining in the guest room or suite. Twenty-four-hour room service.

Facilities: Full-service spa; a Fit Plus package with a fitness profile, lifestyle assessment, body composition analysis and instruction; cardiovascular machines and resistance equipment; personal trainers; beauty salon; 18-hole golf course.

Services & Special Programs: Snorkeling and scuba diving; sportfishing; sailing; kayaking; windsurfing; surfing; desert excursions; horseback riding; sunset cocktail cruises; whale watching; and marine wildlife expeditions.

Rates: $$$

Best Spa Package: The Spa Discovery Package is a three-night program for two that includes accommodations (in a junior suite), round-trip airport transfers, breakfast and dinner daily, private mind/body evaluations, program planning session, and aromatic customization (personally designed essential oils); sage foot bath, neck/shoulder massage, aromatherapy loofah salt glow, aromatherapy facial, moisturizing aloe, tea tree, and lavender wrap, aromatherapy massage, hot oil scalp massage, foot reflexology, two fifty-minute stretch/yoga classes, and use of the spa and gym facilities. $2,900 for two; tax and service additional.

Credit Cards: Most major

Getting There: Major airlines, such as America West, serve the San Jose Del Cabo Airport. Private airport transfers are provided if you book a package.

What's Nearby: Cabo San Lucas with nightclubs, shops, cafes on the sand, and a variety of restaurants.

Bringing an unprecedented level of luxury to Los Cabos, Las Ventanas is a charismatic spa and golf resort with mesmerizing views, nearly perfect weather, and enchanting treatments to lift mind, body, and spirit.

RANCHO LA PUERTA
Baja California

ancho la Puerta, in a small Mexican border town 45 miles east of San Diego, has endeared itself to three generations of health enthusiasts since it was established in 1940 by Edmund and Deborah Szekely. Today this spa, which resembles a quiet Mexican village, accommodates up to 150 guests within its 575 lush acres of gardens and paths.

"Siempre mejor" (always better) is the key to the Rancho's success; there is always something new and better on the agenda, such as the labyrinth, where guests can take a guided meditation walk. Guests come here from all walks of life and from all social and economic levels. Breakfast and lunch are served buffet-style; dinner is served by the waitstaff. You may be seated at a table with an astounding range of spago-ers, from a movie star to a psychiatrist and everyone in between. The ambience is informal; guests dress casu-ally throughout the week-long program, which begins every Saturday.

Each fitness week offers as many as eighty activities. The early-morning hike and exercise program form the cornerstone of the Rancho. There are ten options, including the early-bird hikes, two 6:30 A.M. hikes, and a meadow hike at 7:00 A.M. It's best to view this as a progressive week. Guests are encouraged to start at their own level and partici-

pate gradually in more challenging choices. Many fitness classes are scheduled for the morning so that by lunch you can pat yourself on the back for having already participated. Among those from which to choose are aerobics, power walking, and weight-training. After lunch, which showcases recipes developed by chef Bill Wavrin, it is time to relax with a massage, herbal wrap, facial, or the latest on the massage menu, called the Hot Stone. The new Health Center features spacious treatment rooms, original art, an immaculate locker room, and well-trained therapists.

Guests congregate in the main lounge to sign up for their favorite activities, ranging from an hour with Grandfather Raven (a Native American who talks about casting bones and stones) to the 4-mile vegetable garden breakfast hike, both offered once a week.

The unique accommoda-tions are scattered through-out the property. The Rancho seems immense at first, but every structure is well lit and signed (although new guests still ask directions the first few days). The villa studios and suites, in a lush garden setting, are at the high end of the price range; they include in-room breakfast service in the winter and poolside breakfast service in the summer. The rancheras and haciendas are designed

in Mexican colonial style and, in keeping with all of the buildings, are accented with local arts and crafts. There are single accommodations in this category.

Rancho la Puerta has a loyal following. You might meet guests who've been here twenty times or more (they're recognized at the final dinner). The spa glow seen on the Rancho's guests stems from a harmonious flow of activities, healthy dining, and the upbeat attitude of a caring staff.

An Inner Journey to Personal Bliss

The fitness director at Rancho la Puerta, Phyllis Pilgrim, met the Dalai Lama in 1999. The knowledge she gained from this experience has influenced the tone she sets for her popular class, the "Inner Journey," offered at 4:00 P.M. daily. "Life is short so you must make the most of it," she says. "Think about what you are going to do that will make you feel good at the end of the day. Open your senses daily to appreciate what is around you." Pilgrim encourages guests to appreciate the aromas, the gardens, and the tranquillity of the moment. She believes that a "great metaphor for life" is practicing choice. At the ranch this happens the first day, as the guest may choose among seven group workouts. Pilgrim believes this is practical training for life.

Rancho La Puerta
Tecate, Baja California
Mexico
PO Box 463057
Escondido, CA 92046
Phone: 526–654–1155
Fax: 526–654–1108
Web site: www.rancholapuerta.com
Season: Year-round
General Manager: Jose Manuel Jasso
Fitness Director: Phyllis Pilgrim
Reservations: (760) 744–4222 or (800) 443–7565
Accommodations: Cottages (rancheras and haciendas) with studio bedrooms, private patios and gardens. Villa studios and villa suites are cottages in a parklike garden setting with nearby swimming pool and hot tub; all have fireplaces.
Meals: All meals and snacks are included. Fresh fish twice daily, vegetarian dishes, plenty of greens, legumes, whole grains and other fibers, little fat or salt, and no white flour or refined sugar.
Facilities: The spa offers a comprehensive hiking program on 3,000 acres of rolling, natural terrain; seventy fitness classes; spiritually focused classes in meditation, tai chi, yoga, and more; tennis; volleyball; basketball; gyms; swimming pools; men's and women's health centers with steam rooms, whirlpools, and saunas.
Services & Special Programs: Garden tours and cooking demonstrations; men's fitness program; Pilates; evening programs and movies; couples weeks. Regular services include Hot Stone massage; water massage; salt glows; herbal, seaweed, and aromatherapy wraps; reflexology; facials; beauty salon services; tennis lessons; craft classes.
Rates: $$–$$$
Best Spa Package: The spa offers only one package; the one-week stay includes accommodations, classes, gourmet meals, evening programs, and use of all the facilities, and runs from Saturday to Saturday. Price varies depending on type of accommodation: from $2,307.55 single occupancy or $1,846.68 per person double occupancy to $2,896.75 single occupancy or $2,767.35 per person double occupancy.
Credit Cards: MasterCard, Visa
Getting There: Charter buses operate on Saturdays to and from the San Diego Airport at no charge. If you do not wish to take the bus, other arrangements can be made .
What's Nearby: Beyond its natural setting at the foot of Mount Kuchumaa, sightseeing from Rancho la Puerta is limited to nearby Tecate or other Baja towns. San Diego is only forty-five minutes away, Tijuana is thirty minutes.

EUROPE

ROGNER-BAD BLUMAU
Styria, Austria

reating harmony between body and mind, nature and art, the unique health resort of Rogner-Bad Blumau is both a destination and day spa. Its ten buildings, opened in 1998, are the work of Friedensreich Hundertwasser, an internationally renowned architect. Contemporary inside and out, the spa draws on ancient traditions of an Alpine region richly endowed with thermal waters and cultural centers.

The multicolored, curved buildings initially seem to clash with the pristine meadow in which they are set. Their shapes suggest recumbent dinosaurs; their swooping roofs are covered with grass. Windows are placed haphazardly: rectangles, circles, and squares, their frames painted in natural colors and neon tints. Think of it as the Guggenheim Museum meets EuroDisney. Though disorienting at first, the purpose becomes clear as you explore and experience this architectural wonder.

Treatments and activities, some in English, mostly in German, include such classics as moor mud wraps, nutrition for natural healing, revitalization therapies through sound, and the traditional water cure for purification and detoxification. Since accommodations and spa services are separately priced, your best bet may be to sample what's available on an a la carte basis.

Vacationing here includes all of the above, plus enchanting villages spread out in the direction of Graz (an hour's drive north) and Vienna (two hours south).

Provincial pubs in nearby Blumau tend to have friendly barkeepers who are fairly fluent in English, and knowledgeable about what to see. Golfers can try a circuit that winds through the valley, playing nine different 18-hole courses. And naturally, there are miles of well-tended hiking trails.

As a day spa, Bad Blumau is more thermal water theme park than holistic retreat. Developer Robert Rogner sought to capitalize on thermal springs that gush enough hot water to fill pools that hold the equivalent of 250,000 bathtubs. At times during the summer and holidays, it seems as if that many people are bathing in the outdoor pools, leaping into man-made waves, and enjoying the whirlpool recessed within the main swimming pool. A freshwater pool for children and babies draws lots of families on day trips that have nothing to do with the spa.

But there are private places for spa treatments. Escape to Meditation Island, where you have a choice of saunas— Finnish, Swedish, Turkish, herbal aroma grotto—and a bar called the Klimbin. Or try the FindeDich center, to balance health and mind, or the beauty tower, Wunderschon, with skin care by Biodroga and Decleor.

Staying in the Kunst Haus, you are challenged by the artist/architect's aversion to straight lines. Some rooms, with their smooth, curved walls, evoke a modern-day version of Fred Flintstone's lair. Small but efficient, they are furnished in a modern kind of country style. Foyers hold charming pine armoires, matched by pine-plank

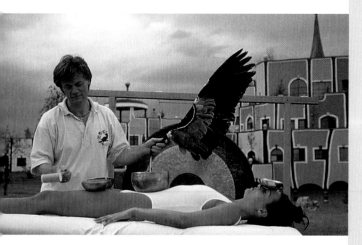

floors. The walls curl gently around corners and archways, painted a restful off-white. Apartments have a balcony and a bathroom with thermal water. Special rooms are reserved for allergy sufferers, nonsmokers, and the physically challenged.

At dusk, steam rises from the outdoor pool, adding to the fantasy of the buildings. With day trippers gone, a meditative mood sets in. Couples cuddle on the concrete banquette that encircles the whirlpool, watching the sun set behind an iridescent golden-onion spire. Natural healing doesn't get much better.

Musical Meditation

Sound therapy with holistic doctor Wolfgang Kolbl gives you a sense of release. It is an intriguing inner adventure accompanied by the sounds of bells and gongs. You lie on a couch while the doctor moves around you, banging huge gongs and tubular bells, waving a buzzard's wing, setting Tibetan prayer bowls resonating on your chakra points, and strumming a monochord under the couch. The fifty-string monochord, all tuned to the same pitch, sends vibrations through your body. The copper bowls on your forehead and stomach vibrate. This symphony of sound is a virtuoso performance, harmonizing body and soul.

Rogner-Bad Blumau
A-8283 Blumau 100
Austria
Phone: 43–3383–5100–0
Fax: 43–3383–5100–808
E-mail: spa.blumau@rogner.com
Web site: www.blumau.com

Season: Year-round

General Manager: Alfred Hackl

Spa Director: Wolfgang Kolbl

Reservations: 800–650–8018 (United States and Canada); 800–13–67–46–81 toll-free from parts of Europe.

Spa Appointments: E-mail: resm@blum.rogner.com

Accommodations: 247 double rooms and twenty-four apartments. Individually detailed, each includes tiled bathroom with shower or tub. Interiors feature unvarnished wood and natural fabrics. Amenities include bathrobe.

Meals: Buffet breakfast, included in room rate, offers muesli, yogurt, fresh fruit, country breads. Lunch and dinner are a la carte, feature local farm produce, Styrian specialties. Vegetarian menu and health food available in main dining room.

Facilities: Holistic health center with extensive selection of hydrotherapy, wraps, and massage; thermal water park; beauty salon for bodywork, skin care; Roman bath, saunas, steam rooms; indoor and outdoor swimming pools; gym with spinning bikes. Recreation includes beach volley ball, streetball, archery, riding, cycling, tennis.

Services & Special Programs: Extensive selection of therapies and water cures. Body wraps include choice of grape residue, hay, aromatherapy oils, or fago. Massage can be Esalen-style, Thai or TuiNa, shiatsu or Swedish. Sound therapy for stress management; kinesi-therapy for muscular or bone problems.

Rates: $$

Best Spa Package: There are occaisonal special weekend packages. For example, $200 for two nights, which includes a mid-priced double room, buffet breakfast, unlimited use of the thermal spa and saunas, bathrobe and towel, and use of the sports and leisure program. Weekday all-day spa passes for the thermal spa and sauna facilities are $18; weekends, $20.

Credit Cards: American Express, MasterCard, Visa

Getting There: From Vienna or Graz, by car or taxi on Autobahn A-2.

What's Nearby: Graz, Salzburg.

LE MERIDIEN LIMASSOL SPA & RESORT
Limossol, Cyprus

he legend of Aphrodite, the goddess of love and beauty, is alive and well on Cyprus in the eastern Mediterranean. According to Greek mythology, Aphrodite was born from the sea near here, emerging from the foam to earn her niche as a celebrated figure symbolizing femininity, beauty, and love. The Greek gods and goddesses chose Cyprus as their destination of choice for indulging pleasure and sport, and Cyprus continues to build on this theme.

The mystique of the gods flourishes on this romantic island. The goal of the resort's French designer was to make Le Meridien Limassol the ultimate spa and resort in Cyprus, dedicated to health, relaxation, therapy, and beauty. The spa was designed to reflect the spirit of the past but uses state-of-the-art engineering to harness the mineral-rich seawater for use in its spa treatments. The seawater, used in treatments with Thalgo Marine products, is thought to have a therapeutic effect on joint and back problems, arthritis, osteoporosis, and water retention.

Le Spa opened just in time to host participants in the Donald Trump Miss Universe 2000 Pageant. With seven seawater pools (three outdoor), an aquarium plunge pool, a heated freshwater pool, an algaeotherapy center, and eleven treatment rooms, this is truly a sybaritic dream.

Enhancing Le Spa are thirteen renovated garden villas with a swimming pool built exclusively for their use. Four villas have private pools. Le Meridien also has two flood-lit tennis courts and a multipurpose, all-

weather training area for football, volleyball, and basketball. Children enjoy the Penguin Village Children's Club with new waterslide and climbing apparatus.

The birth of Le Spa at Le Meridien Limassol Resort, with its thalssaotherapy treatments, is a fitting tribute to the goddess of love and beauty, born from the sea.

Vive La Difference!

More men are enjoying the benefits of spa treatments, according to a recent study conducted by the International Spa Association. It must be right. Just listen to one of our spa colleagues, who, after considerable reluctance, experienced a pedicure and facial for the first time. "I felt so relaxed and wonderful after having my face worked on. I couldn't believe a facial could make my entire body so relaxed. Most men are into their heads and not their bodies. They don't think of their face, feet, or hands. I guess I carry a lot of tension in the facial muscles. The same can be said for feet. We abuse those poor things all day in tight airless shoes, covered with socks. I was proud I had the treatments and felt very good about myself in a new and mysterious way. I looked years younger and felt very relaxed. I should have been enjoying facials and pedicures years ago."

Le Spa at Le Meridien Limassol Resort
Old Limossol-Nicosia Road
PO Box 6560
CY-3308 Limossol
Cyprus
Phone: 357–5–634–000
Fax: 357–5–634–222
E-Mail: meridien@zenon.logos.cy.net
Web Site: www.lemeridien-hotels.com

Season: Year-round

General Manager: John G.C. Wood

Spa Director: George Tavelis

Reservations: 357–5–634–000 or 800–543–4300 (Meridien Hotels)

Accommodations: 222 rooms, including 59 garden suites. Amenities include air-conditioning; balcony or terrace; direct dial telephones; in-house movies; Jacuzzi bath tubs in suites; minibars; safe deposit boxes; and satellite television.

Meals: The three restaurants at the resort offer French gourmet fare at Le Nautile; the open-air Le Vieux Village; and all-day dining at Le Café Fleuri poolside restaurant and terrace with specialty buffets. All have no-smoking sections.

Facilities: Le Spa with four outdoor seawater pools, saunas, whirlpools, plunge pool, heated freshwater pool, algaeotherapy center, and eleven treatment rooms; two tennis courts and an all-weather area for various sports; children's area; art gallery; games room; shopping arcade.

Services & Special Programs: Thalassotherapy, medical checkup, massage, fango, facials.

Rates: $$

Best Spa Package: Helen of Troy Beauty Week includes medical evaluation, anticellulite sea oil treatments, facial, massage, seaweed treatments, mud bath, lymphatic drainage massage, sauna, aroma steam, and herbal tea of the day. $1,150 per person double occupancy. King Zeus Resort Week for men includes medical examination, supervised daily circuit thalassotherapy, use of the sauna and steam rooms, personalized exercise program, and the herbal tea of the day. $1,070 per person double occupancy.

Credit Cards: Most major

Getting There: The resort is on the south side of the island, fifteen minutes from Limassol city center, forty-five minutes from the Larnaca International Airport, and fifty-five minutes from Paphos International Airport.

What's Nearby: The resort sits directly on the beach and is fifteen minutes from the center of the city of Limassol.

THALASSA SPA AT ANASSA

Polis, Cyprus

visit to the mythical birthplace of Aphrodite, the goddess of love and beauty, is a modern legend unfolding. Anassa, a secluded 184-room resort, opened in 1998 on the unspoiled northwestern coast of the Akamas Peninsula. Designed to resemble an island village and built over the cliffs of the Mediterranean, it certainly has the feel of a village, right down to a church, its own organic farm, and a romantic central square with lush gardens. The name Anassa is derived from the classical Greek for queen, and this palatial resort lives up to its name. It is a masterpiece of marble and elegant simplicity, with sophisticated, uncluttered decor and first-class Mediterranean cuisine. The resort is privately owned and family run.

Aphrodite is said to have bathed at this site after entertaining her conquests. Today spa-goers bathe in the luxurious Thalassa Spa. The massages range from an aromatherapy sport-and-fitness massage to a relaxing and deep-cleansing back massage. It is advisable to spread the treatments over three days to fully experience the extensive spa menu.

The resort attracts an international clientele, and the spa, located downstairs behind the church, is per-

petually busy. There is a full-service beauty salon with British staffing. Spa facilities include steam baths, sauna, an indoor pool with poolside snack bar, and several treatment rooms. There are two outdoor, fresh-water multilevel pools, two tennis courts, and one squash court. Water sports abound, from snorkeling and scuba diving to sailing. There is even a private yacht for charter.

Thalassotherapy includes a complete range of baths and showers: algae and mud therapy for local and general application; a warm exercise pool with water jets, saunas, steam baths, and inhalation. Guests are invited to consult with a spa specialist to select the most advantageous treatments.

Accomodations range from spacious garden rooms in the main building to luxurious junior suites with a Mediterranean-inspired lounge area. Several have a private pool on the terrace. Every room or suite has its own personality with stunning views overlooking bay or gardens.

Don't expect spa cuisine. The waitstaff is happy to accommodate special dietary requirements. Pelagos, a casual all-day restaurant where you can sit on the terrace with a view of the bay, is your best bet for spe-

Thalassa Spa at Anassa
PO Box 66006
CY-8830
Polis, Cyprus
Phone: 357–6–888–000 or 357–6–322-800
Fax: 357–6–322–900
Web site: www.thanoshotels.com

Season: Year–round

General Managers: York Brandes and Johnny Mathis

Spa Director: Alkistis Loukides

Reservations: 800–323–7500 (Preferred Hotels)

Spa Appointments: 357–6–888–000

Accommodations: 184 guest rooms, ranging from studio to lavish, each with balcony or terrace, some with private plunge pool or outdoor whirlpool. Room amenities include minibars, color television, international direct-dial phones with two lines, air-conditioning, and hair dryers.

Meals: Four restaurants offer a variety of local and international cuisine.

Facilities: Two outdoor, freshwater multilevel swimming pools with waterfalls and a third with mosaic tile; two tennis courts; a squash court; table tennis; indoor gym; boutique; conference facilities; church. Thalassa Spa: indoor pool, saunas, steam baths, relaxation room, treatment rooms.

Services & Special Programs: A wide range of water sports, including scuba diving and sailing; private beach; live music most nights, barbecues, theme nights; Children's Club with baby-sitting and children's meals; twenty-four-hour room service; laundry and dry cleaning; complimentary shoe shine service; courier services.

Rates: $$$

Best Spa Package: The five-day Rejuvenation Beauty Program includes aromatherapy facial, softening treatment, makeover, hair salon treatment, holistic aromatherapy body treatment, two visits to the marine hydro pool, manicure and pedicure. Rates for luxurious garden view guestrooms start at $399 per night, double occupancy. Spa treatments are a la carte and in addition to room rates.

Credit Cards: Most major

Getting There: The resort is forty-five minutes by car from Pafos Airport and two hours from Larnaca International Airport. Helicopter transfers are available.

What's Nearby: Two 18-hole golf courses, thirty minutes and one hour away.

cialties such as grilled chicken skewers marinated with yogurt and served with oven-roasted tomato and couscous. Amphora serves fresh Mediterranean cuisine; Helios specializes in sophisticated a la carte dining. Basiliko has a menu serving a fusion of Asian and Mediterranean in an intimate, candle-lit setting. The cooking is naturally healthy, made attractive by simplicity in preparation.

Anassa represents a new wave in resort hotels in Cyprus with a range of accommodations, a wealth of activities, and a spa with an international flair.

GRAND HOTEL PUPP—HARP SPA CLINIC

Karlovy Vary, Czech Republic

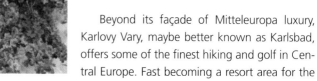

n the grand tradition of the original European spa hotels, the Grand Hotel Pupp in northern Bohemia exudes the charm and grace of the nineteenth century. Elegantly restored, the ballroom and marble atrium create the feeling that crowned heads dance the night away in this magnificent structure.

The grand hotels along the riverwalk here became clinics for citizens from Eastern Bloc countries, who came for free health holidays under their government-paid health plans. Privatization, and a new government in Prague, has encouraged preservation of the traditional water kurs along with new facilities for advanced treatment of stress-related illness. One of the best examples of this new breed is the Harp Spa Clinic at the Grand Hotel Pupp. Housed on two floors of the hotel's garden wing, the clinic offers a full range of treatments under medical supervision. Facilities include underwater massage tubs, mud therapy, massage rooms, facial rooms, and electromagnetic muscular stimulation. Your kur can include lymphatic drainage, reflexology, acupuncture, and hydrotherapy.

Beyond its façade of Mitteleuropa luxury, Karlovy Vary, maybe better known as Karlsbad, offers some of the finest hiking and golf in Central Europe. Fast becoming a resort area for the new moneyed class of Russia and Austria, the old world hotels stayed alongside new condominiums and remnants of communist-era buildings. But if you're not under a doctor's supervision, typically for a three-week kur program, the place to stay is Hotel Pupp. It's a return to the pleasures of a bygone era, with freshly decorated rooms that feature antiques and modern amenities. There are vast restaurants and bars serving Czech and international specialities, not spa cuisine. Concerts are held in the hotel's ballroom, originally opened in 1907, as well as in the city's newly refurbished theater, an 1886 architectural confection. During the annual International Film Festival Karlovy Vary in July, it's not unusual to see Hollywood stars at Hotel Pupp.

The spa is replete with marble columns and mosaic floors and is modeled after ancient Roman baths. On offer daily are massages, saunas, steambaths, whirlpools, and fitness classes. Prices for spa services are about half what you pay at an American spa; appointments can be made by the hotel's concierge when you arrive.

The thermal waters still attract throngs to the town's public springs. According to test results, the warm mineral water contains all the vital minerals your body requires. Said to improve digestion and offer immunity from disease, a daily dose of the waters has been effective in reducing inflamation and for treating lipid disorders. Souvenir mugs with long sipping handles are sold at shops that line the promenade in front of the colonnades where spring water is freely dispensed. Sipping water and strolling, a daily ritual along the riverside located five minutes from the Pupp, visitors snack on waffles—first created here in 1788—and Viennese pastry. There is a museum of handmade glass

Spa Redefines Wine

Symbolizing beauty and harmony, the sculptured harp atop Hotel Pupp celebrates the pleasures of music, food, wine, and health.

"Wine is highly suitable for man if, in sickness and in health, he takes care to drink it with purpose and in proper measure, according to his individual condition." So said Hippocrates, the father of modern medicine. He advocated white wine as a diuretic. This belief in the beneficial powers of wine persists today. According to Michel Montignac, author of *Dine Out and Lose Weight,* wine has been proven to be beneficial to cardiovascular ailments. One glass of wine at the end of a meal is therapeutic, he says. He recommends champagne for rheumatism, pinot noir for weight loss, and dry champagne for bloating. Some spas serve a glass of wine occasionally. Perhaps Hippocrates would say what better way to enjoy spa dining!

from the Moser factory just outside town, where outlet shoppers can find bargains, and a brewery with herbal liqueur samples. Surrounded by forested slopes that make the majestic spa buildings seem even more imposing, the central district of Karlovy Vary conveys a comforting sense of being set apart from the world, a place of health and healing.

Bohemian Traditions Meet Modern Medicine

The Grand Hotel Pupp—Harp Spa Clinic
Mírové námestí 2
360-91 Karlovy Vary, Czech Republic
Phone: 420–0–17–310–91–11
Fax: 420–0–17–322–40–32
E-mail: main@pupp.kpgroup.cz
Web site: www.pupp.cz

Season: Year-round

General Manager: Roman Vacho

Spa Director: Dr. Milada Sarova

Fitness Director: None

Reservations: 420–0–17–310–91–11

Spa Appointments: www.karlsbadspa.cjb.net

Accommodations: 199 luxury guest rooms rebuilt between 1994 and 1996.

Meals: The hotel's main restaurant serves Czech and international specialties.

Facilities: Full-service spa with Roman baths; The Harp Spa medical center; tennis; squash; swimming; horseback riding; volleyball; basketball; conference facilities.

Services & Special Programs: Kur Spa Course (in English) each May, two-week study tour including treatments. Information: Phone 210–822–7238; Fax 208–279–7596.

Rates: $$

Best Spa Package: The Harp Spa and Medical Therapy is custom-designed to meet individual needs. It includes treatment for digestive, metabolic, and motor problems. The cost of the package is relative to the length of stay.

Credit Cards: Most major

Getting There: From Prague by car, Highway. 6 West (90 minutes), by train or bus; airport bus (2 hours.).

What's Nearby: Golf Resort Karlovy Vary; Moser Glassworks; Thun Porcelain; Zen Garden, horse racing course; Dvorak Autumn Music Festival; Marienbad; Plzen (Pilsen Brewery).

NAANTALI SPA HOTEL & RESORT

Naantali, Finland

ome aboard the world's only spa ship! Overlooking the blue Baltic Sea, the Naantali Spa Hotel's new Sunborn Yacht symbolizes the rebirth of a Finnish maritime tradition. Since 1723, health-seekers have come by boat to enjoy the curative powers of the hot springs in Naantali. Now the wedding of a yacht and a modern resort has created a unique destination for health conscious travelers.

With the arrival of its magnificent new Sunborn Yacht Hotel (launched 1998), the resort got a new lease on life. Although treatment facilities are centralized in Naantali Spa Hotel (opened in 1984), guests now have full use of both the yacht and a waterfront complex of shops and restaurants. Staying aboard Sunborn is like being on a deluxe cruise without waves. Permanently docked in the bay, the ship has a covered walkway directly into the spa center. Each of the 102 staterooms is deluxe, similar to small luxury liners built at Finnish shipyards. For the ultimate sauna experience, stay in one of the royal suites that have a private veranda attached to the sauna.

Water is the theme at the main hotel, which has a thermal pool complex stretching toward the sea. Swimming outdoors year-round, even in the snow, you can duck into the hotter Roman pools, two Turkish baths, and four saunas. The fitness center has state-of-the-art exercise equipment, with trainers on hand for personal instruction. In the same area are a gym for group exercise and a sports hall where basketball, volleyball, and badminton games are organized by the activity directors. Don't worry about language problems; English is spoken by all staffers, many of whom are multilingual.

Water also invigorates the spa's treatments. For an antidote to winter darkness, try the Polar Night Bath, a soothing soak in herbal oils while bright-light therapy boosts your mood. Arctic plants and natural blue clay from the region's lakes and forests are used in body treatments to detoxify your body and stimulate your metabolism.

Southwest Finland and its capital city Turku have always had connections with the sea. Located about fifteen minutes by bus or taxi from Naantali, the ancient port has excellent ferry connections with Sweden. A university town, Turku's concert halls and museums add a lively dimension to enjoying the area's natural attractions.

While the spa hotel is a world of its own, a short stroll to Naantali's timbered Old Town reveals the romantic side of Finland. Rows of wooden houses are

perfectly preserved, painted in bright colors, with attractive shops offering handcrafts and antiques. The old Monastery Church, where a summer festival of chamber music is held, and the gardens of the Finnish president's summer retreat, Kultaranta, are open to visitors.

The Baltic Sea's soft embrace makes Naantali an ideal escape from stress.

Sauna's Spiritual Side

The Finns have a spiritual as well as social attitude toward the sauna. It is not simply a place to sweat and douse yourself with water, but a place of healing. Babies were born in saunas, and the dead were laid out in them before funerals. To exorcise the devil, the possessed were taken into the sauna and beaten with a vihta—a whisk made of small birch branches—until the evil spirits departed. Today the sauna ritual is alive in nearly every Finnish home, hotel, and resort. Families gather in them to talk and meditate. After a pause for refreshments and a cooling shower or roll in the snow, it's back to the sauna (pronounced sownah) for another session of healthy sweating.

A Sea Change at Nordic Springs

Naantali Spa Hotel & Resort
21100 Naantali
Finland
Phone: 358-2-44-55-660
Fax: 358-2-44-55-622
E-mail: info@naantalispa.fi
Web site: www.naantalispa.fi

Season: Year-round

General Manager: Heli Virtanen

Spa Director: Ritva Niemi

Spa Appointments: 358-2-44-55-800

Accommodations: 331 rooms and suites, including 227 in the main hotel, 104 on Sunborn Yacht Hotel. All have private bathroom with shower, hair dryer, bathrobes, TV, telephone; most have balcony or sea view. Royal and presidential suites come with private sauna and large terrace.

Meals: Four restaurants and Cafe Roma provide Scandinavian and European specialties. An extensive buffet breakfast is included in hotel rates. Seafood, salads, and organic vegetables are featured. Also available: reindeer steak, pizza, Danish pastry, traditional Finnish rice cake. Special Diet Week with daily menu totaling 1,000 calories.

Facilities: Pool complex indoors and outdoors, saunas, steam baths, hydrotherapy bath, beauty salon. Balneotherapy remedial and galvanic baths, underwater massage, water gymnastics. Solariums.

Services & Special Programs: Aromatherapy massage, zone therapy, lymphatic drainage, reflexology, shiatsu, facials, body wraps and peels. Salon for skin, hair, and nail care. Medically supervised programs for physical rehabilitation, obesity, stress management, and fitness evaluation.

Rates: $$

Best Spa Package: Three-day "Pamper Yourself" holiday includes accommodations, half-board, two treatments, use of facilities. Price per person $252–$339, double; single room supplement $109. (Arrive Sunday or Wednesday).

Credit Cards: Most major.

Getting There: From Helsinki, by train or car to Turku.

What's Nearby: Turku, Helsinki, Valley of the Moomins.

DOMAINE DU ROYAL CLUB EVIAN—
BETTER LIVING INSTITUTE

Evian-les-Bains, France

ien-être. It's French for "well-being," and catering to your well-being is what this legendary spa at a world-class resort is all about.

Nestled between the mountains and Lake Geneva, on a forty-two-acre site with private golf course, century-old trees, and gardens, the Domaine du Royal Club Evian is legendary. Built in 1907 during the Belle Époque for the pleasure of King Edward VII, this 127-room resort at the foot of the awesome Alps has been updated to fulfill the desires of today's spa-goer.

Evian has become a household word for pure drinking water, and this scenic locale in France is its source. While Evian has become synonymous with the ideals of youth, fitness, and beauty, it takes more than sipping this crystal-clear water to turn back the years. All of the ingredients for a spa elixir are found at the Better Living Institute, where treatments include global sensory massage, shiatsu, Thai massage, marine mud wrap, Dead Sea salt peels, hydro massage baths, and fangotherapy.

The wisest way to take in the extensive spa offerings is to select one of the spa packages, which is added on to the cost of accommodations. The resort is a popular venue for conferences and special events, from golf tournaments to music festivals, so it is best to reserve spa packages in advance. Once you've checked in to one of Evian's comfortable rooms, many with mesmerizing pastoral views, it becomes apparent there is much more to do than "spa." There are dozens of activities, depending on the season of your stay. The spa year is basically divided into three seasons: the club season (February through March), the privilege season (April through July), and the royal season (August), which is the most expensive since August is France's traditional vacation month. Highlights at the Club include nine restaurants, the Casino Royal Evian on the shores of Lake Geneva, and a multitude of sports.

The mother-baby program, established over ten years ago, is designed for new mothers with babies between three and nine months old. It includes twenty-six health appointments spread over six days, with such opportunities for bonding as discovering music and swimming. Other classes for new mothers exclusively include a nutrition workshop, gentle massage, fun gym, and exercises to restore muscle tone.

New treatments are regularly added: Try the sensorial touch massage, a hands-on approach for rediscovering energy and body suppleness. The new Turkish-style steam room is for those who enjoy immersing themselves in purifying heat.

The Royal Club Evian may be housed in a nineteenth-century structure, but the spa programs are anything but vintage!

The Diététique Cocktail

The latest rage at European bars is the *diététique* cocktail, thanks to the success of the International Diététique Cocktail Competition, an extravaganza showcasing nonalcoholic cocktails held at the Royal Club Evian. At the competition, creative bartenders whip up over a hundred cocktails splashed with everything but alcohol! In 1994 the winner was Simon Bogarelli, a twenty-three-year-old barman from Switzerland who named his frothy winning cocktail for his mother, calling it "The Carla." You can easily stock your home bar with fresh ingredients such as those used at the Royal Club Evian—pineapples, passion fruit, mango, blueberries, melons, and garden veggies from carrots to cucumbers—to invent your own diététique cocktail.

A Spa at "The Source"

Domaine du Royal Club Evian—Better Living Institute
South Bank of Lake Geneva
74502 Evian-les-Bains
France
Phone: 33–4–50–26–8500
Fax: 33–4–50–75–61–00
Web site: www.royal-evian.com

Season: Year-round

General Manager: Roger Mercier

Spa Director: Evelyne Reygnier; Dr. Sylvie Sheerens

Reservations: (800) 223–6800 (Leading Hotels of the World); (800) 888–4747 (Concord Hotels) or reservations@dommaine-royal.danone.com

Spa Reservations: Same

Accommodations: The resort has 127 guest rooms, including nine suites. The comfortable accommodations offer generous views of Lake Geneva and the park.

Meals: Nine restaurants are on property, including the new La Veranda Rotisserie, featuring a healthful menu; the Toque Royal; the Cafe Royal Gourmandin; Liberta; and Le Jardin des Lys, an elegant dietetic restaurant next to the Better Living Institute.

Facilities: Full-service spa; 18-hole golf course and clubhouse; five tennis courts; four swimming pools; the Casino Royal; archery; squash; climbing; jogging.

Services & Special Programs: The Evian Music Festival; intensive golf program; children's and junior golf; children's clubs; teenagers' club; horseback riding, four-wheel drive tours, paragliding, helicopter trips, cross-country skiing, alpine skiing, dogsled excursions, canoeing, waterskiing, sailing, lake cruises; cooking and patisserie school; gardening classes. A shuttle bus links the hotel to the golf course and casino.

Rates: $$$

Best Spa Package: The Better Living Program includes treatments daily over a six-day period; five water exercise classes, three massages, one algae wrap, one jet shower, one marine wrap for the back, a medical consultation, and dietary advice. Rates range according to season; accommodations are additional. $900.

Credit Cards: Most major

Getting There: The resort is 28 miles from the Geneva Coitrin International Airport and 360 miles from Paris.

What's Nearby: Chateau de Chillon; the Grange au Lac.

INSTITUT DE THALASSOTHERAPIE LOUISON BOBET
AT HOTEL MIRAMAR
Port Crouesty, Arzon, France

Tour de France champion cyclist Louison Bobet experienced a sea change thanks to thalassotherapy forty years ago. Amazed at the good it did his joints after an accident, Bobet and his brother Jean developed a health institute on the coast of southern Brittany. Taking seawater therapy to a higher level, the Institut de Thalassotherapie Louison Bobet at the Hotel Miramar has a cure for all seasons.

Step inside the Miramar Port Crouesty and you might think it's an oceangoing liner. Every detail of the hotel's design suggests a ship, decked out for a luxury cruise. Even the five floors are numbered "ponts," as decks on a French liner. The color scheme of your "cabin" echoes the blue of the sea and sky, and there's a deck chair on the balcony.

This "liner of Good Health" may resemble a ship architecturally, but it is beached in an artificial lake created by recycled seawater from the hotel's thalassotherapy center. Located on a peninsula jutting into the Atlantic Ocean, the sandy beaches at Arzon are protected by environmentalists, so the Miramar's

designers came up with a system to naturally filter water through the sand after it has been treated.

Taking the seaside cure begins with a medical evaluation. A sports medicine doctor checks your heart and general condition, then you head for the Institut to schedule treatments and exercise sessions. Occupying an entire deck of the hotel, the Institute has treatments for chronic aches and pains, fatigue, stress-related disorders, and postnatal body shaping as well as overall fitness programs. Whirlpool baths, jet showers of various kinds, exercise in the water, and massages—plus long walks along the beach and windy cliffs—leave you as tingly-pink as the cheeks of the Bretons.

The hotel has a diététique restaurant offering satisfying seafood dishes calculated at about 300 calories per meal. On the other hand, there is classic cuisine on the *pont supérieur* (the top deck) in a first-class dining room reminiscent of ocean liners. The dazzling Friday night seafood buffet spreads around a top-deck swimming pool—just like being on a cruise.

Thalassotherapy centers come in many sizes and styles—there are nearly fifty on France's Atlantic and Mediterranean coasts—and French law sets the standards. Built in the early 1990s, the Bobet Institute and its sister spa in Biarritz are among top-rated facilities. The nautical ambience at Miramar Crouesty sets it apart from others we have visited, and its location is a plus. Arzon has ancient history and a huge marina at Port Crouesty.

While a "cure" requires a week or more, you can come for a few days and enjoy the beach and indoor seawater swimming pool. The hotel has a well-equipped gymnasium, beauty salon, and sauna. Outings "sportif" by bike and boat are available. Part health club, part seaside resort, the Miramar is managed by Groupe Royal Monceau, known for its prestigious flagship in Paris, Hotel Royal Monceau.

Padding about in bathing suits and fluffy white robes, guests follow the prescribed routine or relax at the rooftop pool, where the glass roof opens on warm days. Everyone carries a tote bag issued at the reception desk; it's likely to be filled with books for reading between bubblings and hosings, sunscreen, and perhaps a pet. After a few days, you'll feel part of the crew, swept away by the beauty of Brittany.

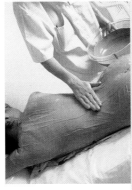

The Seaside Cure

For many people, the scent of sand, sun, and surf is a natural sedative, according to Dr. Alan Hirsch of the Smell and Taste Research Foundation in Chicago. He suggests some reasons for this: vacations mean lower anxiety levels; odors evoke positive memories via chemical reactions in the brain; and odors may work like an olfactory Prozac. Another factor may be negative ions. Studies have yielded conflicting results. Some suggest negatively charged ions wafting off the sea interact with the outer layers of our cells, which in turn alters brain chemistry and is subtly intoxicating. Thalassotherapy, which evolved in France from studies by Dr. Rene Quinton in the late 1800s, combines all these elements in a structured program under medical supervision. The application of seawater and algae to the body, and the simultaneous experience of a bracing seashore climate, has been found to be very beneficial. Thus the French used a Greek word—_thalassa_—meaning the sea to describe the course of treatments in thalassotherapy. Twenty-five centuries ago Euripides wrote: "The sea cures the maladies of man."

Sea Changes in Brittany

Institut de Thalassotherapie Louison Bobet at Hotel Miramar–Crouesty
Port Crouesty
Rue Leen-Vihan (BP 53)
56640 Arzon
France
Phone: 33–49–97–67–68–00
Fax: 33–49–97–67–68–99
E-mail: reservations@miramar-crouesty.com
Web site: www.royalmonceau.com

Season: Year-round

General Manager: Jacques Zartarian

Spa Director: Olivier Vilain

Accommodations: 120 rooms, twelve suites, all with balcony, contemporary furniture, modern bathroom. Amenities include robe and slippers, TV, radio, minibar. All air-conditioned, with sea view.

Meals: Separate dietetic and gourmet dining rooms, fixed-price menu or a la carte. Dinner starters can be fish soup, salad with sea scallops, smoked salmon, or fresh oysters. Grill choices include grilled swordfish, sole, steak, sea scallops, salmon. Specialties include Breton lobster, shellfish, and presalted lamb raised on seaweed and salted herbs. Desert is fruit tart, flan with plums, savarin. Herbal teas and espresso at pool bar.

Facilities: Thalassotherapy exercise pools, indoor seawater swimming pool, hydrotherapy tubs, Vichy shower, foot and hand baths, jet showers, ultrasonic baths, sauna, hammam (steam room), ionization spray, pressotherapy. Beauty salon, gymnasium, medical clinic.

Services & Special Programs: Hydrotherapy baths, showers, massage, seaweed skin care, lymphatic drainage, physical rehabilitation. Postnatal program (seven days). Skin care with LaPrairie products, hair treatments using Rene Furterer method, pedicure, relaxation sessions.

Rates: $$

Best Spa Package: Remise en Forme Six-Night Package Croisière with room and half-board. Price: $1,260–$1,502 per person, double; $1,608–$1,966 single. VAT services included.

Credit Cards: American Express, Diners Club, MasterClub, Visa

Getting There: From Paris, by TGV train to Vannes (two hours), by car Autoroute D–780.

What's Nearby: Belle Isle, Nantes, Vannes.

LES FERMES DE MARIE
Megeve, France

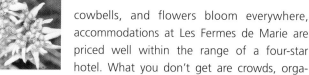

At first sight, the town of Megeve is beyond-belief picturesque: narrow, winding cobblestone streets, tiny squares lined by ivy-covered buildings, and a fourteenth-century church with bulbous bronze-green bell tower. Megeve bans autos in the town center, but has hiking trails and a cable car that ascends to breathtaking 12,600-foot views of Mont Blanc.

A cluster of chalets above a stream outside town, Les Fermes de Marie is more like a mountain village than resort hotel. Created by the owner/manager team of Jean-Louis Sibouet and his wife Jocelyne, it looks ancient, but only opened in 1989. Collected from farms in the area, 300-year-old lumber, carved wooden columns, and antique furniture conceal the resort's concrete infrastructure. There are eight lodges, the restaurant Grand Salle, and a spa building complete with an indoor swimming pool. Furnished in a mix of Savoyard and Ralph Lauren styles, no two rooms are alike.

It's easy to see why the king and queen of Sweden stay here in a private chalet during the ski season. In summer, when the high pastures are alive with tinkling cowbells, and flowers bloom everywhere, accommodations at Les Fermes de Marie are priced well within the range of a four-star hotel. What you don't get are crowds, organized fitness classes, and Americans. Summer clientele are an international mix of Italians, French, and British; only about 4 percent are American. The main attractions are pure mountain air, warm, dry climate, and great food. Families are welcome, although there is no program for kids other than hikes, sports, and a six-day climbing course offered by the Megeve tourism office.

Mountain herbs and flowers infuse the beauty farm with sensory pleasures while you are enjoying an aromatherapy massage or facial. The "all-natural" treatments use beauty care products made from plants, essential oils, and biologically neutral bases. There are ten private treatment rooms in a rabbit-warren below the reception area, all done in wood logs, stone, and terra-cotta tile. For exercise, a small gym offers bikes and treadmills, and there is a glass-walled swimming pool that overlooks an herb garden.

Men are treated to a personalized regimen at the beauty farm. The six-day fitness package alternates sessions of relaxing massage with skin care, hydromassage baths, and seaweed wraps. Other programs for men and women include hydrotherapy and skin care. Altogether, forty-five different treatments are available a la carte.

Lodged in one of the wood-paneled chalets, you will find an array of antiques plus a big soaking tub in the bathroom. Fluffy white bathrobes are provided for lounging on the sunny terrace or balcony. The hotel compound is on several levels, surrounding a small garden where aperitifs and

meals are served. The main dining room, a cozy grill, and a specialty restaurant offer enough variety that you may never need to request the dietetic menu.

Fight Jet Lag with Ginger Tea and Mountain Flowers

Mountain flowers and herbs grow wild in the fields around Les Fermes de Marie. Taking a nature walk with Clotilde Boisvert, founder of L'École des Plantes, a school for nature studies in Paris, you can learn about the healing properties of plants and flowers. As a booster for your immune system, fresh herbs are used as infusions to sip while awaiting spa treatments.

Kim and Cary Collier, an American couple who developed Jamu herbal rituals while living in Indonesia, recommend ginger tea to fight jet lag after a long flight. They find it helps digestion and improves systemic blood circulation, served hot or iced. "Sipping ginger tea while relaxing in a warm bath filled with flower petals is truly one of life's irresistible pleasures," they say.

Les Fermes de Marie
Chemin de Riante Colline
74120 Megeve
France
Phone: 33–4–50–93–03–10
Fax: 33–4–50–93–09–84
E-mail: contact@fermesdemarie.com
Web site: www.fermesdemarie.com

Season: December 15–April 15; June 15–September 5

General Manager: Jocelyne Sibuet

Spa Director: Carole Ravier

Accommodations: Sixty-nine rooms in Alpine lodges for 150 guests. All have private bathroom with modern amenities. Furniture is French-country antiques, wooden armoire, walnut table, rustic bedspread, lounge chairs. TV, telephone, clock/radio are standard; no air-conditioning needed. Dogs and children allowed.

Meals: Gourmet menu served in three restaurants. Breakfast buffet includes eggs cooked to order, cereals, cold meats, cheeses, coffee. Lunch and dinner feature nouvelle cuisine. Dietetic menu on request.

Facilities: Hydrotherapy tubs, Jacuzzi, sauna, steam room, Vichy shower, pressotherapy, exercise studio, indoor heated lap pool.

Services & Special Programs: Swedish massage, Thai massage, shiatsu, reflexology, seaweed wrap, mud packs, body gommage, G5, lymphatic drainage, hydrotherapy bath, jet sprays. Yoga class, excursion for Alpine luncheon, workshop on mountain plants led by a naturalist.

Rates: $$

Best Spa Package: Six-day Balance Program combines skin care and hydrotherapy, two treatments daily, teaching how to take care of yourself. Includes accomadations; buffet breakfast and dinner; lunch at mountain chalet; fitness program; free entrance to pool, sauna, and Jacuzzi; and a basket of beauty products. $986–$1,051 (summer); $1,078–$1,235 (winter). Rate is per person, double occupancy.

Credit Cards: American Express, Diners Club, MasterCard, Visa

Getting There: From Geneva, by car on Autoroute A–40 via Sallanches (sixty minutes). By train from Paris, TGV to Lyon, connection to Sallanches (three hours).

What's Nearby: Chamonix, Le Montenvers, Mer de Glace glacier, Mont Blanc.

LES PRÉS D'EUGÉNIE—LA FERME THERMALE

Eugénie-les-Bains, France

hen food cravings get the better of your fitness program, this is the place to combine both passions. Michel Guérard's three-star restaurant rates among the best in France. A pioneer of *cuisine minceur*, his 500 calorie meals taste like 2,500. Matching the menu's excellence are thermal baths and country-chic accommodations that give new meaning to taking the waters.

La Ferme Thermale at Les Prés d'Eugénie, as the thermal resort complex is known, includes two spa treatment buildings, three hotels, two restaurants, and a cooking school. Clustered on forty acres of parkland planted with an herb garden and shaded by magnolia, plane, and tulip trees, it's in Eugénie-les-Bains, a Belle Époque village that seems to be in a time warp. Each of Les Prés d'Eugénie's hotels has a distinct look and mood, a result of antiques hunts through surrounding farms by Christine Guérard.

La Maison Rose is exclusively for guests who sign up for minceur meals and spa treatments. More modest than lodging at the Couvent des Herbes (a converted convent) or the main hotel, Les Prés d'Eugénie, the thirty-one-room Maison is a shuttered mansion, not a full-service hotel, so the price of accommodations is lower. By 9:00 A.M. spa-goers are up and about, clad in cheerful pink bathrobes and heading across the garden for their morning session. By noon, they will have been tub-soaked, water-massaged, steam-bathed, and mud-packed—a regimen designed to blast away cellulite, eliminate stress, and alleviate a host of other ailments.

The secret of this water therapy is in sulfurous springs that so enthralled Empress Eugénie that she convinced her husband, Napoleon III, to build a posh resort where her society friends could take the waters and be pampered in style. Cold drinking water flows from the *Imperatrice* spring; warm water used for external treatments and baths comes from "Christine Marie"—named after Madame Guérard. There is also a clay bath along with the latest in hydrotherapy, skin care, and antiaging programs.

Designed in the style of a provincial farmhouse, the thermal spa has a covered courtyard tiled in terra-cotta, where you sip a lemon-balm infusion while awaiting treatments. An herbal bath is activated with sprigs of lavender, chamomile, and hawthorn fresh from the garden. In a different version of aromatherapy, oils of lemon, orange, and grapefruit are added to the bath, plus a sachet for scrubbing, filled with rinds of the same fruit—all with thermal spring water that flows at a natural temperature of 102 degrees.

Although the standard cure at La Ferme lasts six days, with four to five daily treatments chosen from a menu of thirteen in consultation with a staff doctor, you can also opt for a single treatment or packages designed for relaxation.

The spa complex has a beauty parlor, gymnasium, indoor and outdoor swimming pools, tennis courts, and bowling.

Located 75 miles northeast of Biarritz, this pastoral pleasure palace is for hedonists who relish good food and the art of the bath.

Chef's Special: Minerals & Mud

Experiments in his kitchen led Michel Guérard to recast more than spa food. A new signature treatment is the mud bath enriched with thermal plankton, said to be an effective skin toner and hair conditioner. Dipped into the vat of white clay, you float weightlessly. The active ingredient is kaolin, a fine-grained clay used to make porcelain and known for its ability to draw toxins from the body. Post-treatment, you recline on a Louis XV daybed amid walls adorned with scenes of French pastoral life.

***Cuisine minceur active* combines hunger-staying fiber with slow-burning carbohydrates. Grains, peas, beans, and lentils appear in various dishes; eggs, cream, sugar, and butter are dirty words. Transferring minerals to food by using Eugénie's thermal water as a cooking medium is another innovation.**

Gourmet Dieting at a Thermal Farm

La Ferme Thermale at Les Prés d'Eugénie
40320 Eugénie-les-Bains
France
Phone: 33–5–58–05–05–05
Fax: 33–5–58–51–10–10

Season: Mid-February–end of December

General Managers: Christine and Michel Guerard

Reservations: 33–5–58–05–05–05

Accommodations: Seventy-four rooms and four suites furnished with antique Turkish rugs, Directoire secretaires, and Louis XVI armoires. Lavishly canopied four-poster beds and modern tiled bathrooms with all rooms. The main hotel, Les Prés d'Eugénie has rows of French doors opening to fanciful wrought-iron balconies. The eight-room Couvent des Herbes, a former convent, is most romantic. French-English colonial antiques, formal restaurant and billiard room. La Ferme aux Grives, once a farmhouse, has four suites and country kitchen restaurant.

Meals: *Cuisine minceur* active meals served at La Maison Rose, table-d'hôte fixed menu: salmon en gelée with capers, eggs with caviar, carpaccio of duck, vegetable risotto, roast venison with spicy quince, crepes with lemon sauce or lemon verbena mock ice cream garnished with strawberries and raspberries. Gourmande meal (included in seven-day package) can begin with morsels of lobster in eggshell or grilled prawns, asparagus tips, osetra caviar, salmon escaloppes with a carrot mousse, ends with pear soufflé.

Facilities: Thermal therapy pool with underwater whirlpool, Vichy shower, mud bath and mud packs, gym, sauna and steam room, beauty parlor, indoor and outdoor swimming pools.

Services & Special Programs: Dietetic drinking cure, weight management weeks, medical team for muscular, arthritis and rheumatism treatments; massage, beauty parlor. Cooking school seminars.

Rates: $$$

Best Spa Package: Semaine Prive (week of peace and quiet), an all-inclusive package with three meals daily, hotel, spa, leisure, sports, outing to local places of interest, optional car rental. Cost: $2,180- $2,510 per person.

Credit Cards: American Express, Diners, Eurocard, Master-Card, Visa

Getting There: From Paris by car, Autoroute A–10 via Bordeaux, Route 64 to Augullon exit (715 kilometers); by Air Inter to Pau; by train, TGV to Pau.

What's Nearby: Lourdes, Biarritz (Atlantic beach resort, Hotel du Palais), Toulouse, Pyrenees mountains, Spain.

LES SOURCES DE CAUDALIE

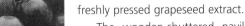

ine lovers have a new reason to visit Bordeaux: a grape escape right in the middle of a Grand Cru vineyard, Chateau Smith Haut Lafitte. With grapevines adorning the lobby, baths in wine barrels, and vintage wines accompanying spa cuisine, this is vinotherapy.

Rising amid undulating vineyards, Les Sources de Caudalie looks more like a winemaker's storage barn than a luxury spa. But that's part of the charm that Mathilde Cathiard-Thomas and Bertrand Thomas achieved by scouring the countryside for battered barn timbers, stone fountains, and handwoven linens. Drawn inside by the overpowering scent of grapes, you discover a "cure" straight from the vines. Spa treatments utilize grapeseed extract from the chateau's cabernet sauvignon crop; mineral water from the estate's thermal spring fills a swimming pool set among the vines; and there are two restaurants overseen by a chef with Michelin star credits. As a bonus, you can tour the cellars of two of France's most honored wineries, Chateau Smith Haut-Lafitte (owned by the Cathiard family) and Chateau Lafitte-Rothschild, which have produced fine vintages since the fourteenth century.

The theory behind vinotherapy is a recent scientific discovery that polyphenols in red grapes help reduce the free radicals responsible for skin aging. Red grapes are rich in polyphenols; voilà, le grape cure!

Mornings begin with walks in the hills of Bordeaux, then a massage with grapeseed oil extract, followed by full-body exfoliation scrub with grapeseed powder. After a high-pressure hosing to reduce cellulite, your therapist suggests rest in the tisanerie, where you sip herbal tea infused with red wine. Next comes a wine-and-honey wrap. Slathered in a gooey paste of wine yeast extracts, you are wrapped in warm blankets to sweat out toxins. The final touch: a bubbling bath in a *barrique* (tub shaped like an oaken barrel), spiked with

freshly pressed grapeseed extract.

The wooden-shuttered pavilion housing the spa contrasts with elegant accommodations in the twenty-nine-room hotel. Amid eighteenth-century antiques and rich fabrics, you can savor the lifestyle of a wine baron. No two rooms are alike, but all have warm provincial furnishings, fluffy duvet on the beds, and Caudalie skin-care products in the big bathroom.

Meals are a la carte or part of the spa package. There are two restaurants (open to the public): Table du Lavoir, which serves brasserie food like steak Bordelaise, and La Grand Vigne, showcasing chef Didier Banyols's new take on spa cuisine. Dinner choices can be lobster with rice and chestnuts, or a health menu that adds of up to 500 calories. Nobody counts calories with food this good: sautéed sea bass with

Les Sources de Caudalie
Chemin de Smith Haut-Lafitte
33650 Bordeaux-Martillac
France
Phone: 888–465–8383
E-mail: sources@sources-caudalie.com
Web site: www.sources-caudalie.com

Season: Year-round

General Managers: Didier and Marie-Louise Banyols

Spa Director: Delphine Duffours

Reservations: sources@sources-caudalie.com or (888) 465–8383

Accommodations: Chateau with six suites, thirteen prestige rooms, ten standard rooms. Individually decorated, all have private bathroom, air-conditioning.

Meals: Southwestern French cuisine served a la carte in two restaurants. Health menu for spa program guests.

Facilities: Barrel bath (*barrique*), indoor and outdoor swimming pools, 3-hole golf, tennis, bicycles, jogging trail, helipad, lounge, terrace.

Services & special programs: Grapeseed wet and dry body care, facials, massage. Grape diet detoxification program, one to seven days (September, October, November). Antiaging, slimming programs, cooking school, wine tastings.

Rates: $$$

Best Spa package: Two-day vinotherapy cure with four treatments, half-board (two meals) $730 per person, double.

Credit Cards: American Express, MasterCard, Visa, Eurocard

Getting There: Bordeaux airport, twenty minutes; TGV train from Paris to Bordeaux (three hours). By car, Autoroute A–10 (five hours from Paris). Located 10 miles south of the city.

What's Nearby: Vineyards, Bordeaux museum, opera, Arachon chateaux.

steamed asparagus and a shaving of truffle as a main course; fruit sorbet accented by strawberry coulis for dessert. Traditional dishes from southwestern France are featured, but portions have been reduced. After dinner, there's conversation and wine by the glass in the Cigar Tower. English is spoken by most hotel staff and spa aestheticians, so the non-French guests have no problem meeting an international mix of spa-goers.

City lights are close enough for a night at the Bordeaux Opera or one of the restaurants for which the area is celebrated along with its wines. Even if you don't take vinotherapy seriously, a glass of vintage cabernet or barrel-aged *Graves* may be just what the doctor ordered.

Vinotherapy vs. Vitamin E

Polyphenols, the basis of vinotherapy, are antioxidants—similar to but more effective than Vitamin E—that help keep arteries in shape and enhance your skin's resistance to free radicals. Although a ton of grape seeds yields only two pounds of polyphenols, Caudalie uses them in skin-care products as well as wraps and baths. Said to be part of the beauty regimen for Madonna, Princess Caroline, and actress Catherine Deneuve, the line can be purchased at Sephora, Bergdorf Goodman, and Barney's.

THALGO LA BAULE THALASSOTHERAPY CENTER

La Baule, Brittany, France

ne of the gems among the thalassotherapy centers that lie along the Atlantic Ocean on the northwest coast of France, the ultramodern Thalgo La Baule, which is linked to the Royal-Thalasso Barrier Hotel, provides a seaside cure par excellence.

Set between the ocean and pine woods, Hotel Royal and the Thalassotherapy Center bring together all the elements for a healthy vacation. Known for its tonic and calming effects, the salty air coming off tidal flats is a taste of things to come when you begin the daily schedule of treatments. Typically the morning includes a bubbling bath in fresh seawater heated to body temperature, exercise in a seawater pool, and massage. Additional water therapies, such as a high-pressure shower of salt water, may be prescribed by the center's medical staff. Following an evaluation, you are pretty much on your own to enjoy the charms of Brittany.

Overlooking the ocean, the spa's saltwater swimming pool is light and airy, no matter what the weather is like. A corridor connects the Center with the hotel, so you only need to dress in the terrycloth robe issued to all guests. But bring your own swimming cap, along with suit and slippers. French sanitary habits require men and women to wear a cap in the pool. A separate exercise pool has underwater jets that work on muscles while you follow an instructor's movements. During warm weather, group exercises on the beach are scheduled.

Afternoons are open for swimming, walking, and touring the area. Bicycles are free for hotel guests, and there is a complimentary car service to the casino and other resort attractions. Throughout your stay the hotel offers golf, horseback riding, tennis, and sailing. The restaurants command a view of the outdoor swimming pool and gardens that slope down to the beach, where windsurfers can be rented for a spin on the bay. Considered one of the most beautiful white-sand beaches in Europe, La Baule is close to small fishing villages and upscale vacation centers that draw families throughout the summer. The rest of the year, beaches are largely deserted, and you can enjoy peace and solitude on walks.

Managed by the Lucien Barriere Group, this four-star hotel has a golden patina associated with Belle Époque hospitality. Meals range from gastronomic to dietetic—the choice is yours—and the services of a nutritionist are available to plan your menus. The Royal Dietetic Restaurant has a special menu of light cuisine,

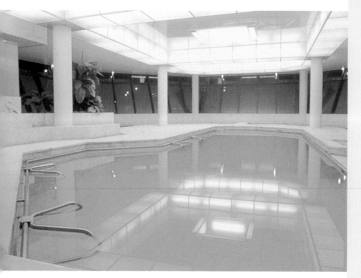

Thalgo La Baule Thalassotherapy Center Royal-Thalasso (Barrier Hotel)
6, avenue Pierre Loti
44500 La Baule
France
Phone: 33–02–40–11–4848
Fax: 33–02–40–11–48–45
Web site: www.lucienbarriere.com

Season: Year-round; Thalasso Center open daily.

General Manager: M. Portiglia

Thalasso Center Director: Yves Treguer, M.D.

Reservations: www.lucienbarriere.com

Accommodations: 91 traditional rooms, three junior suites, six suites. All with private bathroom, air-conditioning.

Meals: Continental or buffet breakfast. Separate dietetic and gastronomic restaurants, beach restaurant.

Facilities: Indoor and outdoor swimming pools, hydrotherapy; access to golf, horseback riding, windsurfers; free bikes, golf lesson, tennis.

Services & Special Programs: Medical consultation, nutrition evaluation, group exercise, massage, sauna, facials, hair and nail care.

Rates: $$$

Best Spa Package: Two-night Thalasso Discovery with three treatments per day, $253.59–$320.61. Six-night Thalasso Freedom, includes medical examination, four treatments per day, breakfast and dinner, free round of golf, $970–$1,241.

Credit Cards: American Express, MasterCard, Visa

Getting There: From Paris, TGV Atlantique (just under three hours); Autoroute Oceane A11 (462 kilometers); Air Inter to Nantes.

What's Nearby: Casino (theater, disco), St.-Nazaire Sea Museum, La Brière Nature Park, Ker Anas Bird Park, Guerande (medieval town), Nantes.

while La Rotonde is devoted to traditional French gastronomy and regional dishes. Naturally the cuisine here features fresh seafood, and the chefs display their talents with a Sunday brunch seafood plateau. Perhaps this will put you in the mood to attend cooking classes at a nearby inn. Whether taking thalasso treatments or simply enjoying a seaside break, you will discover a beautiful side of Brittany.

Seaweed Sources Beneficial Minerals

Marine algae harvested from the sea off Brittany are considered the purest form of minerals and trace elements that can be absorbed by the human body. Selected fucus and lithothammions algae are processed by Thalgo's patented micronization technique for use around the world. In France, however, only fresh seawater and seaweed can be used at certified thalassotherapy centers. Thalgo La Baule earned the distinction of Qualicert, meaning that it is authorized by the French government for the standards of its treatment.

BAD WOERISHOFEN: SPA TOWN

Bavaria, Germany

redited with originating the herbal wrap and a restorative kur program based on hydrotherapy, Sebastian Kneipp then developed a health center in this Bavarian village during the nineteenth century. Kneipp's legacy is alive and well today, thanks to a medical establishment that combines modern technology with botanical knowledge. Completely devoted to Kneipp cures, Bad Woerishofen brings the healing power of nature into the twenty-first century.

Looking like a prosperous resort in the pastoral heart of Bavaria, about an hour's drive from Munich, the village of Bad Woerishofen has dozens of kur hotels, guest houses, campsites, and a shopping mall. There is a country club for golf and tennis, a central park with lake and ducks, and extensive gardens of herbal plants—all designed to get visitors in tune with nature.

The teachings of Pastor Kneipp resonate in the **Sebastianeum,** his original clinic, which is now part of a modern treatment center and hotel, where water therapies, nutrition, and exercise are prescribed for a healthy lifestyle. Forget strenuous exercise—barefoot walks in dewy grass, and pools of alternately warm and cold water, are the favored therapy for circulatory problems. Guided walks, bicycle tours, and dancelike gymnastics are part of a weeklong program for persons with leg problems. Along with massage, relax-

ation training, and fresh country food, Kneipp's naturopathic therapies are as modern as any New Age holistic health retreat.

In Germany, and throughout the world, Kneippness means wellness. Even if you don't speak German, the message is clear: Believe it, we know it works. So when a therapist enters your bedroom at five o'clock in the morning with a hot sack of hay for an herbal wrap, there's little to do but sweat out toxins as you rest. Balancing your nervous system is better done in a resting mode, the doctor explains during a mandatory examination to prescribe your kur course of treatment. Some treatments alternate cold and warm water, either with a high-pressure hose or simply by dipping your arms in basins. Warm baths are infused with essential oils of rosemary, spruce, pine, chamomile, and linden. Strollers in the lovely parks stop at stone fountains to soak their arms and legs. But taking the waters does not mean drinking foul-smelling mineral water; what comes out of the tap here is refreshing, pure, and free.

Kur hotels in Bad Woerishofen are privately owned, but all have similar treatment facilities, outfitted from clinical style to the level of a luxury spa. Standouts among traditional five-star hotels: the **Fontenoy, Tanneck,** and **Residenz.** Family-run, small (averaging sixty rooms), each has private garden with swimming pool, indoor exercise pool, and gymnasium, with full-board meal plan. In 2001 the old-world **Sonnenhof** adds a 200-room resort wing and condominium suites, plus conference facilities managed by Steigenberger. Others specialize: Family-oriented **Hotel Park** treats children and mothers; the **Kurpark Hotel** offers chiropractors, psychologists, and treatments for the ear. At the budget-priced **Sebastianeum,** men and women are housed in separate sections, and there is a Catholic chapel for daily prayers; otherwise, the facilities are similar to first-class hotels. Retreats with original Kneipp treatments are also available at a historic monastery in the center of town. And you can stroll to the Kurhouse for daily concerts. Cafes serve Bavarian

specialties and Kneipp herbal teas; there's a rose garden and several pharmacies that offer a wide range of Kneipp nutrition supplements, herbal and vitamin tablets, and bath products.

Private medical consultation with Kneipp specialists provides an opportunity to learn how natural medicine complements mainstream therapies for aging and chronic disease. Leading researchers include Heinz Leuchtgens, M.D., and Tassilo Albus, M.D., who are part of a European network devoted to classical natural cures for prevention and rehabilitation of degenerative and stress-related diseases. Under their care, language barriers disappear as you focus on feeling healthier.

Bad Woerishofen

Kurdirektion
Postfach 1443
D-86817 Bad Woerishofen
Germany
Phone: 49–8247–969055
Fax: 49–8247–90114
E-mail: info@bad-woerishofen.de
Web site: www.bad-woerishofen.de

Season: Year-round

Spa Director: Alexander von Hohenegg

Accommodations: The central reservation service of the cure administration (Kurdirektion) offers packages that include accommodations at hotels, guest houses, apartments, the sanatorium, or campsites. Information about specific hotels and programs can be secured by e-mail. At a five-star hotel like the Residenz, standard junior suites include a sitting area with TV, balcony, and full bathroom with tub and shower. Two single beds are small but comfortable.

Meals: All five-star hotels include breakfast buffet, lunch, and dinner prepared according to heart-healthy guidelines.

Facilities: Kneipp clinic with hydrotherapy showers and tubs; indoor and outdoor swimming pools, gymnasium.

Services & Special Programs: Daily treatments, Kurhouse concerts, lectures. Excursions to nearby sites by bicycle and guided walks. Special weeks for leg therapy include medical consultation, group exercise, demonstrations of wrapping technique and Kneipp therapies for home use.

Rates: $$

Best Spa Package: Sample Kneipp's natural health concept in a weeklong program that includes accommodations for seven nights, two or three meals daily, medical examination, and transfers from/to Munich Airport. Priced from $700 (U.S.), with upgrades for five-star hotel.

Credit Cards: Most major

Getting There: By train from Munich, Augsburg, Memmingen, or Lindau. By car, from Stuttgart and Wurzburg by way of Ulm (the Autobahn B–18 toward Munich merges into A–96). The nearest international airport is Munich (72 miles/120 kilometers), where limousine, car rental, and taxi service are available.

What's Nearby: The Bavarian Alps (Allgaeu); Munich museums, opera, and historic churches; Neuschwanstein and Hohenschwangau castles (1868–1886) built for King Ludwig II (1845–1889); the Musical Theater Neuschwanstein production of Ludwig II; Fuessen; winter sports in Schwangau; Lake Constance.

BRENNER'S PARK-HOTEL & SPA

Baden-Baden, Germany

ecluded in a fifteen-acre park overlooking the Lichtentaler Allee, Brenner's Park-Hotel dates back to 1872. Over the years there have been additions—a medical clinic and a glass-walled swimming pool—but nothing quite like the spa recently added to the hotel. Forget taking the waters; Brenner's is all about beauty of body and mind.

A personalized program tailored to your needs and time combines elements of new and traditional spa regimes. Themed to the town's Roman origins, the Relaxarium has two whirlpools just big enough for one person; you choose aroma additives to suit your mood. The Frigidarium is an open-air cold-water plunge pool. The fitness center provides cardiovascular workouts on equipment with German and English control panels.

Personal trainers staff the fitness area, conducting classes in a mirrored aerobics studio, and one-on-one stretches outdoors. The fitness lounge has a sports bar that is a comfortable spot for lunch in your spa robe, especially on pleasant days when the garden terrace is open.

Feeling romantic—or want to get away from it all? The luxurious spa suite includes personal attention from a spa butler. For about $500 per day you and up to three guests get pampered privacy: marble bath, radiant-heat Roman sauna with heated benches of green quartzite, and a vitalizing shower where rain, mist, aroma, and light sensors create a relaxing mood. Shoji screens and photos by Karl Lagerfeld set the stage for an East-West indulgent interlude. Relax in a

Japanese steam bath, enriched with jasmine and orchid blossoms, and gaze at the Japanese garden on your private terrace. It's perfect for a candle-lit dinner, and nude sunbathing.

Brenner's remains among the world's truly grand hotels. The main restaurant, aglow with rose pink and sage green damask, offers a choice of classic and lighter cuisine. The breakfast buffet that comes with the daily tariff is huge, an array of fresh fruits and breads, eggs, and smoked salmon, as well as Bavarian ham and local farm cheese. Staff members remember your name and your drink preferences in the lounge, a dress-up place where sedate couples take tea and business deals are made over cognac.

Evenings are made for exercising your luck at the gilded casino, or enjoying opera and concerts at the Festpielhaus. Surrounded by the natural splendor of the Black Forest in southwestern Germany, Baden-Baden retains an old-world ambience while looking to the future as a world-class wellness center.

Brenner's Park-Hotel & Spa
6 Schillerstrasse
D-76530 Baden-Baden
Germany
Phone: 49–7221–900–801
Fax: 49–7221–900–834
E-mail: reservations@brenners.com
Web site: www.brenners.com

Season: Year-round

Managing Director: Frank Marrenbach

Spa Director: Barbara Blint

Reservations: 800–223–6800

Accommodations: One hundred high-ceilinged rooms and suites, individually appointed with antiques and rich fabrics, chandeliers and walnut armoires; each with private bathroom, most with balcony and park view. Amenities include robes and slippers, Anne Sémonin bath products.

Meals: Gourmet menu and spa cuisine menu in main dining room; regional specialties in the bierstube. Full breakfast buffet included in room rate.

Facilities: Spa suite, fitness studio, indoor swimming pool with Finnish sauna, Turkish and bio steam baths, whirlpools, sports bar.

Services & Special Programs: Jet-lag treatment with seaweed and trace elements, facials, massage (Swedish, lomi-lomi, shiatsu), lymphatic drainage, reflexology, G5, body peeling, packs, makeup, hair and nail care.

Rates: $$$

Best Spa Package: Two-day Brenner's Spa Escape includes 3½ hours of beauty treatments, fitness training, pool exercise, gymnastics. Breakfasts, tea, and hotel accommodations come with the program. $1,016 double for two; $604 for single. Taxes and service included.

Credit Cards: Most major

Getting There: From Frankfurt, by car on Autobahn A–4 (two hours), by train from airport (two hours).

What's Nearby: Strasbourg (French Alsace), Heidelberg.

Thermal Traditions

Being rich and famous isn't necessary in today's mass-oriented Baden-Baden. Sweating at the Roman-Irish Bath appeals to traditionalists who enjoy the ornately tiled saunas and pools of thermal water at the Friedrichsbad. Opened by the emperor in 1877, it looks much the way it did when Bismarck and Brahms came for a healthy sweat and scrub. House rules require bathing au natural, so throw modesty to the wind and see one of the grandest bathhouses in the world. Next door, the modern Caracalla Bath was built over a Roman campsite (excavations are visible beneath the building). Busy night and day, this is a waterpark for families who frolic in the steamy open-air pools. Admission tickets are modestly priced; appointments can be made for massage and other treatments.

SCHLOSSHOTEL LERBACH—
LANCASTER BEAUTY FARM
Bergisch-Gladbach, Germany

he fifty-four-room Schlosshotel Lerbach is a handsome estate that has been transformed into a sophisticated yet intimate hotel and conference center enhanced by a luxurious spa, Lancaster Beauty Farm. As you approach along a winding drive, the castle *(schloss)*, with its spires and elegant shuttered windows, looks like a fairy-tale vision right out of the brothers Grimm.

This old-world castle, which traces its history to the fourteenth century, has been thoroughly renovated to impress the most discerning traveler. The ancient exterior is deceiving; inside all has been lovingly restored. The impeccably decorated guest rooms are designer-coordinated from the bedspreads to the drapes and comfortable sofas. Everything from fresh flowers to plumped pillows is perfectly placed. The schloss itself is a favorite venue for conferences. The enchanting gardens are reminiscent of bygone days when guests would promenade each afternoon to see and be seen.

The spa tradition had its roots in Germany, thanks to the legacy of the Romans, and it continues to thrive there. At last count, there were over 300 *bads* (baths), with many offering natural mineral water. Although the famous spas like Baden-Baden continue to attract those seeking a classic three-week cure (bathing, drinking, internal irrigation, and vapor inhalation), Schlosshotel Lerbach has a less structured regime with a decided emphasis on beauty and pampering. The expertly staffed, impressive Lancaster Beauty Farm offers traditional European spa treatments as well as hot stone massage.

Dining at the Schlosshotel Lerbach is an adventure in itself, especially if you are into fine wines and French nouvelle cuisine. The Restaurant Dieter Muller is known for an exquisite menu and wine list; the Schloss-Schanke is less formal, serving regional specialties. Calorie counting is not part of the cure *(kur)* here, but dinner showcases executive chef Dieter Muller's restrained elegance, with plates resembling photos from a gourmet food magazine. This is not the time to worry about a little butter or cream!

For those wanting an intimate spa retreat in the German countryside, the Schlosshotel Lerbach is an ideal choice.

Schlosshotel Lerbach—Lancaster Beauty Farm
Lerbacher Weg
51465 Bergisch-Gladbach
Germany
Phone: 49–22–02–2040
Fax: 49–022–02–204–940
E-mail: lerbach@relaischateaux.fr
Web site: www.relaischateaux.fr

Season: Year-round

General Manager: Kurt Wagner

Spa Director/Owner: Elke Diefendbach-Althoff

Reservations: 49–022–02–2040 or 800–735–2478 (Relais & Chateaux);

Accommodations: Fifty-four guest rooms, including nine suites, decorated in designer-coordinated fabrics and fine furnishings.

Meals: The gourmet Restaurant Dieter Muller, with its exquisite menu and wine list; Schloss-Schanke, less formal and serving regional dishes; and the hotel bar Max Ernst. The spa will cater reduced calorie meals.

Facilities: The Lancaster Beauty Farm with six treatment rooms; indoor swimming pool; sauna and solarium. Conference facilities; seventy acres of parkland with jogging track, tennis court, fish ponds and pathways; bicycle rentals; parking.

Services & Special Programs: Archery, night hikes, cooking classes; concerts; carriage rides, wine tastings.

Rates: $$

Best Spa Package: The three-day Lerbach Program includes accommodations for two nights, breakfast and dinner, body brush massage, two facials, manicure, pedicure, two lymphatic face drainages, one deep body cleaning and peeling, two aromatherapy body treatments, one ocean-tub bath, one makeup consultation. $396 per person; room rates start at $295 per night, which includes breakfast, tax, and service.

Credit Cards: Most major

Getting There: Arriving from the Dusseldorf Airport or by car, take Highway 4 to the Bergisch-Gladbach exit, turning right in the direction of Bensberg Zentrum. Turn left at the junction of Bergisch-Gladbach/Zentrum, and then right in the direction of Kreishaus (street name is Am Rübezahwald; continue to Lerbacher Weg.

What's Nearby: Shopping and sightseeing in Dusseldorf; three golf courses.

Fabulous Footbaths

The footbath is an old-fashioned remedy that has been popular in Germany and Austria for generations. In *Heal Yourself the European Way*, **Betsy Morsher recommends different types of footbath. The alternating hot and cold water bath gives instant energy to a tired body. Sit on the edge of the tub and let hot water run over your feet for two minutes; then switch to cold water. Alternate the hot and cold streams for ten minutes. Or try a mint footbath, used to aid sleep. After a hot day, place a handful of peppermint or spearmint leaves in a tub of hot water and soak your feet for ten minutes. The tension and stress will fade away—feet first! Another type of foot bath helps in cold weather: Dissolve a capful of Epsom salts in hot water and soak your feet and lower legs (up to the knees). Finally, if your feet are swollen or tired (maybe from that long flight to Germany), try the baking soda bath. Pour three table-spoons of baking soda into hot water. After soaking your feet, rub them with witch hazel. Austrian alpine hikers swear by this footbath for relieving body tension.**

TOSKANA THERME
Bad Sulza, Germany

An architectural masterpiece completed just in time for the millennium, the Toskana Therme takes spa-going to new heights. Located in an old spa town near Weimar, the complex includes the Hotel an der Therme, a wellness clinic, and a training school for spa therapists. Both a day spa and a destination spa, this high-tech therme makes taking the waters a unique experience.

Star Trek comes to mind as you approach the domed Toskana Therme. Spanning an entire hillside, the glass-walled structure is a work of art that combines water therapies with music and underwater sound. With six interconnected pools, the main hall is flooded with light, colors, and music. At night, it turns into an aquatic opera house, with dance and band concerts. The audience often gets into the act, floating along rivers of light to the bottom-level swimming pool.

Set amid verdant hills of Thuringia, an area often called the Tuscany of the East, Bad Sulza has been a healing center for more than a century. The saline waters rise from an ancient seabed at 92 degrees Fahrenheit (32–34 degrees Celsius) right under Toskana Therme, constantly circulating fresh, warm mineral water in the pools and baths. Spa-goers can arrange treatments or simply relax. There are saunas, some with panoramic views, and lounges on balconies overlook the pools. Massages, beauty, and kur treatments are available in a wellness center staffed by professionals. Meals and snacks are available on the garden level, where Ristorante il Toskana provides pasta inspired by the chef's homeland.

Orchestrating the various elements of this extraordinary new pleasure palace is a husband-wife team, Klaus Boehm and Marion Schneider. Their arts events turned Bad Sulza from a sleepy East German backwater into something resembling integrative art. Close to the fountainhead of German modern design, the original Bauhaus University in Weimar, the area attracts lovers of the avant-garde with nature-oriented buildings and festivals. Performances in the new Toskana Therme have included a water ballet and live concerts of electronic music as well as works by Bach and Handel's *Water Music*.

The ultimate experience comes in the domed Liquid Sound Temple. Multimedia artist Micky Reimann worked with the architects on an integrated system of underwater sound and projected images that fill the

dome. A session of aqua wellness in the hands of a trained therapist leaves you floating in a sea of color, your body gently moving and vibrating to the rhythms of underwater music. Special evenings are devoted to both live and electronic concerts.

The three-day relaxation program includes accommodations at Hotel an der Therme, a holdover from the days when Bad Sulza served the medical needs of the East German government. This is without a doubt a wellness waterpark for the twenty-first century.

The Art of Liquid Sound

Beneath warm, salty water in a domed pool, a unique technology transforms bathing into a mystical experience. Invented by media artist Micky Reimann, the idea was inspired by encounters with orca whales in the Canadian Pacific. As you float weightlessly in salt water at body temperature, sounds, music, and colors surround you, creating a feeling of release from earthly stress. Video images and colored lights fill the futuristic dome as music wells up from the water. Opera arias, tango, New Age music, even the ur-sound of whales, mix in a burst of creative energy. Blurring the lines between therapy, wellness, and entertainment, the Liquid Sound experience stimulates a relaxation response and a sensory high.

Liquid Sound and Light in a Thermal Springs Temple

Toskana Therme
Wunderwaldstr 2a
D-99518 Bad Sulza
Germany
Phone: 49–36461–91080
Fax: 49–36461–91088
E-mail: toskana@kbs.de
Web site: www.liquid-sound.com

Season: Year-round

General Manager: Klaus Boehm

Spa Director: Marion Schneider

Reservations: E-mail to hoteltherme@aol.com

Accommodations: Eighty-one modern rooms with private bath in Hotel an der Therme have direct access to the spa. Simply furnished, rooms are air-conditioned, have woodland view. Some are equipped for people who are physically challenged; some have four beds. All with private bath, TV, phone.

Meals: The spa cafeteria features Italian specialties from Tuscany, pasta, pizza, and veal. Hotel guests are served breakfast and dinner in a private dining room. Produce from organic farms is used for vegetarian dishes. Seasonal specialties include venison, fish, and modified regional specialties that are low in fat, salt, and sugar.

Facilities: Thermal water pools (four indoor, two outdoor), hydrotherapy baths, fango, foot- and armbaths, exercise studio, saunas, steam bath, medical clinic.

Services & Special Programs: Aqua Wellness (floating water movement and massage); Liquid Sound sessions. Massage, body wrap, mud packs, Kneipp herbal and water therapies; medical consultation.

Rates: $$

Best Spa Package: Half-day program includes classic fity-minute massage, fango mud pack, foot reflexology, plus unlimited use of thermal pools, and private locker ($75). Available only with three-night stay at Hotel an der Therme.

Credit Cards: Visa, Mastercard

Getting There: From Frankfurt, by car on Autobahn A–4 ro Apolda exit, Route B–87 to Bad Sulza turnoff (three hours). By train, to Weimar. Taxi, rental car available.

What's Nearby: Weimar (Goethe house, Bauhaus University), Dresden, Nuremberg, Hanover, Berlin.

THERMAE SYLLA GRAND HOTEL & SPA
Edipsos, Evia Island, Greece

nown by Aristotle, Plutarch, and health-seekers throughout the early Hellenistic period, the waters of Edipsos rise from volcanic springs in the sea. Full of minerals, this constant source of hot water is utilized with state-of-the-art equipment and medical supervision to provide revitalization and wellness programs at the new (1999) Thermae Sylla Spa.

Set on the tip of a popular seaside resort, about 150 kilometers from Athens, Edipsos has connections by ferryboat with some of the most important archaeology sites in Greece. What it does not have is a sandy beach. The new spa makes up for this by mixing seawater with thermal water in the outdoor swimming pool. The water is constantly circulated and requires no chlorine, and can be used year-round.

Given the island's subtropical climate, eucalyptus trees and palms are abundant, shading the pool and used in spa therapy. Relax in a wooden sauna as steam infused with essential oils bathes you. A most magical treatment is the mud chamber ceremony called *rasul*,

where your body is cleansed by natural peeling in a mist of herbal steam and a shower of thermal water from the starry dome. Respiratory problems are treated by inhaling steam of ionized water mixed with extracts of eucalyptus, chamomile, and other plants grown on the island.

All things natural is the key to Thermae Sylla. Geothermal springwater heats the buildings as well as the swimming pools and relaxing whirlpool baths. Physiotherapy under supervision of the spa team takes place in the warm pools, adding extra benefits to exercise for slimming or rehabilitation. Calming showers are combined with massage, and mud mixed with thermal water relieves pain of arthritis, rheumatism, and muscular ailments.

Designed around a secluded garden pool, the new spa complements the original Thermae Sylla Grand Hotel, which first opened in 1897. Newly restored, the hotel offers four-star accommodations with sea views, and new spa rooms overlooking the garden. With interior access to all facilities, this is a self-contained resort, offering destination spa programs, and day spa packages for guests at dozens of hotels nearby.

Mediterranean cuisine comes naturally in the Greek islands, and the Grand Hotel offers a choice of two restaurants with traditional healthy cooking. Special diets for slimming also take advantage of the local seafood and farm products. Combined with massage and physiotherapy, the spa doctors design personalized programs to show results that you can take home.

Nature lovers can explore the Sporades, home of rare seals, and Chalkida, a fishing village noted for restaurants overlooking a rush of tidal waters. Excur-

Thermae Sylla Grand Hotel & Spa
Edipsos, Evia
Greece
Phone. 30–0226–60100
Fax: 30–0226–22055
Web site: www.thermaesylla.gr

Season: Year-round

General Manager: Nikos Trikourakis

Accommodations: 230 rooms in a seafront complex that includes a modern wing adjoining the spa and the original Grand Hotel with high-ceilinged rooms, French doors opening to small balconies. Completely air-conditioned, rooms have king-size or double beds, modern bathroom, some with marble tub. Amenities include robes and slippers, TV, radio, safe, refrigerator.

Meals: Seafood, from giant shrimp to lobster, lamb herbed and cooked with olive oil, are features of the traditional Greek cuisine served in the hotel's two dining rooms. Local farms supply fresh produce year-round, and fruit comes from Mediterranean orchards of Israel and Spain.

Facilities: Gymnasium with exercise equipment, private treatment rooms for clay, mud, and seaweed body masques and facials, Cleopatra Bath with milk and oils, mud bath, underwater massage tubs with ozone, Vichy shower, herbal steam bath, volcanic steam bath, inhalation therapy.

Services & Special Programs: Massage, reflexology, aromatherapy, body wraps, facial. Physiotherapy program, anti-stress program. Tennis, biking, fishing, and water sports. Evening concerts.

Rates: $$

Best Spa Package: Thermae Sylla Energy, a three-day program integrates exercise and relaxation with beauty treatments. Price: $182.84 per person includes half board (buffet breakfast & lunch), taxes, medical exam. Room for two from $118.94 to $288.74.

Credit Cards: Most major

Getting There: From Athens by car, the Lamia Highway to Arkitsa, ferryboat to Edipsos (three hours).

What's Nearby: Delphi, Mount Parnassos, Meteora, Epidaurus Roman coliseum and healing center.

sions to the Byzantine monasteries of Meteora, which cling to rocky cliffs, and offer hospitality from the monks. In winter, there is skiing at Mount Parnassos.

Surrounded by the Aegean sea, Thermae Sylla Spa brings healing waters together with modern technology on an island where time stands still.

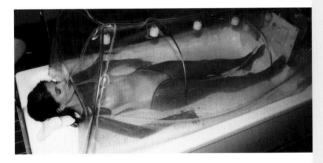

Natural Thalassotherapy

Thalassa is the Greek word for the sea. A French doctor, Rene Quinton, conceived thalassotherapy with fresh seawater and algae. Here seawater is mixed with thermal mineral water. Two layers of water meet in front of the hotel, where steps in the rocks allow you to bathe in the sea. Or have a body wrap with seaweed and special creams said to be effective for body firming. This is thalassotherapy of a different kind.

BUDAPEST: SPA TOWN

Budapest, Hungary

In a city where "taking the waters" is a daily ritual for traditionalists, spa culture can take many forms: medicinal, relaxing, and simply socializing. Therapy-seeking voyagers have trekked here since the time of the Roman Empire. Elaborate bathing establishments built by the city's Ottoman rulers are now open to the public. While the waters certified medicinal are used to treat rheumatic diseases and for physical therapy, a relaxing soak in the buoyant, slightly sulfurous water is also an effective antidote to tourist fatigue.

Back in the 1930s, guests at the St. Gellert Hotel tested the latest in aquatic entertainment: a wave pool where bathing beauties accompanied by a gypsy band faced artificial waves. Every fifteen minutes, a whistle signaled the start of a series of waves pumped from natural hot springs under the hotel. Destroyed by Nazi bombs in 1945, the art deco hotel was rebuilt after the war, complete with wave pool. Now known simply as the **Gellert,** the spa complex has grown to include a family pool and two separate baths, one for men and one for women, each with three plunge pools of varying temperatures, a sauna, and a steam bath. Hotel guests have direct access, and can come in bathrobe; from a side street, the public entrance is busy day and night. Facilities for massage and nail care aren't fancy, but the elaborate

domed pools are a sybaritic fantasy right out of a Fellini movie. Located on the Buda side of the Danube, the hotel looks a bit faded but its old-fashioned rooms are a good value, especially those with a view of the historic Chain Bridge.

Budapest, with its tree-shaded boulevards and Danube venues, retains an air of sophistication. On the Pest side of the river, the city's past splendor is visible in the restored Opera House and the City Park, where a major art museum and famed Gundel restaurant are close to the **Szechenyi Baths** (Allatkerti ut 11). One of Europe's largest bathing establishments when it opened in 1927, Szechenyi offers pools of thermal water inside and out, set among grandiose statuary. Apart from the health care and medical section, its popularity as a recreation center continues today.

The **Kiraly Baths** (Fo ut 84) were built in the mid-1500s on a Roman road still busy with city traffic. Topped by a golden Turkish crescent and domed roof, the interior is dark and foreboding. Pin-pricks of colored glass permit light through the dome. Alternate days are allotted for men and women, and unlike the Gellert, bathing is au naturel. Ask for a massage and you will be soaped, pummeled, rubbed, and smacked, and leave feeling good!

Modern thermal hotels cluster around **Margaret Island** (Margitsziget), where

you have a choice of destination spa or day spa programs. A giant park in the Danube, with rose gardens and jogging paths, Margaret Island's two spa hotels are linked underground to thermal pools of such intensely hot waters that a checkup with the medical director is required before you bathe. The 206-room **Margitsziget Hotel,** rated five-star, has full medical and dental clinics; the more charming, 163-room

Danubius Grand Hotel dates from 1873. Both hotels feature dietetic and Hungarian cuisine. Sharing the island's spring water and facilities, **Thermal Hotel Helia** (262 rooms) on the Pest embankment, and **Thermal Hotel Aquincum** (312 rooms) on the Buda shore, are oriented to leisure vacations and conventions, and offer Finnish saunas, gymnasium, and indoor swimming pools.

Forget Modesty

Bathing au naturel is the traditional way to get in touch with your outer self at the old bathhouses. Tickets for the furdo (baths) cost about $3.00; if you want massage, point to a menu posted over the ticket booth. Bring a bathing cap (mandatory); modesty is served by an apron available in the locker room. No matter what shape you're in, all are equal when naked. Get a free neck massage under spouts of water that constantly refresh the pools. Exposure to thermal water can't hurt you, but skeptics question medical benefits. Simply soaking, however, will put a spring in your step.

Taking the Waters in an Ancient City of Thermal Springs

Hungarian Hotels
6033 West Century Boulevard
Los Angeles, CA 90045
Phone: (213) 649–5960 or (800) 649–5960
Fax: (213) 649–5852
E-mail: Tradesco@ix.netcom.com
Web site: www.gotohungary.com
Reservations: 800–448–4321
Rates: $$

Getting There: International airlines serving Budapest include Malev, British Airways, and Lufthansa. Train service from the airport to downtown, then taxi.

What's Nearby: Lake Heviz (thermal springs); Lake Balaton (sailing, camping); Sarvar (thermal springs); Eger (wineries, Lippizan horse farm).

THE LODGE & SPA AT INCHYDONEY ISLAND
West Cork, Ireland

f you enjoy walking along a secluded beach, listening to the sounds of crashing waves, and inhaling brisk ocean air, the Lodge and Spa at Inchydoney Island is the spot for you. The pristine environment on this mystical island off the coast of West Cork is the perfect location for a thalassotherapy spa—it's free of pollution, offers expansive areas for exercise and relaxation, and, importantly, an abundant supply of seawater. This is a retreat where the word *stress* is unwelcome and virtually unknown.

This luxury spa, opened in 1999, is a full service thalassotherapy center, Ireland's first and only such center. The Blue Flag Beaches stretching out to the south from the Virgin Mary Bank benefit from the Gulf Stream water, making this a natural choice for a thalassotherapy cure—and adding solitude to this dramatic location.

The Lodge was designed to reflect the environment in subtle ways. Natural simplicity is evident in all areas of the building, from the foyer, with its stunning natural slate floor and limestone fireplace, to the guest quarters.

Within the stunning heated seawater pool are a geyser spa, a waterfall, a counter-current swimming area, underwater jets, an aqua gymnastic area, neck showers, microbubble seats, and an airy spa. The sheer delight of the wondrous edifice to seawater should be experienced in a leisurely fashion.

The pool serves as an introduction to the thalassotherapy treatments, which are based on the fundamentals of the French seawater cure. The spa has eleven treatment rooms offering a complete range of therapies, including balneotherapy, brumisation, hydrojet therapy, and algeotherapy. The spa offerings are further enhanced by pressotherapy, cryotherapy, electrolysis, massage, relfexology, yoga, body stretch, toning, beach walking, and beauty treatments. Espa products are used for facial, body, scalp, foot, and nail treatments.

The diet plan is creative and ambitious. Executive chef Chris Farrell has designed a sensible program based on 50 percent carbohydrates; 30 percent fat (with polysaturated olive and fish oils, avocados, and nuts); and 20 percent protein. You will find fresh fruits and vegetables, plus cereals and grains on the menu, which includes information on calorie and fat content.

The Lodge's guest rooms and suites are spacious and comfortable, and all capture majestic views of the ocean. They are equipped with satellite television and direct-dial phones. Fortunate spa-goers here enjoy the benefits of a thalassotherapy cure at one of Ireland's premier resorts.

The Seawater Cure Comes of Age

To specialize in thalassotherapy, a spa must meet six rules which were established by the French government in June 1997. The thalassa spa must have an exceptional location by the sea; it must use natural seawater and elements derived from the sea, such as seaweed, sea mud, and sand; there must be permanent medical supervision; there must be professionally trained staff; there must be permanent concern for hygiene and security; and there must be specialized, well-maintained equipment. Thalassotherapy has been known to be effective in treatments for headaches, menopause, leg problems, stress, and insomnia; it also induces relaxation and slimming.

Spa Setting an Inspiration for Poets

The Lodge & Spa at Inchydoney Island
Clonakilty
West Cork, Ireland
Phone: 353–23–33143
Fax: 353–23–35229
E-mail: reservations@inchydoneyisland.com
Web site: www.inchydoneyisland.com

Season: Year-round

General Manager: Michael Knox-Johnston

Spa Director: Dr. Christian Jost

Reservations: 00–353–23–33143 or 800–888–4747 (from the United States only) or by e-mail (above)

Accommodations: Sixty-three double- or twin-bed ocean-view rooms; three suites with conservatory sitting rooms overlooking both beaches; one junior suite; eighteen two-bedroom apartments and two four-bedroom apartments. All accommodations face the famous Inchydoney beaches.

Meals: The resort has two restaurants, the Gulfstream Restaurant and Contented Plaice at Dunes Pub.

Facilities: Hydrotherapy; skincare; fitness center; lounge and library; snooker room; gymnasium.

Services & Special Programs: Wellness week, weight management; golf at Bandon and at the unique Lisselan 6-hole course; horseback riding at Clonakity Equestrian Center; deep-sea fishing; salmon and trout fishing; off-road driving; clay pigeon shooting and archery; diving; and twenty-four-hour room service.

Rates: $$

Best Spa Package: The Sejour Specifique Experience is seven nights and includes accommodations, seven Irish breakfasts, seven dinners, and twenty-four thalasso treatments. The rates start at $1,806, double occupancy (per room) in the low season, September through April. Add to this a 10% service charge.

Credit Cards: Most major

Getting There: British Airways to London with a connecting flight to the Cork Airport, forty-five minutes from the resort. By train from the Cork Rail Station, fifty-five minutes away.

What's Nearby: Golf at the Old Head of Kinsale Golf Links; fishing in the Gulf Stream waters; Mallow races; wreck of the Luisitania, thirty minutes offshore; the West Cork Museum; Animal Park; Park Collins Memorial Homestead; Lisselan Gardens.

CAPRI BEAUTY FARM AT THE PALACE HOTEL

Capri, Italy

Since ancient times, Capri has been considered the ideal place to reunite with nature. Thanks to the island's mild Mediterranean climate and lush surroundings, the Capri Beauty Farm provides the perfect environment for a memorable spa vacation.

Perched atop one of the highest hills on Capri, the Palace Hotel is surrounded by stunning views of the Gulf of Naples, Vesuvius, and the Amalfi coast. After breakfast in a garden suite, or on your balcony overlooking the sea, stroll to the hotel's intimate Capri Beauty Farm for a morning of ritual renewal. Water therapies are emphasized here: seawater invigorates your workout at the indoor pool; there is a hydrotherapy bath with seaweed and algae and a saltwater Kneipp circuit. Hydrotherapy baths are prescribed for inflammations or chronic problems associated with muscular and bone structure, plus a full range of hydrokinestherapy (motion and exercise), electrical stimulation, and massage. Personal trainers and a medical staff work as a team with each guest.

Treatments feature thalassotherapy based on French technology and marine products. Housed in a recently expanded two-story wing of the hotel, serenely quiet and private, the Beauty Farm is a favorite hangout of Hollywood celebrities like Julia Roberts and Harrison Ford, as well as fashion designers from Milan, Saudi royalty, and the king and queen of Sweden.

The highly professional staff at Capri Beauty Farm is led by Francesco Canonanco, a medical doctor and specialist in food science, immunology, and aesthetic medicine. With a full range of face and body treatments prescribed in what the doctor describes as a logical and progressive sequence, aesthetics becomes a science here. The new terme marine program offers fango treatments with sea mud, inhalations, and seaweed body wraps.

Capri Beauty Farm at the Palace Hotel
Via Capodimonte, 2
80071 Anacapri
Capri, Italy
Phone: 39–081–837–3800
Fax: 39–081–837–3191
E-mail: palacehotel@italyhotel.com
Web site: www.capri-palace.com

Season: Year-round

General Manager: Tonino Cacace

Spa Director: Francesco Canonaco, M.D.

Reservations: 800–223–5652

Accommodations: Eighty rooms, including twenty-two junior suites (four with private garden and heated plunge pool) amid Moorish arches, whitewashed walls. Mediterranean-modern look of bedrooms features tile floor, baldachino-style beds (four-poster draped in white linen), wicker, and wood furniture. Travertine marble bathroom with robes, full-size bathtub, shower. Completely air-conditioned, rooms have ceiling fans, minibar, safe. Penthouse suite has hanging gardens, private swimming pool.

Meals: Buffet breakfast included in room rate. Main dining room serves a la carte lunch and dinner with salad bar, a selection of heart-healthy food, and a low-fat Mediterranean diet of that uses lots of grains, olive-oil, and fish.

Facilities: Beauty farm with private hydrotherapy tubs, indoor exercise pool with salt water, outdoor Kneipp walk, pressotherapy leggings, Turkish steambath, solarium, hair salon, gymnasium. Medical clinic for laser therapy, electrocardiogram, laboratory tests.

Services & Special Programs: Cosmetology facials, aerosol inhalation, marine algae baths and body wraps, hairstyling, manicure/pedicure, massage, shiatsu, Vodder manual lymphatic drainage, ayurvedic massage. Special program for tired legs includes massage, diet food, medicated wraps.

Rates: $$$

Best Spa Package: Terme Marine, a seven-day program with half board (breakfast and dinner), medical checkup, Kneipp therapies for vascular system, algotherapies, massage, seawater aerosol inhalations, clay facial and hair treatments, gymnastics in pool, guided walks. From $1,691.51.

Credit Cards: Most major

Getting There: From Naples or Sorrento, slow ferries or fast hydrofoil to Marina Grande (forty minutes). Hotel sends porter and car to pier on request.

What's Nearby: Blue Grotto, Villa San Michele museum, Punta Carena lighthouse and beach club.

The island's sun-splashed environment gets you in the mood to relax once your medical checkup is complete. Located in Anacapri, steps from a hiking trail and cable cars on Monte Solaro, the Palace is a convenient base for sightseeing. Unless you're trying to escape paparazzi, take a taxi or public bus down hairpin-curved roads to the port. After the last ferries full of day-trippers leave Marina Piccola, walk along a cliffside path to Fontelina, a club set in the rocks of an ancient Roman landing place. Among yachts and cafes is a swimming hole called Da Luigi. Night is the best time to explore Capri town, midway up the mountain, and to people-watch on Capri's version of Rodeo Drive.

A style-setter in the 1960s, the five-star Palace Hotel has gotten a new lease on life under owner Tonino Cacace, whose parents liked the location even though it was on the unfashionable side of the island. Beyond the souvenir stands and pizzerias, this is a small gem where even the police wear designer shades.

GRAND HOTEL TERME ABANO

Abano Terme, Italy

urrounded by the Euganean hills an hour from Venice, Abano is a spa town like no other. Fango, a medicinal mud dug from the hills, is the main attraction. More than 135 hotels in the valley offer fango treatments for arthritis, rheumatism, osteoporosis, gout, and sciatica. Doctors use mud therapy for patients recuperating from surgery and accidents. Mixed with hot thermal mineral spring water to simmer and mature in open-air vats, fango's ingredients include algae, minerals, and trace elements. It's as natural a cure for aches and pains as you can find.

Following a routine prescribed by the hotel's resident doctor, fango treatments are relaxing and help to sweat out toxins. Spread on linen sheets by a fanghini therapist who tucks you in, then applies a cool cloth to your sweating brow, the warm mud opens pores, allowing heat and minerals to penetrate the body. With little to do but meditate, think about the Romans who discovered this place, named *aponus* from the Greek for "to relieve pain." Legend says temples to Hercules were built here, and some archeological sites

have been excavated in the center of town. The Doges of Venice had villas in the valley, and Lord Byron visited in the 1800s. Just when you feel stuck in the mud, your fanghini says shower off and soak in a bathtub full of bubbling ozonated mineral water. Following a rest period and massage, you're ready for breakfast.

A personal program is planned by a coordinator at the hotel first—your heart is checked and medical condition discussed with a staff doctor. Contraindications: fango is not allowed for pregnant women and people with certain medical conditions. Diet and nutrition complement the cure program, and consultation can be arranged to set up special meals. Alternative therapies also are discussed by the doctor before you begin a "cure." Recommended for best benefits: twelve-day stay with daily treatments.

At the new five-star Grand Hotel Terme Abano, traditional fango cures mix with today's spa trends in beauty and well-being. Set in landscaped, semitropical gardens, the hotel has an atmosphere of elegance and exclusivity. Crystal chandeliers, marble floors, and Ori-

Grand Hotel Terme Abano
Via V. Flacco
35031 Abano Terme (Padova)
Italy
Phone: 390–49–8248100
Fax: 390–49–8669994
E-mail: ghabano@gbhotels.it
Web site: www.gbhotels.it

Season: Year-round

Managing Director: Chiara Borile

Spa Director: Maurizio Grassetto, M.D.

Accommodations: 189 rooms, twelve junior suites, and eight suites. Some are nonsmoking. All have balcony, full modern bathroom with tub and shower, hair dryer, decorated in marble. Furnished with antique reproductions, rooms are air-conditioned, have TV, telephone, spacious closet, linens and robes by Frette.

Meals: Full board includes breakfast buffet with eggs to order; lunch and dinner in the main dining room. Health menu at no extra charge, based on 1,000 calories.

Facilities: Thirty-three private rooms for fango thermal therapy; beauty salon; gymnasium; two outdoor swimming pools (one with whirlpool and jets) with thermal mineral water; indoor swimming pool and whirlpool; Kneipp water walk; sauna grotto; steam room.

Services & Special Programs: Massage, shiatsu, Thai massage, facial mud pack, inhalation therapy, ayurvedic scalp treatment, lymphatic drainage, hydromassage. Programs include anti-stress, anticellulite, body firming.

Rate: $$$

Best Spa Package: *Remise en Forme,* a week with varied treatments daily, including facial grommage, body peeling, collagen treatment, massage. The program starts with a medical examination at the hotel and includes checkups as needed. Daily group gymnastics in the swimming pools or gymnasium, plus an evening infusion drink. Priced at approximately $775, this package does not include meals and accommodations.

Credit Cards: Most major

Getting There: By car from Milan, Autostrada (highway) A–4, exit Padua west. By train to Terme Euganee or Padua stations; taxi, car rental, or bus. Nearest airports: Venice or Verona.

What's Nearby: Four championship 18-hole golf courses; Venice, Verona, Padua; Palladio's Vicenza villas.

ental rugs decorate the lobby. Created by the privately-held GB Hotels Group, and managed by the Borile family, this is more than a hotel. Two floors are dedicated to health and beauty. Separate from the fango department, and not requiring medical supervision, an entire floor is devoted to beauty treatments. All guests have access to the fitness equipment, gymnasium, steam room, and huge sauna designed to resemble a mountainside grotto.

Excursions by private bus are scheduled, and the hotel has bicycles for guided trips in the region. Concerts in the town garden and opera evenings at the hotel are free of charge.

Doing the Fango

All mud therapy sessions are composed of four fundamentals: the body wrap; bathing in mineral water; the sweat reaction; and, finally, massage, with its tonic action on the muscular and nervous system. The therapeutic properties of the mud combine with the mineral water's chemical composition (bromine-iodine) and temperature to benefit the skin. The doctor may also prescribe sessions in a steam bath or "sweat grotto" for treatment of obesity, gout, and diabetes.

GROTTA GIUSTI TERME
Monsummano Terme, Tuscany, Italy

eneath this hillside hotel is a grotto called the Inferno. This ancient natural vapor cave, the largest thermal grotto in the world, provides a place to cleanse body and mind.

Terme in Tuscany come in many sizes, from traditional hot springs to sophisticated resorts. Grotta Giusti is neither the largest nor the grandest, but it has a combination of comfortable lodging and affordable treatments that make it among the best buys in Italy. Basics include thermal mud baths and facials, consultation with dermatology specialists, and choice of treatments designed to activate musculoskeletal and circulatory systems. Add the grand country villa ambience and personalized service of a four-star hotel, and you have an affordable escape.

Both a day spa and destination spa, Grotta Giusti offers three-day revitalization packages with the adjoining hotel of the same name. Guest rooms are functional-modern, rather than posh old-world. Surrounded by extensive gardens, tall parasol pines, and chestnut trees, it is an enchanted place where time seems to stand still. The villa's history goes back to the nineteenth century, when the poet Giuseppe Giusti had the hillside estate created. Today you don a spa robe in your room and walk down the hall directly into the reception area.

A physical checkup is in order prior to any heat-based treatment, so an English-speaking hostess escorts new arrivals to the medical department. Once your appointments are programmed into the computer, red-coated hostesses help you get oriented. Spa clothing appears in your room: a long white cotton tunic for relaxing in the grotto, a hooded woolen robe for warmth, and plastic shower shoes.

Group activity is minimal, but meeting people is no problem. The dining room host speaks four languages and seats you in a section of the room where menus are in the appropriate language. Join a morning exercise group or walk in the park to make new friends. In the palestra, an airy aerobics studio with sprung-wood floor, aerobics, tai chi, and back muscle stretches alternate with sessions of yoga. Your daily routine might include a sweat in the grotto, a massage, or inhalation therapy.

Save one morning to take the waters in Montecatini at the grandest spa park in the world, Tettucio Springs. As an orchestra plays operatic arias and waltzes under a classical rotunda, stroll to ornately tiled

Grotta Giusti Terme
Via Grotta Giusti, 171
51015 Monsummano Terme
Italy
Phone. 39–572–51165
Fax: 39–572–51269
E-mail: info@grottagiustispa.com
Web site: www.grottagiustispa.com

Season: April–November

General Manager: Aldo Pollastri

Spa Director: Antonino Di Pietro, M.D.

Spa Appointments: 39–572–51008

Accommodations: Seventy air-conditioned rooms with basic modern furniture, small shower or full bathtub. Room rate varies according to view: park or hillside, standard or superior. Amenities include satellite color TV, direct-dial telephone, minibar, safe.

Meals: Breakfast buffet included in daily hotel room rate. Lunch and dinner offer low-calorie alternative menu, typical Tuscan dishes. Specialties include gnocchi in tomato sauce, veal scaloppini with braised fennel, and risotto. Salads, fish, and steak included in the fixed menu. Dessert can be cream cake or baked apple.

Facilities: Hydrotherapy, inhalations, indoor thermal exercise pool, aerobics studio, thermal steam grotto.

Services & Special Programs: Body wraps, facials, massage, shiatsu, reflexology, facials. Dermatology clinic and medical consultation.

Rates: $$

Best Spa Package: Star VIP anti-stress revitalization program with three-night hotel accommodation and full board. Treatments by dermatologist include glycolic acid peeling, rebalancing, and cellular therapy. Two physiotherapy massages, shiatsu, and daily thermal steam bath. Take-home gift of anti-fatigue bath gel made with Grotta Giusti thermal water. $870 per person, double; $1,068 single.

Credit Cards: MasterCard, Visa

Getting There: From Florence or Pisa by car, Autostrada E–76 to exit Montecatini-Monsummano. By train, commuter service Florence-Montecatini.

What's Nearby: Pisa, Florence, Lucca, Viareggio beach resorts.

Note: Major renovations planned for Spring 2002.

fountains and try a cup of sulfurous, salty water. Famous for helping to repair the damage of overindulging in the good life, Tettuccio's waters have been praised for their purgative powers. Since all shops and spa services shut down each day from noon to 3:00 P.M., and all day on Sunday, complimentary van service is provided by Grotta Giusti to get you back to your hillside hideaway in time for lunch, a swim in the outdoor pool, and perhaps a nap before dinner.

Antidote to La Dolce Vita

As an antidote to la dolce vita, the grotto at Grotta Giusti ranks among the best spa experiences. Robed and hooded, you join a monklike group on stone ramps leading to subterranean caves and an underground lake. Handed towels, you recline on wooden chairs, meditate, and sweat out toxins. An eerie beauty pervades the vaulted rocky chambers of Inferno. Heat increases as you descend past dripping stalactites and a transluscent pool called Lake of Limbo, where scuba divers explore on weekends. Arriving at Purgatorio, your tunic soaked in sweat, it's hard to keep track of time. But an attendant brings towels and a dry tunic just in time to head back up for a shower and massage Paradiso!

PALAZZO ARZAGA HOTEL—SATURNIA SPA

Brescia, Italy

Imagine having an herbal wrap in a fifteenth-century monastery, the Palazzo Arzaga, just twenty-five minutes outside of Verona. An ambitious renovation has transformed this once austere abbey into a luxurious golf and spa resort.

Designed with golfers in mind, there is a morning warm-up and stretch program endorsed by PGA Europe, as well as a variety of massage therapies under medical supervision designed especially for golfers. For those who want to assess their muscle contraction and posture (which might affect swing or cause pain), a kinesiologist is on staff to solve the problem. And for those who simply wish to "spa," the holistic skin and body treatments span the Saturnia product range, with antiaging facials, biopeeling, reflexology, and aromatherapy.

The Palazzo is for those who are comfortable at a resort where the outside world is held at bay (thanks in part to excellent security). In many ways the ambience is that of an upscale American spa and golf resort. There are year-round tournaments at the Jack Nicklaus II 18-hole, par 72 golf course, and a golf academy for those who want to improve their game.

The guest rooms are among the most unusual in Italy, with the original monastery frescoes still intact and integrated into the decor, some appearing in the luxurious bathrooms and others on walls. Every room has a distinct personality: eighteenth-century Venetian and nineteenth-century Lombardy furnishings, sumptuous fabrics, marble bathrooms, fireplaces, hand-painted and timbered ceilings, and such modern amenities as satellite television, minibars, and hair dryers. Guests choose not only from a superb collection of rooms in the hotel but also from thirteen chapel rooms near the church and others that overlook the golf course. From their windows, guests may view the serene inner courtyard and chapel, the original orchard behind the hotel, or the Palazzo's terrace.

Pistachio gelato and penne pasta aside, there is a weight program integrating the Arzaga light menu (low sugar and low-fat ingredients) with a personalized exercise program. Together they afford a gentle way to induce weight loss.

Unique in Italy, the resort's Slim & Tonic Pool contains water formulated with mineral, marine, and thermal salts that are thought to have an impact on metabolism and circulation. Magnesium, potassium, bromine sodium, and iodine are added to the pool to stimulate venous and lymphatic circulation, important for the treatment of cellulitis and general circulatory problems, according to spa director Dr. Marco Merlin.

Situated in the tranquil Italian countryside combined with a beautifully restored palazzo, Saturnia Spa, championship golf courses, and acres of gardens,

the Palazzo Arzaga is one of Europe's finest resorts, one where the spa experience has been taken "religiously."

An Italian Olive Oil Bath to Soften Skin

Roman aristocrats did more than cook with olive oil. When they reclined in their lavish marble bathtubs in about A.D. 212, it was olive oil they used to soften their skin. Roman soldiers, who often returned from battle with dry skin, added olive oil to their baths, too. Today olive oil is an ingredient of many skin-care products, but you can recreate an authentic olive oil bath at home or when you travel by following this easy recipe. Betsy Morsher, author of *Heal Yourself the European Way*, recommends the following as an excellent skin moisturizer: ½ cup of sesame oil, ½ cup of olive oil, 1 tablespoon of liquid detergent or shampoo, and ½ teaspoon of your favorite perfume or essential oil. Pour the oil, shampoo, and perfume or essential oil into a bottle and shake vigorously. Add two tablespoons to your bath as the warm water is running. Add a few scented candles, play some soft music, and relax.

Italy's Answer to the Perfect Marriage of Golf and Spa

Palazzo Arzaga Hotel—Saturnia Spa
25080 Carzago di Calvagese della Riviera
Brescia
Italy
Phone: 39-30-680600
Fax: 39-30–6806168
E-mail: info@palazzoarzaga.com
Web site: www.palazzoarzaga.com

Season: Year-round

General Manager: Kenyon Price

Spa Director: Marco Merlin, M.D.

Reservations: 39–30–680600 or (800) 323–7500 (Preferred Hotels & Resorts Worldwide)

Accommodations: Eighty-four guest rooms and five suites. Antiques, hand-painted ceilings, some fireplaces, marble bathrooms, minibars, in-room safes, air-conditioning, satellite television, hair dryers.

Meals: Five restaurants and bars. La Taverna, the hotel's original fourteenth-century cellar, specializes in Italian wines.

Facilities: Full-service spa; indoor mineral pool; cardiovascular equipment; aerobics and water exercise classes; indoor and outdoor swimming pools; massage; herbal wraps and beauty treatments; professional trainers; hiking trails; jogging track; 18-hole Jack Nicklaus II course and 9-hole Gary Player course; driving range; golf academy; two tennis courts; boutique; pro shop.

Services & Special Programs: Physician-guided program for golfers; cooking school; chapel concerts; day trips (wine tastings, tea in Venice); sailing; biking on site through seventy acres of hills and gardens; concierge; twenty-four-hour room service.

Rates: $$$

Best Spa Package: The five-night classic Total Relaxation includes accommodations, breakfast, lunch, and dinner daily, plus seven treatments and the Slim & Tonic Pool. The cost ranges from $1,250 to $1,600 per person double occupancy, depending on the season.

Credit Cards: Most major

Getting There: Getting to Palazzo Arzaga is streamlined if you fly into Brescia or Verona, just twenty-five minutes away. The concierge can arrange for a car to meet you at either airport. Rental cars available as well. Those arriving in Milan should request a private car transfer, as the directions tend to be confusing for those unaccustomed to driving in Italy.

What's Nearby: Cremona, where Stradivarius made his violins, and home of Torrone nougat candy.

SPA'DEUS

Tuscany, Italy

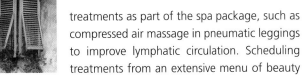

nspired by visiting California health spas, Christina Newburgh created Italy's first and only American-style wellness program in Tuscany. Located in Chianciano Terme, a town noted for medicinal mineral water therapy, Spa'Deus offers hydrotherapy treatments, aquacize, and three bottles of mineral water daily. This unique destination spa program teaches that doing away with old habits and learning to move freely are the keys to living well.

The main attractions at Spa'Deus, which sits atop the town's highest hill, are walks in the scenic hills of Tuscany, with meals to match. Serious workouts are balanced by relaxation time, pampering treatments, and excursions to historic hill towns.

What makes Spa'Deus a true destination spa is the camaraderie that develops among the guests. Coming from many nations and backgrounds, they form a happy group of hikers. English is a common bond; the program attracts single women and men, a sprinkling of Milanese and Manhattan fashion models, London business executives, and couples from Rome. Personal attention by the multilingual staff, including American and European fitness trainers, helps newcomers learn where to go for treatments and exercise classes. Awaiting you are a sweatsuit, robe, and slippers, so the main thing to bring is walking shoes.

Every day starts with stretches and aerobics to get you revved up for an hourlong walk. Driven to back-roads and private estates, you discover the real Tuscany. Vistas of vineyard-covered hills, ancient towns, and valleys covered in a patchwork of flowers and farms make each morning an adventure. Sometimes the hike ends at a country inn where the spa's kitchen has sent breakfast.

Returning to the hotel in high spirits, the group splits into three aerobics studios, where spinning sessions on stationary bikes, stretching, dance exercise, and FitBall training are scheduled. Everyone gets basic

treatments as part of the spa package, such as compressed air massage in pneumatic leggings to improve lymphatic circulation. Scheduling treatments from an extensive menu of beauty and skin-care services requires a visit with the spa programmer, which is charged to your account. Choices include ayurvedic massage synchronized by two therapists, massage with hot and cold stones placed on your body's pressure points to relieve stress, rhythmic lomi-lomi massage from Hawaii, and water-borne massage. Several of these treatments are exclusive to Spa'Deus, not available elsewhere in Italy. Others require attention by the resident doctor and nurse, such as a water cleansing of the colon.

Getting weighed and measured daily encourages progress in shedding pounds (kilos here), which proves surprisingly easy if you stick to the spa menu. The dining room manager suavely offers choices: diet or maintenance, with pasta, eggs, and fish, or simply

Spa'Deus
Via le Piane, 35
53042 Chianciano Terme
Italy
Phone: 39–05–78–63232
Fax: 39–05–78–64329
E-mail: info@spadeus.it
Web site: www.spadeus.it

Season: March–October

General Manager: Christina Newburgh

Accommodations: Thirty spacious rooms with private bathroom and balcony in three-story hotel furnished in an eclectic mix of antique rugs and contemporary Italian art.

Meals: Three meals daily are served at communal tables. Breakfast can be fruit, an egg, multigrain bread, and plum jam. Lunch features include Tuscan baked chicken, salmon baked in a bread crust, and homemade pasta with tomato sauce. Salads, yogurt, herbal tea, and coffee substitute available at all times.

Facilities: Gymnasium with extensive selection of exercise equipment, large indoor swimming pool, climbing wall, spinal traction pool, underwater exercise equipment, hydrotherapy tubs.

Services & Special Programs: Massage, shiatsu, reflexology, facial, thalasso bath, CO_2 bath to promote circulation, underwater massage bath, oxygen inhalation, yoga. Medical checkup, colonic.

Rates: $$

Best Spa Package: All inclusive rejuvenation week $1,885 per person, double; $2,159 single.

Credit Cards: American Express, MasterCard, Visa

Getting There: From Florence, train or taxi to Chiusi (one hour). By car, Autostrada A–1.

What's Nearby: Siena, Montepulciano.

vegetarian. Some meals include salad; most of the time you are served the posted menu, plus fruit drink, herbal tea, or coffee substitute. One day lunch might be at a farm villa, complete with piano player; another outing takes in a wine tasting. Tuscany couldn't be better.

Herbal Supplements Enhance Spa Treatments

Prepare yourself for the intensive program at Spa'Deus by going on a daily regimen of herbal tea. Served in the morning prior to the daily walk, the tisane is available throughout the day. Or bring along herbal preparation for the barman to fix: kava-kava (from Fiji) and noni (from Tahiti) are effective as a sleeping aid and also help boost your immune system after a long trip. Don't forget nail and hair nutrients. Specific formulas can be purchased at Italian and American pharmacies. Don't isolate spa treatments from your life; make them part of your daily routine, enhanced by herbal teas and nutrients.

TERME DI SATURNIA RESORT

Tuscany, Italy

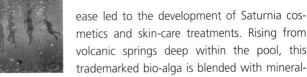

n a grove of plane-top pine trees and cypress, the thermal springs of Saturnia have attracted health-seekers since the Etruscans built temples. Scientific cosmetology and thermal medicine enrich the spa experience at the newly expanded Terme di Saturnia Resort. Harmonizing fire, earth, and water, this is a place of mystical energy.

The rolling hills of the Maremma region in southern Tuscany give little hint of volcanic springs or a modern resort hotel. As you leave the autostrada, about two hours from Rome, the earthy feel of old Toscana makes you breathe a sigh of relaxation.

Hotel guests are received in an ancient stone building. From the lobby bar you can see a lake-size swimming pool and vast lawns where the waters cascade into stone-walled baths and pools.

As you enter the sulfurous water from the canopied doors of the locker rooms, the first thing you notice are blobs of black plankton. Its therapeutic use for skin disease led to the development of Saturnia cosmetics and skin-care treatments. Rising from volcanic springs deep within the pool, this trademarked bio-alga is blended with mineral-rich mud for facials and body wraps. The water bubbles up at a constant 98.6 degrees (37 degrees Celsius)—the same as your body temperature—working its soothing magic on a tired traveler. Getting a Watsu treatment in one of the small outdoor pools is like being in the womb of mother nature. Or try the new Thermalion capsule, which combines steam and heat.

The resort can be a busy place on a warm day. Hundreds of day-trippers take up spots on the lawn. Spa appointments have to be made early. (A new building scheduled to open in 2002 will more than double facilities.) Programs range from revitalizing an aging complexion to improving the appearance of sensitive skin. Best bet: day spa package includes your choice of four hydrotherapy treatments, plus free use of pool.

Saturnia doesn't stint on food. Diet, you are informed, means knowing how to live well. A nutritionist is on staff to evaluate your body structure and energy needs, and special diets are served to guests seated as far as possible from the copious buffets. Avoiding wine or alcohol, though, takes self-control. Most of the diners are here to enjoy Tuscany's bounty of fresh produce, game, and pasta. After dinner there is espresso, followed by drinks and dancing in the lounge, where bar manager Umberto has a special menu of nonalcoholic cocktails.

A morning jog with the Italian-American fitness team helps work

off calories and gives you a chance to learn about the area's sports, wineries, olive oil makers, and cultural attractions. The hilltop town of Saturnia is a short distance from the resort. Saturnia Country Club provides horseback riding, fishing, archery, meals, and lodging. But the waters will draw you back.

Healing Waters

Thermal water is extremely relaxing and boosts the immune system, says Saturnia medical director N. A. Fortunati. By increasing resistance to illnesses, Dr. Fortunati explains, thermal water stimulates three functions that link body and mind: the involuntary nervous system, the glands, and the immune system. Saturnia's warm sulfurous waters are enriched with beneficial plant and mineral substances while passing through the volcanic subsoil. The secret of their healing and reinvigorating properties lies in the water's sulfuric-carbonic composition and temperature. Benefits can be experienced on your skin, in your respiratory system, and in enhanced muscular movement.

Soaking Up Vitality and Beauty in Tuscany

Hotel Terme di Saturnia Resort
58050 Saturnia (GR)
Italy
Phone: 39–0564–601601
Fax: 39–0564–601266
E-mail: info@termedisaturnia.it
Web site: www.termedisaturnia.com

Season: Year-round

General Manager: Glauco San Giovanni

Medical Director: Nicola Angelo Fortunati, M.D.

Fitness Directors: Kirk W. Lemley, Rocco Caloro

Reservations: 800–16–32–50

Accommodations: 160 rooms and seventy-eight suites in three buildings, plus nearby lodges with thirty-four rooms. Standard rooms in the original hotel are compact, have modern furniture, full-size bed, bathroom with shower. All are air-conditioned, have satellite TV and VCR, minibar, telephone. Amenities include robe, slippers, and cotton workout clothing.

Meals: Extensive breakfast buffet included with room rate. Villa Montepaldi restaurant table d'hôte fixed-price menu includes pasta, fish, and meat courses, antipasto buffet, and dessert.

Facilities: Institute of Scientific Cosmetology, thermal pools, water walk, sauna, steam room, hydromassage, whirlpools, gymnasium with exercise equipment. Golf driving range, all-weather tennis courts (lit at night), bocce, mountain bikes.

Services & Special Programs: Seven-day fitness and anti-stress program. Program includes medical checkup, massage, multijet showers. Treatments booked individually include massage, watsu, shiatsu, LaStone therapy, fango, reflexology, Vodder manual lymphatic drainage, aerosol inhalations, facial with glycolic acid, dermatology micro-surgery, laser epilation, body gommage, manicure, and pedicure. Fitness classes and personal training, yoga, and postural gymnastics charged per session.

Rates: $$

Best Spa Package: Thermal Week hydrotherapy and fangotherapy with exercise includes full board. From $821, double; $946, single.

Credit Cards: Most major.

Getting There: From Rome, by car via Civitavechia on Autostrada to Montalto, Manciano (170 kilometers); scheduled van service from Rome International Airport.

What's Nearby: Perugia, Pitigliano, Tyrrhenian Sea beach resorts, Siena.

VILLA D'ESTE

Lake Como, Italy

Located on the south shore of Lake Como, the grand old estate of Villa d'Este has been transformed into a twenty-first century resort and sports club. Breathtaking views of the lake complement the spa's refreshingly spacious treatment rooms and will inspire your workouts. Located less than an hour's drive from Milan, Villa d'Este is a combination of contemporary design and sixteenth-century architecture.

Cool in slate gray and green tones, the spa's six treatment rooms are a soothing cocoon. Floral arrangements in green and white match the decor, and there are Frette linens on extralong massage beds. (Tall people will appreciate the leg room.) Therapists are multilingual, conversant with *massagi* techniques like reflexology, shiatsu, and lymphatic drainage. There are hydrotherapy tubs for *tonificante* baths infused with essential oils, to be followed by gentle application of moisturizing milk from the spa's signature line of skincare products.

Well-being goes hand in hand with exercise at the Sporting Club. An underground passage leads directly from the spa to an indoor Olympic-size swimming pool, squash court, locker rooms, and sauna/Turkish steam room. So come in your robe or workout clothes. You can sign up for water sports, tennis on eight outdoor courts, and golf at nearby courses. Scheduled to be renovated by 2001, the club has cardiovascular and strength-training equipment and an electronic golf simulator and real putting green, with clubs and balls to loan. Guest membership in the club is complimentary for hotel guests, and charges for sports facilities can be signed to your room account.

Transformed from classic palazzo to stylish resort, Villa d'Este is more than the sum of its parts. The main building glitters with crystal chandeliers, cocktail lounges, and a glass-walled restaurant where the low-calorie menu complements market-fresh selections.

Style is everything here: During fashion weeks in Milan, the lobby can be filled with buyers in jeans, examining fabric swatches from Como textile makers or setting off on shopping sprees for silks at designer discount stores; groups of Japanese tourists, heading for a sushi restaurant in the gardens; and American vacationers.

Although this grand establishment has welcomed the rich and famous for several centuries, anyone with

Villa d'Este
Lago di Como
22012 Cernobbio
Italy
Phone: 39–031–348–1
Fax: 39–031–348–844
E-mail: info@villadeste.it
Web site: www.villadeste.com

Season: March–mid-November
General Manager: Claudio Ceccherelli
Spa Director: Francesca Tozzi

Accommodations: 164 rooms and suites in two buildings. Decorated with antiques, crystal chandeliers, and damask drapery, all have marble bathroom with Jacuzzi tub, and ample closet space.

Meals: Breakfast, lunch, and dinner are a la carte. The dinner menu has a buffet of vegetables and seasonal salads, choice of sea bass or turbot, and mixed grilled fish. The menu dietetico offers calorie-counted selections. Informal dining (dinner only) in the Grill and Kisho; lunch at the pool bar.

Facilities: The Spa offers private rooms for massage with en-suite shower, hydrotherapy tubs, and beauty treatments for face and body. At the Sporting Club, there is an open-air heated swimming pool; separate pool for children, and indoor swimming pool with steam/sauna. Sports include outdoor tennis (six clay courts, two grass), jogging track, mountain bikes (free), windsurfing, waterskiing, canoeing, sailing, motorboat rental, putting green; indoor electronic golf simulator, squash court. Aerobic gym and fitness room.

Services & Special Programs: Group exercise at indoor pool, aerobics in gym, and guided jogging in the park. Massage, hydrotherapy baths, aromatherapy, body mask, pressotherapy, anticellulite wraps, and beauty treatments.

Rates: $$$

Best Spa Package: Beauty and Relax on the Lake, a four-night stay with six spa treatments on face and body, three massages, three hydrotherapy treatments, buffet breakfast at the Verandah daily, free use of Sporting Club, service and taxes. Available spring and fall, $1,140 per person sharing double room.

Credit Cards: Most major

Getting There: By car from Milan, Autostrada A–9, exit Como North (nord), 5 kilometers (three miles) to Cernobbio (one hour). By train to Como, taxi and rental car available at station.

What's Nearby: Bellagio, Villa Carlotta gardens, Lake Lugano, Casino of Campione; Milan: La Scala, the Duomo (cathedral), fashion boutiques.

a large bank account is welcome. Don't count on a room with a view of the lake unless confirmed in writing; they are fully booked in high season. Day spa packages at Villa d'Este may be the best bargain, but be sure to call or fax in advance for confirmed appointments.

Surrounded by ten acres of private park and hillside walks, Villa d'Este provides old-fashioned service and a contemporary approach to *salute e benessere*—health and well-being, Italian-style.

Herbal Healing and Cooking

Set on the hill behind the hotel, a botanical garden supplies fresh herbs for aromatherapy in the spa as well as for the chefs' culinary creations. With more than 150 herbs under cultivation, the garden is open for visits. Follow the path to a statue of Hercules and enjoy a panoramic view of the lake. Sample aromatic herbs like lavender and rosemary for a soak in your bath. In addition to treatments, a selection of herbs is on sale in the spa and hotel gift shops. At the bar, try an infusion with fresh herbs from the garden.

SAN LAWRENZ RESORT

Gozo, Malta

n an island steeped in history, the new San Lawrenz Resort provides the latest in sea-inspired treatments to help you de-stress and rejuvenate. An exclusive Thalgo marine cure center offers the full range of European body care, facials, and hydrotherapy. Combined with extensive recreational facilities, this is a resort where you can bring children, enjoy hikes and bike rides on unspoiled seaside roads, and simply get back to nature.

Legend has it that the first settlers were a religious cult that worshiped the Earth Mother. Remains of temples predate the pyramids in Egypt. Built of giant boulders in circles similar to Stonehenge, the megalithic temples of Ggantija are a mysterious reminder of nature's power to stir the imagination.

The Knights of Malta, renowned for their hospital on the main island, harvested a healing fungus from rocks near the resort. Known as fungus gaulitanus, this rare plant was prized for medical treatments. Set in a deep recess in the rocky coastline, the fungus rock is part of an area called the inland sea of Dwejra, a magnet for scuba divers and sightseers.

Inspired by the architecture of traditional Maltese country estates, the resort is in a picturesque valley that is still being developed with upscale vacation homes. From the marble lobby you walk onto a spacious terrace overlooking eight acres of landscaped gardens and a free-form swimming pool. At garden level, the marine cure center brings the sea indoors, with a pool for relaxation and exercise—only here, springwater has been infused with micronized algae imported from France.

The French cosmetic firm Thalgo teamed up with the resort's developers to create a contemporary healing center that uses products made with seaweed and algae. Body wraps are "rich in minerals, vitamins, and micronutrients." The treatment is said to activate circulation, relieve aches and pains, detoxify, and restore metabolic balance. And it is completely relaxing. Other treatments include a cold marine mask that oxy-

San Lawrenz Resort
Triq ir-Rokon, San Lawrenz GRB 104
Gozo, Malta
Phone: 356–558640
Fax: 356–562977
E-mail: info@sanlawrenz.com
Web site: www.sanlawrenz.com

Season: Year-round

General Manager: Joseph Baldacchino

Spa Director: Alfred Fiteni

Accommodations: 106 rooms, virtually all suites, furnished in contemporary style. Rooms have terra-cotta tile floors, separate sitting area with balcony. All have air-conditioning and ceiling fan, coffeemaker, large-screen TV, hair dryer, and ironing board and iron.

Meals: Mediterranean cuisine in the main restaurant, a la carte. Included in room rate is breakfast buffet. Special dinners in the Wine Boutique.

Facilities: Two-floor Thalgo marine cure center with fitness room, hydrotherapy pool, Vichy shower, Blitz shower, pressotherapy, balneo bathtubs. Two private tennis courts, two squash courts, two outdoor swimming pools, indoor pool.

Services & Special Programs: Massage, facials, body and skin care, manicure and pedicure.

Rates: $$

Best Spa Package: Six-day Relaxing Program includes twenty-four treatments. Priced at $358, the daily program offers four treatments for total relaxation. Services range from an algae wrap to Vichy shower. (Hotel accommodation not included.)

Credit Cards: Most major

Getting There: From Valletta, Malta International Airport, helicopter transfer to Gozo can be arranged by Air Malta. By car, daily ferry from the main island (thirty minutes). The resort is on the southern shore road.

What's Nearby: Victoria, fortified medieval city, with cathedral, opera house (courtesy bus from resort), Ggantija temples, Calypso's Cave, Comino (by ferry).

genates the skin, tightening and smoothing stress signs. There are relaxing baths with marine salts, algae, and essential oils, as well as expert massage.

Although there is a well-equipped gym, organized exercise is minimal. The hydrotherapy pool has underwater jets to massage parts of your body and can be used for physical therapy sessions with a local specialist. An indoor swimming pool and whirlpool adjoin the Thalgo center, open to all resort guests. At the outdoor pool (unheated), bar service is available during warm months. Both pools are freshwater; for a swim in the sea, the resort's courtesy bus takes you to nearby sandy and rocky beaches during summer.

Getting a Thalgo treatment here is the next best thing to being in France. And only half as expensive.

Calypso's Cave Lures Lovers

Overlooking the red sands of Gozo's finest beach, Ramla l-Hamra, is the cave assumed to be the home of Calypso, the legendary nymph mentioned in Homer's *Odyssey*. Here the beautiful sea-maiden kept Odysseus as a "prisoner of love" for seven years. Odysseus escaped and returned to his faithful wife, Penelope. Climbing the rocky cliff to see the cave is challenging, and the view is breathtaking.

LES THERMES MARINS DE MONTE-CARLO

Monte Carlo, Monaco

verlooking the Mediterranean Sea and Monte Carlo, this lavish, modern seawater spa draws entrepreneurs and deal-makers—at poolside by day, in the casino at night.

Les Thermes Marins is more than a thalassotherapy center; facilities include two beauty salons associated with renowned hairstylists, therapy pools staffed by specialists in restoring equilibrium after childbirth or an accident, a full circuit of LifeFitness exercise equipment, and, of course, seafood restaurant with dietetic menu. Created in 1995 by Prince Rainier's hotel group, La Société des Bains de Mer, this spectacular seaswept aerie is so spacious that a complete vacation can be planned around a day here. And you don't need a princely budget; there are day spa packages as well as overnight programs with Monaco's four top hotels.

Staying at the Hotel de Paris or Hotel Hermitage gives you direct access to Les Thermes via a marble-walled tunnel. Dip into the largest indoor seawater swimming pool on the Riviera coast. Sea and sky illuminate the shell-shaped pool through tall glass windows, creating the effect of a Botticelli painting. Off to the side are a Turkish steam bath (hammam), cabanas, and the bar. On the terrace, chaise longues fill up quickly, as the lunch crowd arrives early and stays late, cell phones beeping constantly.

Spa package guests get free use of all facilities, plus breakfast in the seaview dining room. Holistic programs are tailored to counteract the stress of modern life and enhance your feeling of well-being. Medical, nutrition, and physiotherapy services can be combined with massage and facials.

Taking a thalassotherapy cure, or course of treatments, is considered medical therapy and requires approval from one of the staff doctors. Once past the medical review, a mutilingual hostess guides you to treatments in the four-floor building. Four treatments are scheduled daily, usually a full morning: hydromassage bath, algae or seaweed bath, body wrap, and massage. Exercise sessions in a seawater pool heated to body temperature are led by staff members who pay special attention to physical limitations of participants; sessions last about forty minutes.

Monaco's glamorous entertainment, shopping, dining, museums, and sports are within minutes of Les Thermes Marins. The place to be seen is Hotel de Paris, which faces the historic casino and opera house. The more low-key Hotel Hermitage is ideal as a romantic hideaway, has heated (mosaic-tile) bathroom floors, and a winter garden designed by Eiffel with Tiffany-style

glass ceiling. In addition to free use of the pool and fitness equipment, hotel guests get a VIP "passport" for dining and shopping discounts, and admission to golf and tennis clubs. Take a walk or jog in the casino gardens, down to the yacht-filled harbor, or up to the Grimaldi castle. Monaco is a grande dame who knows how to enjoy life.

Getting the Rhythm for Shapeups

Seawater workouts at the aqua-fitness center are not only for physical exercise and relaxation; they are prescribed as an indispensable complement for the cures. Lipo-training is a slimming method recently developed by the spa team, tailored to each person's body weight and composition. Workouts in the pool are done at a pleasant rhythm, tuned to the best individual rate for burning fat and boosting metabolism. Prior to starting sessions in the cardio-strength training studio, a treadmill test measures your consumption of oxygen. Based on the fitness team's evaluation, your best cardiac working frequency will be the basis for a training program.

Thalassotherapy Fit for Royalty

Les Thermes Marins de Monte-Carlo
2, Avenue de Monte-Carlo (B.P. 215)
MC 980004 Monaco Cedex
Phone. 377–92–16–40–40
Fax: 377–92–16–49–49
E-mail: thermes@sbm.mc
Web site: www.montecarloresort.com

Season: Year-round

General Manager: Fabienne Guillot-Farneti

Reservations: 800–221–4708 or
e-mail: office@sbm.ny.com

Accommodations: The 227-room Hotel Hermitage and 197-room Hotel de Paris are five-star properties. Rooms with sea view have balcony. All air-conditioned, with TV, full bath, robes and slippers. Service is formal, dress code to match.

Meals: Dietetic menu available in the spa's restaurant L'Hirondelle. Low-calorie desserts, herbal teas, and mineral water are available throughout the day at the spa pool. In the hotel dining rooms, dietetic selections appear on menus, or you can indulge in Alain Ducasse's cuisine at Le Louis XV. The rooftop restaurant at Hotel de Paris, Le Grill, offers a perfect blend of dining and ambience.

Facilities: Seawater therapy in baths, showers, and pools; marine aerosol inhalations, and pressure therapy to stimulate muscles; fitness center with LifeFitness equipment and personal trainers; Turkish steam bath, saunas, beauty salons.

Services & Special Programs: Medical and nutrition consultation, physical rehabilitation in the pool. Weeklong programs for stress control, slimming, anticellulite, leg problems, wellness. Massage, shiatsu, reflexology, guided stress control, aromatherapy, hydrotherapy bath and affusion massage with seawater, algae, mud.

Rates: $$$

Best Spa Package: Well-Being program, three or six nights, includes dietetic continental breakfast daily, twelve to twenty-four treatments, medical checkup, hotel accommodation. Approximately $400 per day.

Credit Cards: Most major

Getting There: From Nice, frequent express bus schedule at International Airport Côte d'Azur (one hour); helicopter (fifteen minutes); train (forty-five minutes). Limousine and rental car available.

What's Nearby: Eze (artist colony), Matisse and Chagall museums, Fondation Maeght museum and gardens (contemporary art), Italian riviera.

VILALARA THALASSO
Algarve, Portugal

"he sea cures man's diseases," Euripides said. That this belief is still held thousands of years later is evident in the number of spas specializing in thalassotherapy—seawater cure. One such is Vilalara, located in the Algarve, a chic resort area on Portugal's legendary sun-drenched coastline noted for having an average of 300 sunny days annually. The spa's secluded ninety-one suites and seven self-contained apartments make this an ideal destination for those interested in a luxurious spa experience at one of the most popular beach resort areas in Europe.

This spa resort with its private beach is under Swiss ownership and management, providing both luxury and efficient Swiss hospitality, and setting it apart from others in this region. The suites, restaurants, and spa are comparable to those found in a four- or five-star Swiss hotel. Vilalara's impressive thalassotherapy center includes heated swimming pools, individual hydromassages, jet showers, bubbling baths, and submarine jet-stream pools, housed in a spacious building with access to the hotel.

The cures are focused on specific problem areas; three of these can be booked as packages: Body Slimming (for the upper body, hips, buttocks, and thighs); the weeklong Anti-Cellulite Cure; and the six-day Anti-Tobacco Cure. An osteopathic treatment, under the direction of Dr. Bernard Gabarel, deals with such problems as headaches, tennis elbow, and lumbago, and may also be reserved. The fitness program takes a back seat to the cures here, so don't expect any 6:00 A.M. hikes followed by step aerobics. However, the equipment is state of the art, and the ambience is one of understated elegance.

Spa cuisine served in the *dietetico* restaurant is decidedly lower in calories than what you'll find in the resort's gourmet restaurant.

The heart of the spa experience here is the thalassotherapy treatments, whose ingredients are based on mud, seaweed, and algae. In Europe these ingredients are respected for their relaxing and restorative powers, and the cure is taken seriously. The clientele is mainly well-heeled Europeans, but English is spoken and readily understood, thanks to a large British population that has retired in this area.

As in all serious spas, the goal here is to bring your mind, body, and soul into a natural balance and harmony. There are abundant opportunities in the Algarve for sightseeing, golf (Vilamoura, Vila Sol and Pin-

Vilalara Thalasso
Praia Das Gauoiths
8365-909 Armacao de Pera
Algarve, Portugal
Phone: 351–282–320–000
Fax: 351–282–314–956
E-mail: vilalara@ip.pt
Web site: www.vilalara.com

Season: Year-round

General Manager: Pierre Castera

Spa Director: Beatrice Fabrizzi

Reservations: 351–282–320–000 or call Small Luxury Hotels, 800–525–4800

Spa Appointments: 351–282–320–000

Accommodations: Suites and apartments set in parklike grounds. Each unit has air-conditioning, satellite television, and private terrace.

Meals: The poolside grill offers informal dining; the gourmet restaurant is known for fine dining; and healthy, low-calorie yet imaginative cuisine can be found in the *dietetico* restaurant. Snacks are available at the poolside bars.

Facilities: Heated swimming pools; submarine jet-stream pools; jet showers; jet-stream bathtubs; submarine showers; saunas; Turkish baths; fitness center; gym; hairdresser; beach.

Services & Special Programs: Marine mud treatments; algotherapy; lymph drainages; massage; shiatzu; pediluve; ionisation; pressotherapy; ultrasound treatments; acupuncture; osteopathy; and special treatments for cellulitis, stretch marks and tired legs, slimming, and smoking cessation.

Rates: $$

Best Spa Package: The seven-night package includes accommodations, three meals daily, a medical checkup, six days of treatments (about 2½ hours daily), use of spa facilities for bathing, and perks such as a VIP welcome treatment and thalasso gift pack. There are four seasons of costs, the lowest being from November through February. Rates start at $1,362; room rates start at about $185 per night, double occupancy and include breakfast, tax, service.

Credit Cards: Most major

Getting There: Faro International Airport is 45 kilometers (28 miles), or a forty minute ride from the resort. By limousine, $40 one-way.

What's Nearby: Lisbon, Seville, historic Silves.

heieros are nearby), and tennis. But the lure of Vilalara, with its secluded bay and pristine white sand beach, is a spa experience for those who love the luxury of thalassotherapy without a challenging fitness program.

Cure for Smoking in Paradise

This clifftop setting overlooking a pristine beach and bay offers tranquillity and seclusion, making it an almost idyllic spot to once and for all stop smoking. Indeed, Vilalara Thalasso calls itself "the ideal place to free yourself of the harmful smoking habit," and its six-day smoking cure is claiming success. Guests in the program are given auriculo-therapy (which acts on reflex zones of the ear); an acupuncture treatment; marine aerosol sprays (to treat the bronchial and pulmonary zones); respiratory and relaxing exercises; and a homeopathic detoxifying treatment.

STUREBADET

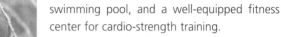

ecret spas are rare, but we've found one in the center of Stockholm that never advertises. The country that brought you ABBA and the Saab keeps Sturebadet to itself. Not exactly a secret—there are 4,000 members—it's the place in Stockholm to work out, get a massage, and enjoy spa cuisine. So here's how to experience Sweden's oldest and grandest spa.

Don't be put off by the location—in a shopping mall called Sturegallerian. The original Sturebadet stood here, opened in 1885 as a communal bathhouse. Destroyed a century later, the new building recreates Sturebadet in all its Nordic Art Nouveau glory. There are Moorish arches and Arabic grottoes, two floors of galleries for massage and skin care around the

swimming pool, and a well-equipped fitness center for cardio-strength training.

The decor inspires mixed reactions: One member describes it as what a temple to the Vikings might have looked like to an Ottoman sultan. Restoration involved carving antique pine timber for the galleries, adding a warm note to the granite fountain that fills one end of the pool area. Skylights illuminate the pool, a nice touch in winter when members gather in bathrobes at the cafe/restaurant on the fifth-floor gallery, overlooking the pool.

Busy day and night, the club attracts the young, professional, high-energy, and stressed. Visitors are welcome when space is available for treatments, or you can drop in to swim and exercise by paying for a

day pass ($15). Check in at a reception desk on the mall level, collect a robe and locker key, then take the elevator to the locker rooms. An aerobics studio pulses with classes throughout the day, some high-impact, others listed for various levels. In the gymnasium, you may have to wait if your favorite treadmill or StairMaster is in use, but there are rowing machines, bicycles, and free weights. An instructor is always present; if you don't speak Swedish, the locals are fluent in English and other languages.

With all the high-energy workouts, getting a Swedish massage here is worth taking the next SAS flight. Because therapists are trained for three years at professional schools like the Axellsson Institute, the classic massage strokes are mixed with new techniques that set up a synergy between masseuse and recipient. The spa department also provides facials, body scrub, manicure and pedicure, and the latest herbal treatments by Kerstin Florian. Treatment cabins surround the pool on all sides, and demand for appointments is so heavy that there is a Web site for members to snag last-minute cancellations.

Two hotels in the area have branches of Sturebadet, where getting treatments may be more convenient. If you stay at the recently built Radisson SAS Royal Park or the historic Grand Hotel opposite the Royal Palace, you can use facilities at all three club spas. But nowhere else can you combine a historic bathhouse with an aromatherapy kur.

Kerstin's Kur

Healthy complexions are a Swedish tradition that's very much alive at Sturebadet. Swedish-born skin-care specialist Kerstin Florian creates some of the spa world's most innovative products for her California-based company, then comes home to Stockholm every summer for workshops and personal training with spa aestheticians. The Kerstin Florian range of products includes Austrian moor mud, Hungarian thermal mineral bath crystals, and German herbal krauter bath oils. Based on the European kur, a centuries-old ritual of renewal and exercise combined with treatment for the face and body, Florian created the kur program to integrate spa treatments at Sturebadet and leading American spas. Scientific use of advanced phytotherapy (therapeutic plant extracts) with marine and mineral elements, combined with essential oils used in aromatherapy, maintains the natural balance, elasticity, and appearance of healthy youthful skin. The result is a complete skin-care system.

A Viking Temple of Health

Sturebadet
Sturegallerian 36
SE 114 46 Stockholm
Sweden
Phone: 46–8–545–01500
Fax: 46–8–545–01510
E-mail: info@sturebadet.se
Web site: www.sturebadet.se

Season: Year-round

Accommodations: SAS Royal Park Hotel

Meals: Sturebadet Restaurant offers full-service menu of spa cuisine, breakfast through dinner, every day. Marble-top tables reflect simplicity in food presentation. Fish, vegetable, and pasta dishes change daily.

Facilities: Cardio-strength training fitness center with equipment by Cybex, StairMaster, and free weights; private cabins for spa treatments; hydrotherapy tubs; aerobics studio.

Services & Special Programs: Massage, facials, manicure, pedicure, body scrub, body wraps with aroma oils or moor mud, algae wrap, kur bath, waxing, eye treatments. Chiropractic treatments.

Rates: $

Best Spa package: Sturebadet half-day Kur, $215, includes body scrub, kur bath, twenty-five-minute massage, facial, manicure or pedicure, and full use of club facilities, robes.

Credit Cards: American Express, MasterCard, Visa

Getting There: From center of Stockholm, T-underground train to Ostermalmstorg or Hotorget station, entrance on Stureplan.

What's Nearby: Food halls, Kungsgatan gardens, Vasa museum (1628 royal warship), Old Town.

GRAND HOTELS BAD RAGAZ
Bad Ragaz, Switzerland

his grande dame of the Swiss spa world is synonymous with "taking the waters." Located in the Alpine foothills in the canton of St. Gallen, the resort has long been a destination for rejuvenation and for relief from rheumatism, arthritis, and other debilitating ills.

The resort consists of two hotels, the chic five-star Grand Hotel Quellenhof and the slightly less expensive, four-star Grand Hotel Hof Ragaz. The elegant Quellenhof underwent a major renovation between 1990 and 1992, transforming it from a rather stodgy old-world bastion attracting a rather sickly crowd to an upbeat, trend-setting spa oasis. Although both hotels remain a symbol of the elegant spas of the nineteenth and early twentieth centuries, they have reinvented themselves to reflect today's interest in wellness and preventive health, all the while continuing to maintain their uncompromising standards.

The spa experience Quellenhof-style is a singular one. There are performance diagnostic tests, fitness checkups, massages, and beauty programs. In the well-equipped gym you'll find bicycle ergometers, stepping and rowing machines, Skywalkers, and four-teen training machines. Daily exercise classes include FitBall, stretching, pool workout, and qi gong. In some respects the overall program is similar to that found at a traditional American spa, but when it comes to water, the Swiss get serious. The classic water cure has been taken to the next level with some of the most impressive technology in Europe.

The Tamina Gorge, an imposing reconstruction of granite cliffs and waterfall, is used for the Kneipp course—a specialized water therapy that originated in Bad Woerishofen, Germany. The Roman influence prevails in the Thermarium (classical steam bath) and the Finnish influence in the coed Sauna Landscape (private saunas are available on request). The cold-water, open-air pool will toughen you up; there are also four individual whirlpools and a large swimming pool. But the heart of this grand European spa is the Helena Bath, the thermal Roman bathing temple adjacent to a Roman-Irish cycle (alternating steam and water baths).

Enhancing the water therapy is the Beauty Oasis for face and body care. A clinic called "Prevention of Skin Aging" offers the latest therapy—myo-lifting.

Myo-lifting is ionotherapy using ampoules of active ingredients. Carita, a French skin-care line, is used for specialized facials. Body treatments using thalassotherapy products are designed to improve circulation, refine, and tone. Slimming and cellulite treatments use partial and whole-body packs, underwater massage, and low-temperature leg treatments.

The Grand Hotels Ragaz represents the new wave of Swiss spas with state-of-the-art technology, a progressive fitness program, a beauty farm, sports, and luxury—all showcasing the efficiency and grace of Swiss hospitality.

Grand Hotels Bad Ragaz
CH-7310 Bad Ragaz
Switzerland
Phone: 4181–303–30–30
Fax: 0041–81–303–30–33
E-mail: resortragaz@bluewin.ch
Web site: www.resortragaz.ch

Season: Year-round

General Manager: Hans Geiger

Spa Director: Corrine Denzler

Fitness Director: Brigitte Hallwachs, M.D.

Reservations: 800–223–6800 (Leading Hotels of the World) or 0041–81–303–30–30

Spa Appointments: 41–81–303–20–60

Accommodations: Grand Hotel Quellenhof offers ninety-six junior suites, eight suites and a royal suite; all guest accommodations are spacious, decorated in a blue and yellow color scheme, with luxurious baths and balconies with Alpine views. Amenities include remote cable television, direct-dial telephones, in-room safe, robes, and fresh flowers.

Meals: Restaurant Bel-Air, with sunny terrace, offers popular summer barbecues and spa cuisine; the Dorfbeiz Zollstube serves typical Swiss dishes; the Terrace Café Winter Garden offers snacks; and the Golf Club Restaurant has a garden terrace. Gourmet restaurant, Aebtestube.

Facilities: Eighteen-hole golf course with two-story driving range, indoor range, and putting green; six tennis courts (four outdoor, two indoor); two squash courts; two badminton courts; beauty salon; thermal indoor and outdoor pools; complete health club; spa; mountain bikes; shopping arcade; casino; meeting facilities; and hiking trails.

Services & Special Programs: Car rental; laundry/dry cleaning; limousine service; dogs permitted; valet parking; twenty-four-hour room service; business services; children's programs; health and beauty packages; golf packages.

Rates: $$$

Best Spa Package: The His-and-Her Lifestyle Week, with accommodations for six nights, half board (breakfast and dinner), the Fitness & Wellness Experience, daily fitness classes, and the Lifestyle Program (massage, facial, manicure, pedicure, body exfoliation, wave bath, and marine algae gel pack). Price at the Grand Hotel Quellenhof is $1677 per person double occupancy in winter (January 2 through May 1).

Credit Cards: Most major

Getting There: The resort is one hour from the Zurich-Kloten International Airport and three hours from Munich or Milan. Rail service and limousine transfers are available.

HOTEL LES SOURCES DES ALPES
Leukerbad, Valais, Switzerland

inner of the Best Swiss Health Farm Award, this twenty-two room, eight-suite retreat in an Alpine ski resort provides an intimate spa setting for those seeking rest and relaxation. The journey to Leukerbad alone is worth the trip, taking you through such picturesque towns as Martigny, Sion, and Sierre. As you reach the higher altitudes, the pristine Alpine air and the charming village of Leukerbad combine their spell to gently reduce stress and jet lag.

The thermal water has been historically recognized as therapeutic (and the Swiss take their thermal water seriously). During your stay, which can be for any number of nights, consider a daily bath, either in the glass-enclosed indoor pool or in the outdoor pool. With accommodations hosting no more than sixty guests, there is never crowding or lines. Service is always personal and attentive. Because of this, the clientele is loyal; reservations should be made at least a month in advance.

Fitness opportunities range from training and bodybuilding to stretching and water exercise. In the summer hiking is superb with well-marked trails. In winter Leukerbad is a haven for skiers.

Restaurant LaMalvoisie serves sophisticated spa-style cuisine artfully presented, all enhanced by a serious wine cellar. This is a European spa in every sense of the word, with a fairly formal attitude toward dining. The waitstaff wears tuxedos. Don't go to dinner in leotards or a warmup suit. Casual elegance is the rule here. You'll find a silver bud vase at your bedside

The beauty center offers treatments using the Clarins line of products. In addition to body treatments, such as a full-body exfoliation, a slimming treatment, and a back treatment, there are three types of facials.

All treatments take place in the thermal center, which is decorated in relaxing shades of blue. Treatment rooms are tiled and equipped with the latest spa technology. The spa is immaculate, almost sterile. The therapists must meet strict professional requirements.

Three packages are available: Beauty, Anti-Stress, and Vitality, each designed for either three or six nights. All include accommodations, breakfast, and dinner. You can also opt for the nightly rate and schedule your spa services a la carte. There is no minimum or maximum length of stay.

Leukerbad is in a French-speaking canton of Switzerland, but English is widely understood. The international clientele consists mainly of well-heeled, middle-aged professionals and business owners, with some mixture of couples, singles, and mothers and daughters. Although there

Hotel Les Sources des Alpes
CH-3954 Loeche-les-Bains
Leukerbad, Valais
Switzerland
Phone: 41–27–472–2000
Fax: 41–27–472–2001 or 401–854–1612 (Relais & Chateaux)
E-mail: sources@relaischateaux.fr
Web site: www.relaischateaux.ch/sources

Season: Year-round; annual closing November 12 to December 15

General Manager: Marianne and Marco Colombo

Spa Director: Roland Mayor

Fitness Director: Roland Mayor

Reservations: 41–27–472–2000 or 800–735–2478 (Relais & Chateaux)

Spa Appointments: 41–27–472–2000

Accommodations: Twenty-two guest rooms, including eight suites. Luxurious, traditional decor.

Meals: Restaurant LaMalvoisie for casual elegance and high-quality cuisine.

Facilities: Indoor and outdoor thermal pools; beauty center; thermal center.

Services & Special Programs: Beauty center offers facials, body treatments, makeup, nail care, hair removal; thermal center treatments include massages, various baths, fango packs, Vichy showers, aqua gymnastics, herbal inhalation, and fitness training.

Rates: $$$

Best Spa Package: The six-night Beauty Week includes breakfast and dinner, a facial, brush massage, almond bath, full body exfoliations, makeup consultation, body treatment, herbal compress, herbal bath, Vichy shower, manicure, and a water exercise class daily. Price per person, double occupancy, ranges from $1,280 to $1,493, depending on the season.

Credit Cards: Most major

Getting There: From Geneva, about 160 miles by car, or the hotel can arrange transfers. From Lausanne, highway towards Simplon-Brig to Sion, Sierre, then Susteu.

are undoubtedly some celebrities and well-known personalities staying here, the ambience remains discreet and private. Les Sources des Alpes is Swiss spa elegance at its finest.

VICTORIA-JUNGFRAU GRAND HOTEL & SPA

Interlaken, Switzerland

he luxury five-star, 220-room Victoria-Jungfrau Grand Hotel, with stunning views of the Jungfrau mountain range in the heart of Interlaken, opened in 1865 and has hosted the likes of Mark Twain and other visiting dignitaries over the course of its 135-year history. Now the hotel is home to a spa that measures up to its traditional high standards. The ultramodern design of the state-of-the-art Spa Interlaken harmonizes with the venerable hotel, despite the disparity in age. The centerpiece of the spa is a swimming pool meant to evoke the grandeur of a Roman bath.

The spa complex includes a saltwater Jacuzzi, Turkish steam bath, Finnish sauna, bio-saunas with active-light therapy, a solarium, and a relaxation area. The "aqua-fun" water exercises are designed to aid the circulatory system. Foot reflexology, lymphatic drainage, and combined massages are guaranteed to induce relaxation.

Setting this spa apart from the other hotel-based facilities is its medical-fitness program created through the cooperation of physicians and therapists. Each guest is prescribed an exercise regimen based on their strength, stamina, speed, mobility, and coordination. The program begins with the Victoria-Jungfrau Fit Test, which takes one hour to administer. Those in the program can use the Cybex 6000 equipment under supervision, and can also select electrotherapy, heat and cold treatments, hydrotherapy, and manual therapy. The medical fitness program is combined with an evenly balanced nutritional program of *cuisine minceur* (1,500 calories daily, including a small glass of wine).

At the Victoria-Jungfrau beauty center, an analysis of skin type precedes the selection of a

facial. Additional services at the center include anticellulite treatments, personal makeup, and hairstyling.

Hiking, golf, and tennis can be added to your program. There are seven tennis courts (four indoor, three outdoor) and an indoor golf facility. You'll be fit to scale the Jungfrau after this precision-driven Swiss body tune-up.

Few Calories, Lots of Nutrition

The spa's *cuisine minceur* program is very low in calories—just 1,400 to 1,500 per day—but high in nutritional benefits. The aim is to maintain and enhance good health and general well-being, and to prevent nutrition-related illnesses. In addition to breakfast, lunch, and dinner, those following the program get three snacks and a small glass of wine. The theory at Victoria-Jungfrau is that spa cuisine should be a culinary delight rather than a duty; it should satisfy even the most discerning gourmets.

A State-of-the-Art Approach to Alpine Wellness

Victoria-Jungfrau Grand Hotel & Spa
CH-3800 Interlaken
Switzerland
Phone: 33–828–26–36
Fax: 33–828–28–44
E-mail: interlaken@victoria-jungfrau.ch
Web site: www.victoria-jungfrau.ch

Season: Year-round

General Manager: Emanuel Berger

Reservations: 33–828–28–28 or 800–223–6800

Spa Appointments: 33–828–28–28 or 800–223–6800

Accommodations: Classic elegance is captured in 220 guest rooms, junior suites and duplex suites, all with private bath, direct-dial phones, radio, television, and minibar.

Meals: The hotel offers eight distinctive restaurants or bars. Among them: The informal Jungfrau-Stube offers typical Swiss meals and summer barbecues; La Terrasse features elegant dining with piano music; international artists appear at the Cabaret, a private nightclub; and the Victoria Bar is good spot for cocktails and dancing.

Facilities: Indoor heated swimming pool; seven tennis courts; fitness center; spa; health and beauty center; indoor golf; billiards; conference rooms; hotel garage parking; boutique.

Services & Special Programs: Sightseeing excursions, hiking weeks, adventure packages; various spa packages; numerous family and children's events and programs; complimentary hotel kindergarten.

Rates: $$$

Best Spa Package: The Spa Deluxe six-night package includes a spa fitness test, private training with a qualified instructor, massage, and nutritional counseling. $1,340 per person, double occupancy.

Credit Cards: Most major

Getting There: Two-hour drive from Zurich and Geneva airports and one-half hour from Bern airport. Direct train connections are available; limousine service can be arranged through the hotel.

What's Nearby: Shopping; 18-hole golf course; horseback riding; wide range of sports from downhill and cross-country skiing to hiking and mountain biking; William Tell Open-Air Theatre.

KLASSIS RESORT HOTEL & COUNTRY CLUB

Istanbul, Turkey

seaside retreat and conference center, the Klassis resort harbors two spas, two hotels, an 18-hole golf course, and a country club with tennis, bowling, ice rink, and gym. As a family-oriented resort, the range of sports and training for children is extensive, from horseback riding to golf. But the spas are an adult-only oasis, featuring French marine care for face and body.

As the mosques and minarets of old Istanbul fade into a pastoral landscape of farms and vineyards, the Sea of Marmara comes into view. In a country where East meets West and Europe and Asia straddle the Bosporus, it seems perfectly natural to have a Turkish hotel spa that features French products. The ornate Greek-Ottoman style of the Klassis Resort Hotel adds to the mood of fantasy at the Lavinium Spa and Clarins Institute. The inner sanctum of the spa's marble-walled steam rooms, which recall ancient Turkish hammams, is where you are scrubbed and bathed, massaged and oiled. Clarins face and body care adds the finishing touch, at prices less than half the cost of similar treatments in Paris. Staying in a luxurious villa or standard room, you have full access to all sports and the spa at both hotels and the country club.

Klassis changes personality with the seasons; summer—resort for families, and executive escape from Istanbul; winter—golf and tennis in the balmy luxury of the country club's slow season, indoor ice-skating, squash, bowling, and cooking classes. Built on a monumental scale, both the hotel and country club are under the same management, linked by free shuttle bus. Day trips to Istanbul museums and archaeological sites, as well as to shopping bazaars, are regularly scheduled through the concierge desk.

Sports and spa can be combined at Klassis Golf & Country Club. The Thalgo Health Farm offers a broad selection of treatments with marine products harvested in the Atlantic ocean: Slimming wraps, face mask, leg wraps, sun care, and body care with flower and fruit extracts are among offerings in spacious, private treatment rooms. Equipped with the latest French technology, the two-floor Thalgo center is a private enclave within the country club, but nonresidents are welcome to enjoy a day spa package.

Diet programs at the country club are developed jointly by the nutritionist, chefs, and fitness trainers.

Klassis Resort Hotel & Country Club
34930 Silviri, Istanbul
Turkey
Phone: 90–212–727–40–50
Fax: 90–212–727–40–49
E-mail: bilgi@klassis-hotel.com
Web site: www.klassis.com.tr

Season: Year-round
General Manager: Handan Boyce
Spa Director: Recep Ozbudak
Accommodations: Hotel with 303 rooms, fourteen suites, and twenty-four private garden and pool villas; country club and golf course with one hundred standard rooms, seven suites, private villas. Rooms are modern, with marble-tiled bath, full-size tub and shower. Amenities include robes, hair dryer, TV, air-conditioning, sea view.
Meals: Specialty restaurants feature Turkish, Thracean, and European menus, with selected low-calorie items. Summer barbecues and terrace dining. Special diet meals on request.
Facilities: Lavinium Spa in the hotel has Clarins Institute, fitness studio, exercise pool with underwater jets, Jacuzzi, sauna/steam rooms. Thalgo Health Farm at the country club has hydrotherapy tubs and indoor saltwater pool, sauna/steam rooms, pressotherapy, Rasul, Jacuzzi. Indoor and outdoor swimming pools.
Services & Special Programs: Massage, shiatsu, pressotherapy, aromatherapy, underwater massage, jet shower, leg wrapping, body mineralizing mask, peeling, hydrotherapy bath, seaweed face masque, eye care, soft-pack water bed, ionized saltwater inhalation, anticellulite electrical toning, lymphatic drainage. Anti-stress program (seven days), weekend revitalizing (two days), slimming (six days).
Rates: $$
Best Spa Package: Classical Slimming Program (six days) includes medical consultation, daily treatments and personalized exercise, three massages, baths, and mechanical massage bed treatments. $260 per person, plus hotel accommodations.
Credit Cards: All major
Getting There: From Ataturk Airport by car (50 kilometers) on E–5 expressway or Highway TEM (one hour).
What's Nearby: Istanbul (Topkapi Palace, Dolmabhace Palace, Hagia Sofia (museum), Blue Mosque, Suleyman mosque, Yerebatan Saray underground water cistern of Ottoman era, Grand Bazaar, Pergamum, Aphrodisias, Ephesus, Smyrna.

Not on the dining room menu, dietetic meals are designed and served to add eye-appeal and flavor while reducing fat, salt, and sugar. A personalized program is developed after the medical checkup that comes with the slimming program, which includes Thalgo's patented anticellulite wraps and baths.

Exercise complements spa services in several packages. Facilities are mainly used one-on-one with a trainer, in scheduled sessions of group aerobics and at your leisure. Seawater fills one of the hotel's huge outdoor swimming pools, filtered and heated for year-round use. Indoor pools exclusively for spa guests are used for group exercise and relaxation. The hotel's huge glass-covered swimming pool has a waterslide that keeps kids happy.

Classy in every way, the resort is a taste of two worlds: modern facilities and old-world hospitality.

CHAMPNEYS HEALTH RESORT & SPA

Tring, Hertfordshire, England

destination spa providing more than twenty daily activities, over one hundred treatments, holistic health services, and gourmet meals, Champneys is England's version of California's Golden Door. Founded over sixty years ago by a naturopath, the resort has evolved with the times and currently emphasizes organic food, a balanced regimen of exercise and stress management, state-of-the-art treatments, and the simple pleasures of country walks. Recently given a facelift, new restaurant, and additional guest rooms, the resort attracts a lively mix of fitness-oriented and stressed-out men and women.

Arriving at the mansion, about an hour from London, you are welcomed and escorted to registration. The mansion's Victorian elegance and sunny garden

terraces immediately create an air of relaxation. Beyond an oaken door to the drawing room, is a bar that serves herbal teas, mineral water, and after-dinner coffee. There's also a quiet music room, as well as a games room with snooker (pool) table and smoking room. In the west wing are exercise studios equipped for strength training and cardiovascular workouts.

Champneys is on the cutting edge of preventive medicine, holistic health, and stress management. At the spa, skin care and hair treatments feature products by Clarins, Decleor, Guinot, Aromatherapy Associates, Jessica, Lamour, and O-Lys. The staff outnumber guests by two to one, and it doesn't take them long to make a visitor from abroad feel at home. On arrival, you meet a nurse (called "sister" in England) to go over any health problems and plan a personal program. Appointments will be made for the bath or wrap and massage, which are included in the daily fee. Beyond that, treatments are a la carte or part of packages for two to five nights, and you are free to join scheduled group exercise or simply relax.

Dieting here has an elegant edge: Meals are served on Wedgwood china, and dinner can include wine in crystal goblets. Selections are rated by fat and fiber content and you can chose from the fixed light diet menu or an elaborate salad bar and hot buffet of local game, trout, sea bass, or salmon, and vegetarian pasta. In warm weather you can dine on the terrace. Meet people at the Champneys table reserved for single guests.

Set on 170 acres of sweeping lawns and colorful flower beds, the mansion, which was once owned by the British branch of the Rothschilds, is an ideal getaway spa. Country house informality encourages dressing down during the day (jogging suits are fine; some guests wear a dressing gown or the robe and slippers supplied in your room). Sturdy walking shoes or boots are advised for exploring the Chiltern hills,

where horseback riding, golf, and guided walks are offered daily. Bring rain gear; the concierge supplies Wellies (high rubber boots).

This twenty-first century wellness center, which can be traced back to 1307 when the estate was owned by the Champeneys family, brings together the best of Europe and America.

Shedding Light on Facials

Exposure to light treatments using O-Lys equipment and products is said to increase your body's production of vitamin D, thus aiding the natural absorption of calcium, phosphorus, and magnesium. Focused by a specially trained aesthetician, the equipment concentrates light, with no laser burn. Other modes improve muscle function (including that of the heart), lower blood pressure, and help those suffering sleep disorders or jet lag. Try it in conjunction with reflexology for a head-to-toe rejuvenating experience. Another blend of light and color therapy, called aura-soma, stimulates natural healing and self-discovery based on your selection of bottled herbal extracts, essential oils, gems, and crystals that reveal energy auras.

Country Pleasures for Mind, Body, and Soul

Champneys
Wigginton, Tring, Hertfordshire HP23 6HY
England
Phone: 44–01–442–291111
Fax: 44–01–442–291112
E-mail: reservations@champneys.co.uk
Web site: www.champneys.com

Season: All year, except Christmas week

General Manager: Jonathan R. Stapleton

Spa Manager: Mette Haxthausen

Accommodations: Seventy-eight rooms, including eight suites in mansion. All with en-suite bathroom, except fourteen budget rooms in west wing. Modern rooms facing gardens have traditional pine furniture, chintz fabrics. Spacious suites Nos. 17–19 on second floor of mansion consist of a living-dining area, elaborately draped king-size bed facing bay window overlooking garden, marble-walled bathroom with whirlpool tub. Centrally heated and air-conditioned, with phones.

Meals: Included in daily tariff. Choice of menu in dining room: Light diet or gourmet cuisine a la carte, with vegetarian option.

Facilities: Fitness center with advanced cardiovascular equipment, StairMaster, VersaClimber, stationary bikes. Separate spa baths for men and women, forty-four treatment rooms. Indoor swimming pool and squash court; whirlpool indoors and outside, croquet lawn, three tennis courts, mountain bikes, snooker table, volleyball and badminton, darts; art studio, aerobics gym.

Services & Special Programs: Over one hundred treatments offered a la carte, including acupuncture, shiatsu, LaStone massage, aura-soma, homeopathy. Nutrition consultation, cooking demonstrations; holistic health programs; breast examination. Art instruction and craft workshops.

Rates: $$$

Best Spa Package: Two-night package with daily massage and heat treatment, three meals daily, choice of group exercise. $784–$1,200 per person.

Credit Cards: Most major

Getting There: Train to Berkhamsted from London Euston Station; taxi or limousine meet trains and planes, on request. By car, the M–1 from London, exit 8, follow A–4147 to A–41.

What's Nearby: Windsor Castle, Stratford-upon-Avon, Oxford, Henley, Woburn Abbey, Dunstable Downs Gliding Club, Tring Museum.

CLIVEDEN—THE PAVILION SPA

Taplow, Berkshire, England

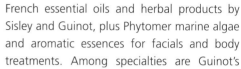

tately homes don't come much grander than Cliveden, the former country estate of the Astor family. Set amid 375 acres of parkland bordered by the River Thames, about an hour from London, the mansion and formal gardens are listed by the National Trust. Staying here is like being a guest at a fabulous country party. And discreetly tucked into a garden pavilion is a surprisingly complete spa.

A gravel path leads to the Pavilion Spa, where a large swimming pool with ozonated water is the centerpiece. Austere (some might say cold), the spa is a small gem among Cliveden's many treasures. Not a place for fitness buffs, but a place to be savored like fine wine, by enjoying walks and jogging paths, outings on the river aboard vintage wooden boats, and dining in splendid rooms overlooking gardens rated among the best in Britain.

There are seven treatment rooms, an exercise equipment room, whirlpool and cold plunge pools, separate sauna and steam room in the locker areas, and the Conservatory Cafe, which serves spa cuisine and afternoon tea. Holistic therapies come with French essential oils and herbal products by Sisley and Guinot, plus Phytomer marine algae and aromatic essences for facials and body treatments. Among specialties are Guinot's Cathiodermie, an intensive facial enhanced by galvanic current to treat deeper layers of the skin, and an ayurvedic head massage that restores energy and vitality to body and mind.

Walks tell much about the estate's history if you rent an audio-guide tape machine. Lord Astor bought the place at the end of the nineteenth century, when he was the richest man in America. He built it into his country seat and then served in Parliament, followed by his Virginia-born wife, Nancy, who was the first woman elected to the House of Commons. You can play tennis on Nancy's indoor court, an innovation when built in 1911, as well as outdoors. Today's Viscount Astor, Lord Crathorne, is a director of Cliveden Limited, and one of the investors is Bill Gates.

Footmen in formal livery greet guests, and you are escorted through the great hall, where tea and cocktails are served daily in front of a massive fireplace from

a Renaissance palace in Italy. Accommodations are in two wings added early in the twentieth century. With just twenty-two standard rooms and sixteen suites, privacy and quiet are assured. Large tiled bathrooms come with full-length tub and shower (handheld as well as wall-mounted), heated towel rack, and bidet. The dressing room contains rain gear, even a portable radio for picnic outings. Standard throughout the house are a media cabinet with CD and video players, TV, bar setup, and fluffy duvets and Irish linen sheets on beds. Staffed by students from some of Europe's leading hotel schools, as well as by highly professional hoteliers, Cliveden is a living monument to the good life.

The Bespoke Retreat

Cliveden's tradition of personal service allows guests to take full advantage of the estate. Romantic river outings in vintage wooden boats come with a picnic hamper full of your favorite food and wine. Honeymooners often reserve Nancy Astor's bedroom; it's big enough for a party or intimate dinners and has a private terrace to enjoy on fine days. Lord Astor commissioned the outdoor swimming pool within the Pavilion's walled garden for Lady Astor to deter her from swimming in the River Thames. The pool is heated and used year-round. Time spent there immediately creates a sense of calm and harmony. For the best of both worlds, combine a London stay at the Cliveden Town House on Cadogan Gardens, where attentive service and lodging are in the Astor tradition.

Upstairs / Downstairs in the Grand Manor

Cliveden—The Pavilion Spa
Taplow, Berkshire SL6 OJF
England
Phone: 01628–668561
Fax: 01628–661837; toll-free (800) 747–6918 (in U.S.), 0800–454–064 (in U.K.)
E-mail: reservations@clivedenhouse.co.uk
Web site: www.clivedenhouse.co.uk

Season: Year-round

General Manager: Stephen Carter

Reservations: 0800–454–063 (in U.K.); 800–747–6917 (in U.S.)

Accommodations: Twenty-two standard rooms with private bath, sixteen suites with sitting room and gas fireplace, large tiled bathroom with full-size tub and shower. A riverbank cottage can be reserved for families or two couples.

Meals: Breakfast is continental or full buffet. A prix fixe menu is served nightly (except Sunday and Monday) downstairs in the cozy Waldo's.

Facilities: Treatment rooms have heated massage tables, dry flotation bed, baths; salon for hair and nail care, makeup consultation, and waxing. Hiking and walking trails; boating on the river; tennis courts, squash, and croquet. Nearby are horseback riding, fishing, and shooting. Indoor and outdoor swimming pools.

Services & Special Programs: Aromatherapy massage, reflexology, Indian head massage, sports massage, seaweed wrap, remineralizing oil bath or wrap, facials, Guinot's Cathiodermie facial. Two packages are offered, subject to availability: the Cliveden Weekend (two nights) and the Cliveden Experience (five nights).

Rates: $$$

Best Spa Package: The Cliveden Experience (Sunday through Thursday): two nights for two, includes two hours of treatments, two breakfasts, dinner allowance. Price from $1,082 for two.

Credit Cards: Most major

Getting There: From London Paddington Station, Thames Trains to Burnham (thirty minutes); call ahead for Cliveden's complimentary transfer, or take a taxi for 2 miles. Heathrow Airport is twenty minutes by car, Gatwick Airport fifty minutes; airport transfers by chauffeured Jaguar can be arranged.

What's Nearby: Stratford-upon-Avon, Bath, Reading, Maidenhead.

THE DORCHESTER
London, England

he Dorchester, a London landmark hotel, has basked in glory since its establishment in 1931. It was the site of Philip Mountbatten's celebration on the eve of his wedding to Princess (now Queen) Elizabeth in 1947, and it was here that General Dwight D. Eisenhower planned the invasion of Normandy in World War II. The Dorchester is repeatedly ranked among the world's most prestigious hotels in industry surveys. With such illustrious credentials, it's little surprise that the Dorchester's spa is also top-of-the-line. Hotel guests enjoy complimentary use of the spa; others pay the day rate (currently $50) for a one-day pass.

Located on the ground floor of the hotel, the art deco spa offers privacy and pampering. As you enter, the colors, shapes, and textures create a sumptuous ambience. An opulent fountain whose bronze water lilies gush water commands attention, as does a Lalique-style glass screen by Clifford Rainey. The decor sets the stage for an uncompromising spa menu featuring E'Spa products, created by Susan Harmsworth, as well as Eve Lom and Thalgo skin-care regimens.

The spa focuses on releasing stress and rebalancing the body. The jet shower treatment is a serious, effective antidote to jet lag. Add to this an aromatic massage and reflexology, and you will forget the twenty-hour flight before you can say "take me to the Tower of London." Or if you feel the aches and pains of sitting too long in an airplane, the paraffin wax body wrap, a warming treatment with heated wax, will relieve discomfort while softening the skin. The pan-thermal bath was designed to rejuvenate tired bodies in need of some revving up: You are bathed in ionized steam at body temperature to encourage perspiration. Then pure oxygen and an aromatic mist are used for a refreshing boost. The one-hour treatment concludes with a water-jet massage. The hand and nail care services at the spa feature Jessica nail products and

include a soothing hand massage and a paraffin wax treatment with the one-hour appointment.

The spa serves a light cuisine, and it is recommended you schedule your treatments to take advantage of lunch. The vegetarian, low-calorie fare features low-fat entrees. Even if you must stay an extra day, don't deny yourself afternoon tea at the Dorchester. A special teatime chef and crew of twenty-four pastry chefs ensure that all the breads, muffins, biscuits, quiches, chocolates, and pastries are perfection.

The Dorchester is known for a celebrity clientele, but that doesn't mean you'll rub shoulders with Barbra

The Dorchester
Park Lane
London W1A 2HJ
England
Phone: 44–20–7629–888
Fax: 44–20–7409–0114
E-mail: reservations@dorchesterhotel.com
Web Site: www.dorchesterhotel.com

Season: Year-round

General Manager: David Wilkinson

Spa Director: Wayne Devlery

Reservations: 44–20–7629–8888 or 800–727–9820 or Leading Hotels of the World at 800–223–6800

Spa Appointments: 0171–495–7335

Accommodations: 195 guest rooms, including forty-nine suites and four roof-garden suites. All rooms are individually decorated and have individual climate control and air-conditioning, as well as dedicated private telephone and fax lines. Guest rooms are decorated in Georgian country house–style with generous use of silks, brocade, and Irish linens; four-poster beds are swagged in brocades or hung with chintz. Rooms have satellite television.

Meals: The hotel offers four choices for dining: the Orchid Room, noted for the blue-and-white Wedgwood color scheme; the Grill Room, modeled after an old Spanish palace; the Oriental Restaurant, with decoration themes reflective of India, Thailand, and China; and the Dorchester Bar, specializing in Italian fare. The Promenade serves afternoon tea. The Dorchester's wine list includes approximately 460 wines, some going back to the 1920s.

Facilities: Spa: steam and sauna rooms, whirlpool baths, massage and beauty services, fully equipped gym with free weights, Stairmasters, rowers; beauty salon and barbershop.

Services & Special Programs: Twenty-four-hour room service; business center; limousine service; mobile phone rental; shopping gallery; handicapped accessibility.

Rates: $$$

Best Spa Package: Thalgo Day includes hydrotherapy bath, panthermal bath, stress-relieving massage, and a Thalgo facial, in addition to the steam and sauna. The cost is $230. A special health breakfast, served daily, is $32. Guest rooms range from $520 to $765 (higher for for suites). This is the ideal antidote for jet lag; book it before you arrive.

Credit Cards: Most major

Getting There: A limousine can be arranged to and from Heathrow International Airport.

What's Nearby: The hotel is close to the theater district, fine shopping, and Hyde Park.

Streisand or Brad Pitt in the locker room. If your favorite celeb looks great, though, chances are he or she has spent a few hours at the Dorchester's spa having a pure collagen velvet facial or a micronized marine algae seaweed body wrap. You can do the same.

Some "Not Too Hot" Tips for Unwinding

The spa at the Dorchester recommends that after a grueling and stressful day, you head to the bathtub for some much needed unwinding. Run a warm bath (not too hot), adding a few drops of E'Spa Soothing Oil to the running water. Massage your hair and scalp with a generous amount of E'Spa Pink Hair and Scalp Mud. Soak two cotton pads with E'Spa Soothing Lotion, light a few candles, and put on some relaxing music. Step into the bath, apply the soaked cotton pads to your eyes, lie back, and relax. Leave the hair and scalp mud in overnight (wrap your head in a towel and cover your pillow). You'll get a great night's sleep and awake refreshed and relaxed. Wash your hair and bathe as usual. You're ready for another day!

FOREST MERE HEALTH FARM
Liphook, Hampshire, England

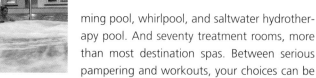

he English countryside is a perfect counterpoint to the luxuries of Forest Mere. Natural beauty surrounds this classic country manor set amid farms on 120 acres of tranquil woodland about an hour south of London. But the beauty within comes from treatments with top European brands of skin care and cosmetic products.

New Age energy meets old English charm in the spa department. Reservationists check you into comfortably appointed lounge areas; then it's up to you to plan a program or simply relax. With two aerobics studios offering unlimited free group workouts and a gymnasium full of LifeFitness equipment and free weights, the ambience is much like that at an American resort. Then you discover the pools: a glass-walled ozonated 25-meter (half–Olympic length) indoor swim-

ming pool, whirlpool, and saltwater hydrotherapy pool. And seventy treatment rooms, more than most destination spas. Between serious pampering and workouts, your choices can be the most difficult exercise.

In addition to traditional treatments, alternative medicine specialists offer Chinese herbal care for many illnesses, hypnotherapy, and osteopathy. In the hands of therapists who are credentialed and caring, you are quickly lulled into a state of serenity.

How about trying something exotic? Aromatherapy is practically a necessity for the stressed young executives who make up a large portion of Forest Mere regulars. Try a full body massage with essential oils on the acupuncture points for relaxation or stimulation. Then there are seaweed and mud wraps, and a dry flotation bed where you relax cocooned in the seaweed wrap. For sensual luxury, there is a Cleopatra milk float, and an evening primrose oil float. Plus the pièce de résistance, a mud treatment in the Serail-Bad, an oriental steam room with brightly tiled walls, a fountain that puffs herbal mist, and a selection of muds for gentle exfoliation.

British-style thalassotherapy starts with group exercise in a huge saltwater hydrotherapy pool. Led by a staffer and supported by the saltwater (the pool has a mix of spring water and sea salts—a first for the U.K.), you move through a series of underwater jets and overhead cascades that add a watery massage to the experience.

Just outside the grounds are two championship golf courses. Nearby is the Pilgrims' Way, a 100-mile path that traces the route believed to have been taken in the fourteenth century by pilgrims headed for Canterbury, immortalized by Geoffrey Chaucer in *The Canterbury Tales*. Join a guided hike or cycling group to explore the peaceful byways and vast green fields populated with fluffy white sheep. Sometimes a gentle mist provides nature's facial. And there's always a pub at the next crossroad.

Meals add another dimension to this British version of healthy living. With an executive chef who trained at some of London's trendy new restaurants, health farm cooking is based on organic, fresh, locally-grown British produce. Simple cooking, basic ingredients, and favorites like pasta and fish make each meal a show-case for healthy options.

The informality of a country house quickly sets you at ease. Robes can be worn in the dining room for breakfast and lunch. Afternoon tea is a good time for socializing over a cup of tea. A hostess or concierge is on hand to arrange transport for sightseeing or to help you catch the train for London. Created by the owners of Henlow Grange and Springs Health Farm, Forest Mere, with its innovative combination of destination spa and lifestyle programs, was honored as Spa of the Year by the British Beauty Awards in 1999.

Health Farm Harvest of Well-Being

Forest Mere Health Farm
Liphook, Hampshire GU30 7JQ
England
Phone: 44–1428–726000
Fax: 44–1428–723501
E-mail: enquiries@henlowgrange.co.uk
Web site: www.healthfarms.co.uk

General Manager: Stephen Purdew

Spa Director: Haley Neech

Accommodations: Seventy-seven rooms done in country-style wooden furniture, flowered chintz, and fluffy pillows, private (en suite) bathroom. Most rooms are in garden-level wings that connect to the main house and dining rooms. Suites have French doors that open to a terrace. All are air-conditioned and have TV and phone.

Meals: Three meals included in daily tariff. Extensive breakfast and lunch buffets. Cooked vegetarian breakfast available for supplementary charge. Dinner menu includes gravlax, wild mushroom soup, sole with mock hollandaise sauce, chargrilled marinated vegetables. Vegan, kosher, and detox diets available. Wine by bottle or glass, mineral water, soft drinks.

Facilities: Beauty farm with seventy treatment rooms, aerobics studios with sprung floors, gymnasium with computerized cardiovascular and strength training equipment, Pilates studio, indoor and outdoor swimming pools, men's and women's locker rooms with sauna, steam room, cold plunge pool; outdoor tennis court, bicycles. Smoking lounge. Robe hire.

Services & Special Programs: Comprehensive range of traditional and alternative therapies, skin care, bodywork, and exercise. Saltwater hydrotherapy pool. Hair salon. Programs for stress management, weight loss. Personal training in Pilates, tai chi, and healing circles.

Rates: $$

Best Spa Package: Four-night Break package includes two massages, facial, algae wraps, thalassotherapy pool session, unlimited use of facilities and exercise classes, all meals, evening talks. Single: $635–$1,313; double (for two): $721.12–$1,456.73. Upgrade to premier service includes robe, treatments in private area.

Credit Cards: Most major

Getting There: By train from London Waterloo station to Liphook (one hour) on Portsmouth line; by car, A–3 south-bound toward Portsmouth, exit after Hindhead on B–2131 to B–2070.

What's Nearby: Chichester, Guildford, Portsmouth

THE ROYAL CRESCENT HOTEL—THE BATH HOUSE

Bath, England

elebrated by the Romans for healing waters, Bath has been Britain's greatest spa town since ancient times. But tucked away in the garden of The Royal Crescent Hotel in Bath is a state-of-the-art spa, the Bath House, that is more Japanese than Roman.

An easy walk from the center of town and its tourist throngs, the hotel is in a crescent-shaped residential block built just before the American Revolution, when classical architecture set the style under King George III. Facing a pretty park where hot-air balloon ascensions are staged, the hotel has no sign. Savvy spa-goers phone ahead to make appointments: Certain times are exclusively for women or men, but otherwise all hotel guests can use the Bath House facilities from 8:00 A.M. to 8:00 P.M.

A garden path leads to the former carriage house that now serves as a spa. The ground floor has a long lap pool embedded in black slate and soaking pools sheathed in teak. There is a tiny sauna and steam room, called karahafus. The menu of Bath House services is extensive, from aromatherapy facials and body wraps to nail care and hairstyling. A range of massage is offered, including Watsu in the water and reiki. The holistic approach starts with a consultation to evaluate your nutritional needs and general health and well-being. Tailored to treat specific areas of tension, your program can include yoga and deep-relaxation exercises. Simply being here is relaxing, the elements of wood,

bamboo, stone, and water forming an airy environment.

Tranquillity is the essence of Royal Crescent accommodations. Many rooms have four-poster beds with a specially designed Cliveden mattress that's extra-firm. Tall windows draped in heavy silk look out on the garden or park. For extra privacy, two suites are tucked into a garden villa, each with its own plunge pool. Two restaurants offer heart-healthy cuisine: Pimpernel's within the mansion has a menu influenced by the Far East; in the garden is an informal brasserie where breakfast is also served.

The town of Bath centers on a Roman temple honoring the goddess Minerva, which was built over the healing springs in A.D. 43. Excavated and partially rebuilt, the large complex of pools and heated relaxariums is a museum that traces water cults to the Celts and their deity Sul. Transformed by Richard "Beau" Nash, a "bon viveur" who became the city's official master of ceremonies in 1705, Bath's assembly rooms became the center of fashionable society, now displayed in a costume museum.

Bath is alive and well today. Visitors still queue up for a cup of the foul-smelling mineral water, or dine while a string trio provides gentle strains of yesteryear, at the Pump Room.

Thanks to modern technology, the hot springs that filled the vast Roman baths have been tapped for a new hydrotherapy center and day spa, scheduled to open in 2003.

The Royal Crescent Hotel—The Bath House
16 Royal Crescent, Bath BA1 2LS
England
Phone: 01225–823333
Fax: 01225–339401
E-mail: reservations@royalcrescent.co.uk
Web site: www.royalcrescent.co.uk

Season: Year-round

General Manager: Laurence Beere

Reservations: 0800–9800987 (U.K.); 888–295–4710 (U.S.)

Accommodations: Forty-five bedrooms and spacious suites, decorated with Georgian antiques, period beds and rich drapery; bathroom has claw-foot tub, hand-painted tiles. Fireplace in all suites. Garden Villa with two suites, plunge pool. Completely air-conditioned.

Meals: Full English breakfast included in daily tariff. Lunch and dinner a la carte.

Facilities: The Bath House indoor lap pool, two plunge tubs, steam room and sauna, dry flotation bed, garden, hot-air balloon, yacht.

Services & Special Programs: The Bath House Treatment, aromatherapy massage, wrap, facial, shiatsu, watsu, Thai massage, reiki, reflexology, movement and meditation, nutritional evaluation; group classes in yoga, pilates, tai chi, aquatics. Salon for hair and nail care. Retreats.

Rates: $$$

Best Spa Package: Two-day residential retreat with treatment, massage, breakfast and lunch, from $1,140 per person.

Credit Cards: Most major

Getting There: By train from London (Paddington Station), eighty minutes; by car from London, M–4 (exit 18) to A–46 to Bath, two hours; by air, Heathrow International Airport, two hours, London Gatwick, three hours.

What's Nearby: Stratford-upon-Avon (Shakespeare Theater), Oxford, Cotswolds walks, Roman York and Chester, Fairleigh Hungerford Castle, Thames river cruise, golf.

Bathing in Bath

New arrivals at the Bath House are advised to begin with a coordinated treatment that combines a sequence of bathing and cleansing with a relaxing massage. This two-hour package ($94) begins with swimming laps, followed by the karahafus dry and wet heat rooms, and a plunge in teak-lined soaking tubs, heated or cool. After a cleansing exfoliation, you enjoy a fifty-minute full-body massage.

TURNBERRY HOTEL, GOLF COURSES, AND SPA

Ayrshire, Scotland

orld-class golf meets a world-class spa at the hallowed grounds of Turnberry, an Edwardian-style country house dating back to 1906, now a Westin resort. The opening of the Turnberry Health Spa in 1991 symbolized a new era for this landmark golf resort. The legendary Ailsa course has hosted the British Open three times. The spa is located in a long complex adjoining the main hotel. The natural coastline and wild countryside, once ruled by Robert the Bruce, now has a civilized spa where golfers and spa-goers alike may enjoy it all, from a challenging aerobics class to squash to an aromatherapy massage.

The weather in this corner of Scotland is famous for mild temperatures and sunshine. That, plus exclusive spa treatments, championship golf on two courses, and the highly touted cuisine of chef Stewart Cameron makes Turnberry a popular destination. The Westin resort is rated five stars by both the Scottish Tourist Board and the Royal Automobile Club.

Sue Harmsworth launched her successul product line E'Spa here, with the goal of promoting guests' well-being. As with the golf, the spa here is already a legend with an outstanding range of treatments for both men and women. Aromatherapy is the spa's specialty, with treatments such as the aromatherapy total body, which includes a total skin brushing of face, scalp, and body designed to induce total relaxation. The spa's centerpiece is a magnificent 20-meter pool with breathtaking views across the Irish Sea to the island of Ailsa Craig.

The spa has its own restaurant with Mediterranean-inspired dishes, as well as two other fine restaurants. The bright and airy guest rooms are all individually decorated and extend the feel of a fine old country estate.

As you approach, Turnberry is like a vision from a vintage etching. The two-level white edifice with red

tile roof cries out to be photographed. In the evening, as the sun sets over the heather, a lone bagpiper dressed in full tartan plays his bagpipes. Another idyllic day has passed at Turnberry.

Skin as Smooth as a Scottish Morn

The Turnberry Spa's approach to healthy skin is a holistic one—your skin reflects your inner well-being. Treatment at the spa begins with a lifestyle consultation to detect such underlying problems as stress, hormonal changes, or erratic sleep patterns. This is followed by a purity program, based on the belief that the key to body balance is regular purifying. The program includes a jet blitz to increase circulation and improve skin tone; a hydrotherapy bath using an infusion of detoxifying mineral sea salts, seaweed, and essential aromatherapy oils; an aromatherapy massage for relaxation of mind and body; and home care advice on products to ensure that the benefits of purification last well after the trip to the spa is over.

A Scottish Spa Amid Heavenly Golf and Heather-Studded Hills

Turnberry Hotel, Golf Courses, and Spa
Ayrshire KA26 9LT
Scotland
Phone: 44–1655–331–000
Fax: 44–0–1655–331–706
E-Mail: turnberry@westin.com
Web Site: www.turnberry.co.uk or www.westin.com

Season: Year round

General Manager: Stuart Selbie

Spa Director: Vicky Pearson

Fitness Director: Peter Conlan

Reservations: 44–0–1655–331–000 or 800–325–3535 or 800–WESTIN–1

Spa Appointments: 44–0–1655–331–000

Accommodations: 132 guest rooms, all individually decorated.

Meals: The resort offers three restaurants. The Turnberry Restaurant, the main dining room, features local produce and fish as well as French delicacies. The Clubhouse restaurant strides off the eighteeth green of the Ailsa course. The Spa restaurant serves health-conscious, low-fat entrees.

Facilities: Full-service, 50,000-square-foot spa with six treatment rooms and spa-side Jacuzzi; 65-foot pool with views across the Irish Sea to Ailsa Craig; two hydrotherapy rooms; fully equipped gym; beauty salon; two squash courts; saunas; two championship golf courses; private landing strip; helicopter pad.

Services & Special Programs: Chauffeur-driven car service; business services; golf clinics; one-on-one personal fitness training.

Rates: $$$

Best Spa Package: The half-day Total Relaxation package includes a body polish, full-body massage, facial, and skin-softening treatment for hands and feet (about $175). You may schedule other treatments on an a la carte basis.

Credit Cards: Most major

Getting There: Glasgow Airport is forty-five minutes away by car; a private landing strip and helicopter pad are located on the premises.

What's Nearby: Culzean Castle; Burns Country (poet Robert); Castle Kennedy ruins and gardens, 35 miles away; Bargany Gardens, 9 miles from the resort; and Dunure Castle, just 8 miles away.

THE CELTIC MANOR RESORT—FORUM HEALTH CLUB AND SPA

Newport, Wales

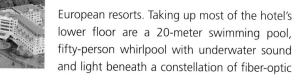

pened in 1999 on a 1,400-acre estate rich with scenery and history, the Forum Health Club and Spa capped development of the most complete resort in Wales. Combining exceptional golf, leisure, and convention facilities, the Celtic Manor Resort traces its heritage in Roman and Celtic themes throughout the 400-room hotel and its three championship golf courses.

Crossing the Severn estuary on a dramatic new bridge, you can't miss the Manor. An in-your-face newly built megalith dominating the M–4 motorway, the resort is all about thinking big. Canadian telecommunications tycoon Terry Matthews invited golf course designer Robert Trent Jones Sr.—both born in Wales—to launch the project in 1995. At its center is the nineteenth century manor-turned-maternity home where Matthews was born. Set into a hillside, the hotel's soaring central atrium links three wings of bedrooms to the spa and leisure club, and to a high-tech convention center.

The Forum Health Club and Spa surpasses many

European resorts. Taking up most of the hotel's lower floor are a 20-meter swimming pool, fifty-person whirlpool with underwater sound and light beneath a constellation of fiber-optic stars, and luxurious changing rooms with their own sauna and steam room, plunge pool, and whirlpool. The sixteen therapy rooms are spacious and well-equipped for a range of treatments by Clarins, Elemis, and Guinot, including sports massage and skin care for men. Perhaps the most unique feature is a Rasul chamber, where mud-caked guests socialize as they steam out impurities under a star-studded dome.

Spacious and elegantly appointed, the Forum's wide corridors, high ceilings, and light-filled exercise studios are a pleasant environment, even when the weather isn't. The fifty-four-station gym allows you to watch TV or enjoy music while you work out on cross-trainers, steppers, bikes, rowers, free weights, and treadmills. Personal trainers are on hand, and scheduled sessions of yoga and aerobics are held in a wood-floored studio. The gym also offers fitness assessment and counseling packages from Fitech. Kids up to age fifteen have their own Hideaway Club, with gym, swimming pool, whirlpool, computer, and cinema. Taking care of the entire family are an Aveda concept hair salon, run by local-TV celeb Philip Mungeam, and a spa cafe.

At the golf clubhouse, open to the public as well as members, a second health club called Dylans offers an aerobics studio, gym, indoor swimming pool, and treatment rooms. The focus here is on sports medicine, osteopathy, and physiotherapy. Shape up your game at the golf academy and its twenty-four bay

driving range, floodlit for evening use.

Secluded amid woodlands and valleys, the resort has views of nearby Cardiff and industrial developments. Tennis, mountain biking, riding, walks, and hiking are on offer, as well as pony trekking, clay pigeon shooting, archery, and off-road driving. Elegant restaurants offer Welsh fusion cuisine and Mediterranean classics. Legendary Wales has a new star.

Detox Dome Is Muddy Marvelous

Rasul, an ancient cleansing ceremony originated by Eastern healers, debuts here in a lushly tiled chamber. Seated under a blue dome twinkling with fiber-optic stars, you apply mud mixed for your skin type. Steam rises through herbs in a central pillar, gradually increasing the humidity and temperature of the chamber. After showering off the mud you are coated with nourishing oils by a therapist. Four friends can share the experience, au naturel, or borrow disposable knickers. Cost: $29 per person.

The Celtic Manor Resort—Forum Health Club and Spa
Coldra Woods, Newport
Gwent NP18 1HQ
Wales
Phone: 44–0–1633–413–000
Fax 44–0–1633–412–912
E-mail: postbox@celtic-manor.com
Web site: www.celtic-manor.com

Season: Year-round

General Manager: Robert Church

Sports and Leisure Manager: Ian Phillips

Reservations: 800–223–6800

Accommodations: 400 luxury rooms, thirty-two suites in contemporary hotel, most with balcony. All have private bath and shower, air-conditioning, speaker phone with voice mail, desk with fax modem and dual voltage power, CD player, TV. Amenities include hair dryer, trouser press, iron and board, tea- and coffeemakers, robe, toiletries. Library lounge.

Meals: A la carte menu in two restaurants and spa cafe. Also available at golf clubhouse, conservatory and terrace, games room and library, and piano bar.

Facilities: Two indoor swimming pools and whirlpools, sixteen treatment rooms including hydrotherapy, dry flotation bed, Rasul chamber, two fitness centers with cardiovascular and strength equipment, aerobics/dance studios, men's and women's changing rooms with sauna/steam rooms, plunge pool. Hideaway Club for kids. Admission is free to hotel guests.

Services & Special Programs: Skin care, facials, massage, G5 machine massage, body wrap, aromatherapy, Cathiodermie, hair and nail care; jet shower, hydrotherapy tubs. Fitness evaluation, personal trainers.

Rates: $$$$

Best Spa Package: Elemis aromatherapy, top-to-toe, two-hour treatment for $72, plus gratuity.

Credit Cards: Most major

Getting There: By train to Cardiff/Newport from London Paddington Station on Great Western (two hours); by car, M–4 to Severn Bridge, Junction 24 (approximately two hours).

What's Nearby: Cardiff Bay, Wentwood Forest, Caernarfon Castle, Tintern Abbey.

INDIA & AFRICA

RAJVILAS

Jaipur, India

I n the perfumed gardens of a maharaja's palace, a cool retreat blends Eastern and Western wellness treatments. At Rajvilas, ritual purification, a centuries-old tradition in India, is reinterpreted through herbal body care, aromatherapy massage, and deep-cleansing facials.

The destination says it all: Jaipur. A city of storybook forts and palaces; of polo-playing maharajas and colorful desert people; and the source of ayurveda—traditional natural healing for purity of body and mind.

This sumptuous palace was built in 1727, amid parched, pale desert. Restored in 1995 as the jewel in the crown of the Oberoi Hotel Group, the stunning public rooms and guest suites are nothing less than regal. Rajvilas brings past and present together in a glorious fusion of styles.

Water gardens that would have delighted Mogul princesses now harbor a lavish spa complex devoted to soothing body and soul. The spa is a private hideaway for hotel guests. The setting is graced by a 250-year-old Shiva temple surrounded by a lotus pond, fragrant herb garden, and 25-meter lap pool. Drawing on Mogul influences absorbed by the rulers of Jaipur, the spa is housed in the original building on the site, a classic Rajasthani mansion, called a haveli. The ornate interior features treatment rooms for both holistic Western and ayurvedic relaxation and pampering, a whirlpool in an open-to-the-sky courtyard, shaded terraces for meditation, and an air-conditioned gymnasium outfitted with the very latest exercise equipment.

Enhancing your enjoyment of the spa are ready supplies of cold towels, fresh juices, herbal teas, and a light cuisine. There are massage suites with private lounge and recreation areas, individual Finnish saunas, steam rooms, separate hot and cold plunge pools, and showers for men and women.

Guest rooms are an architectural amalgam of traditional Rajasthani flat-roofed houses and havelis.

Clustered around courtyards, each building is hand-decorated with colorful frescoes depicting tropical birds and flowers. The rooms are an eclectic blend of colonial and Indian influences, furnished with four-posters, dhurrie rugs, and wicker. Sunken marble baths look onto secluded gardens. Dramatically lit at night by flaming torches, the fort's central courtyard has a dais for performances of traditional dances while you dine in an open-air section of the restaurant.

Rajvilas
Goner Road, Jaipur 303 012
India
Phone: 91–141–64–0101
Fax: 91–141–640202
E-mail: rchopra@oberoidel.com
Web site: www.oberoihotels.com

Season: Year-round

General Manager: Vikram Oberoi

Accommodations: Seventy-one rooms in small clusters of traditional houses and tents. Private villas (three) have swimming pool. All are air-conditioned, with marble bathroom, sunken tub.

Meals: Gourmet European and Indian cuisine served in the Surya Mahal Restaurant. Spa menu available a la carte or as part of package.

Facilities: Separate wings for men and women, each containing changing and rest rooms, sauna, steam room, plunge pool, therapy rooms. Gymnasium with Cybex and LifeFitness equipment. Salon for hair and nail care. Recreation: Tennis on two floodlit courts, heated swimming pool.

Services & Special Programs: Yoga, meditation, massage, ayurvedic full-body massage, body wrap, facial, shirodhara (head massage), Swedish massage, aromatherapy, eye treatments.

Rates: $$$

Best Spa Package: The Serenity Retreat includes two nights and three days accommodation in a deluxe room, spa breakfast and dinners for two, daily spa treatment, guided yoga and meditation. Chauffeur-driven limousine transfers on arrival and departure. $700 per person, double occupancy, including tax.

Credit Cards: American Express, Diners Club, MasterCard, Visa

Getting There: Jaipur can be accessed either by rail, air, or road from Delhi or Bombay. Complimentary transfers to hotel from airport or railway station. A helipad is on the grounds.

What's Nearby: The Amber Fort, Jagarth Fort, the "Pink City" of Jaipur, Ramgarth.

For a touch of desert living, you can stay in a tent that a prince might have used while on safari. Appointed with teak floors and campaign chests, as well as cool white and beige block-print fabrics, these cloistered tents are perhaps the most distinctive accommodations in Oberoi hotels, which can be found from Bali to Lombok, London to Hong Kong.

Rajvilas offers an exotic retreat, complete with elephant ride at the Amber Fort. Located thirty minutes from the Jaipur airport, it is another world.

Ayurvedic Rejuvenation

Ayurvedic methods of relaxation, massage, and herbal treatments are the core of the Rajvilas experience. With treatments based on ayurvedic principles to relax the mind and promote well-being, the spa uses therapeutic essential oils developed in America by Aveda. Aromaveda experiences include such traditional treatments as massage, shirodhara, and kati-basti. Using local ingredients, a shirodhara therapist drizzles a fine stream of warm sesame oil or buttermilk onto your "third eye" (the center of your forehead) to help calm and clear the mind. Or a therapist may prepare you for massage with an herbal "ubtan"—a body polish using sandalwood and rose powder to slough off dead cells that leaves your skin soft, smooth, and glowing.

SÉRÉNITÉ WELLNESS CENTRE
Constantia Valley, South Africa

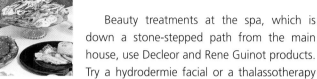

his intimate eleven-room retreat in the verdant forest of the Cape's Constantia Valley is a jewel among spas. It has been recognized as the finest in South Africa, an admirable accomplishment, since Sérénité Wellness Centre opened only in 1998.

This is the epitome of a personalized spa experience, with a successful hands-on approach achieved by owners Axel and Elizabeth Brandt. They have developed five programs that focus on holistic health, rejuvenation, executive de-stressing, detox and weight loss, and beauty.

The owners guide you into the best program for your needs, but the one called the Sérénité Experience is often a sensible choice for first-time spa-goers. All wellness packages include treatments along with classes, such as yoga and tai chi. There are also mountain walks, swimming, and gym sessions available. About half of the guests here are men (many drawn by the special de-stress program), a much higher percentage than in most world-class spas.

Beauty treatments at the spa, which is down a stone-stepped path from the main house, use Decleor and Rene Guinot products. Try a hydrodermie facial or a thalassotherapy treatment with stress-relieving seaweed.

The Brandts' team approach to wellness underscores individuality; there are no ready-made cures or cookie-cutter approaches to programming guests' treatments. The best way to start a program here is by completing a health assessment administered by Dr. David Green, the resident physician. The examination includes tests for blood pressure, lung and heart function, cholesterol, and diabetes. Based on an evaluation of the tests, a customized program is prepared, with input from a dietitian and personal trainer. The Brandts report that the most common symptoms diagnosed are stress-related, from migraines to backaches. The antidote for stress is a program encompassing relaxation therapy, tai chi, reiki, shiatsu, yoga, and, for those in need of some soul-searching, meditation.

The peaceful and mesmerizing views, stretching out to False Bay, aid in the recovery process. The Sérénité ambience is sensuous: Bursts of flowers—roses, hibiscus, bougainvillea, and petunias—create a panoply of color. The sensory delights of Sérénité extend to the spa cuisine, which emphasizes fresh ingredients and original recipes. Not a drop of wine is served here, but who needs it? The experience is totally intoxicating.

Serene Spa Moments

As you might expect from its name, at Sérénité Wellness Center the emphasis is on "serenity." With the mountain air as a catalyst, Elizabeth and Axel Brandt have provided wide-open spaces, peaceful pleasures, and a "beautiful silence." Small ponds surround a meditation area, and from the hill you can enjoy views of Cape Town's harbor and city lights. Sérénité accommodates no more than eighteen guests at a time. The Brandts believe that they are better able to change attitudes about health when working with such a small group. Adding to the sense of serenity are classes such as yoga and treatments such as the two-hour facial that includes paraffin-dipped warming mitts for hands and feet.

Elegance and Intimacy at a Secluded Spa

Sérénité Wellness Centre
16 Debaren Close
Constantia, Cape Town 7945
South Africa
PO Box 30097
Tokai 7966
South Africa
Phone: 27–021–713–1760
Fax: 27–021–713–0049
E-mail: info@serenite.co.za
Web site: www.serenite.co.za

Season: Year-round

General Manager: Axel and Elizabeth Brandt

Reservations: 27–021–713–1760

Spa Appointments: 27–021–713–1760

Accommodations: Eleven elegant guest rooms, each individually decorated and featuring down feather duvets, air-conditioning, CD player, satellite television, and fireplace.

Meals: All meals are included. The accent is on low-calorie, healthful food; most of the vegetables and herbs come from the resort's own garden.

Facilities: Two outdoor heated pools; an indoor heated pool; two tennis courts; fully equipped fitness center, saunas, steam baths, and meditation sanctuary.

Services & Special Programs: Horseback riding and golf nearby may be arranged; customized wellness programs; booking of South African excursions; fresh flowers and fruit in the rooms; lectures and concerts; guided mountain and forest walks.

Rates: $$

Best Spa Package: The two-night Break-A-Way package includes accommodations, all meals, daily water aerobics, a yoga relaxation, tai chi, two massages, a Vichy shower and mineral exfoliation, hydrotherapy tub, and a facial or body wrap treatment. $340 per person double occupancy or $465 single occupancy.

Credit Cards: Most major

Getting There: Airport transfers are arranged from Cape Town.

What's Nearby: The wine country and several wineries, a botanical garden, and the penguins on Boulders Beach.

HOTEL HASDRUBAL THALASSA—
VITAL CENTER THALGO
Hammamet, Tunisia

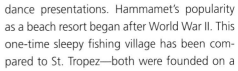

From the moment you arrive at the regal gates of Hasdrubal Thalassa, a palatial 222-suite resort hotel along the Mediterranean shore, it is evident that it will take nearly a week to explore the grounds, restaurants, and, ultimately, the Vital Center Thalgo, which features spa treatments with a sensory twist.

This five-star hotel is the most impressive of many in this now booming tourist area. According to the Tunisian National Tourism Office, forty new hotels are planned, with the goal of accommodating up to 40,000 visitors. The area first began attracting travelers in the 1920s and 1930s, when Georges Sebastion, a Romanian millionaire, built a home here called Dar Sebastion, which attracted many artists, writers, and politicians. Today Dar Sebastion is an international cultural center and the site of the Hammamet International Festival each summer, with jazz, theater, and dance presentations. Hammamet's popularity as a beach resort began after World War II. This one-time sleepy fishing village has been compared to St. Tropez—both were founded on a gulf, are guarded by sixteenth-century citadels, expanded around a fishing port, and, thanks to the jet set, became fashionable seaside resorts.

If you are spa jaded and yearn for something out of the ordinary, the Vital Center Thalgo at Hasdrubal Thalassa is a perfect choice. The clientele is mainly European and Middle Eastern, with a smattering of British. English is understood, but brush up on your French before you come. Tunisia is deeply influenced by the French culture, and, if you speak French, you won't have any difficulty differentiating a *douche à jet* from a *massage spécifique aux huiles essentielles*.

The bi-level Vital Center Thalgo is in its own wing and offers hydrobaths, algae wraps, and seawater

showers to rev up the body. There's also Swedish massage, electrotherapy (using different currents to relax stressed muscles), and a special treatment to improve capillary circulation that uses water jet streams with varying temperatures and jet showers.

At the center guests are encouraged to fine-tune their senses through a variety of highly unique treatments. Smell is revitalized through aromatherapeutic use of essential oils; hearing through subaquatic music therapy (sound waves infused directly in water); touch through exposure to seawater mist and diffused essential oils in hot and cold waves. A better sense of taste is stimulated by drinking tisanes,

Hotel Hasdrubal Thalassa—Vital Center Thalgo
Zone Touristique-Yasmine
Hammamet, Tunisia
Phone: 216–2–248–800
Fax: 216–2–248–923
E-mail: hasdrubal.thala@planet.tn

Season: Year-round

General Manager: Hyekal Akrout

Spa Director: Ezzadine Lakhouaja

Fitness Director: Kaothar Meddeb

Reservations: 216–2–248–800 or through Leading Hotels of the World at 800–223–6800

Spa Appointments: 216–2–248–800

Accommodations: 220 luxurious suites, including a presidential suite.

Meals: Four restaurants, featuring Tunisian, Italian, international, and dietetic cuisine, serve casual to gourmet meals, as well as spa cuisine.

Facilities: A full-service 16,404-square-foot spa; two seawater swimming pools (indoor and outdoor pools); fully equipped gym; treatment rooms; Jacques Dessange Hair Salon; private beach; indoor and outdoor pools; sauna; Turkish baths; conference room; games, bridge room; tennis courts.

Services & Special Programs: Twenty-four-hour room service, fully equipped business center, private sandy beach, outdoor sporting activities. Sightseeing and shopping in Hammamet.

Rates: $$

Best Spa Package: Spa packages are added onto room rates. The six-day Thalgo Vital program includes four treatments daily, selected from a menu that includes a medically supervised marine back treatment, a slimming treatment, an anti-stress treatment, a leg stimulation treatment, a biolifting beauty treatment, and a daily fitness class. $780 per person, double occupancy.

Credit Cards: American Express, Eurocard, MasterCard, Visa

Getting There: Fly into Tunis-Carthage International Airport or the Monastir/Sousse Bourguiba International Airport. The hotel can arrange for a private limousine transfer. British Airways operates flights between London and Tunis; flying time is approximately two hours and forty-five minutes.

What's Nearby: The Kasbah, a sixteenth-century restored fort; Tataouine (which inspired the name of the planet Tatooine in the *Star Wars* saga); the Cyrus 18-hole golf course designed by Ronald Fream.

a range of herbal infusion teas. The sense of sight is stimulated by wearing special alpha wave generating glasses. At this "festival of the body," the thalasso therapy is less medically oriented than in France and more focused toward overall health and well-being. And the accommodating staff won't make a fuss if you are ten minutes late for a treatment.

Guest rooms at the resort are dramatic, with king-size beds on platforms. The accommodations are a step above luxury, with original works of art, marble bathrooms, generous terraces overlooking the Mediterranean, air-conditioning, sitting areas, television, and minibars. Some suites are nonsmoking.

Hasdrubal Thalassa is a luxurious spa getaway with sun, seawater, and a sumptuous setting.

Bubbling Baths for Relaxation

The resort's baths, Niagara and Thalasso, are recommended for both relaxation and good blood circulation. The treatments immerse the entire body in a seawater bath with massaging jets. A rain shower combined with a manual massage induces even greater relaxation. Following that, a revitalizing jet shower adds controlled pressure all over the body. An underwater massage by hydrotherapists relieves muscular pain and improve body circulation. The experience is not to be missed.

THE RESIDENCE—PHYTOMER SPA
La Marsa, Carthage, Tunisia

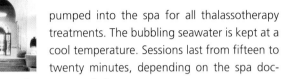

unisia is forging ahead with an ambitious master plan to attract tourists, and the fabulous Phytomer Spa at the luxurious Residence resort is destined to put this North African country on every spa-lover's map. And plan a few days before or after your visit to explore this legendary country sandwiched between Algeria and Libya.

The spa with its spectacular dome-covered pool offers massage, lymphatic drainage, skin care, hydromassage, bubbling seawater massage, circular showers with affusion, and seaweed therapy—all in a luxurious setting of arches, columns, balustrades, cupolas, arcades, fountains, urns, and sculptures. There are thirty treatment rooms, and the staff is expertly trained.

The thalasso-based spa complies with the French standards of thalassotherapy, but goes well beyond them as well. Water from the Mediterranean, highly charged with sodium chloride and magnesium, is pumped into the spa for all thalassotherapy treatments. The bubbling seawater is kept at a cool temperature. Sessions last from fifteen to twenty minutes, depending on the spa doctor's recommendations.

Speaking French is helpful here, but not necessary. The multi-lingual spa director can arrange your appointments. The beauty salon has limited hours. There is a lovely spa restaurant with an excellent luncheon buffet and juice bar.

Guest rooms are brochure-perfect, with private balconies overlooking the sea and all of the amenities imaginable, from satellite television to minibar refrigerators. The elegant, oversized baths are decorated in red and black marble and feature dressing tables, telephones, bathrobes, and slippers.

The Residence is ideal for the spa-goer who seeks a world-class spa in one of the most exotic settings in the world.

The Residence—Phytomer Spa
Les Cotes de Carthage
Boîte Postale 697
2070 La Marsa
Tunisia
Phone: 216–1–910–101
Fax: 216–1–910–144
E-mail: residence.tun@gnet.tn
Web site: www.theresidence.com

Season: Year-round

General Manager: M. Jean-Pierre Auriol

Spa Director: Emna Bouchoucha

Reservations: 800–223–6800 (Leading Hotels of the World); 800–SICILY–1 (Amelia Tours).

Accommodations: 161 rooms and nine suites, most suites with sea views. All accommodations are double, furnished with king-size beds or two double beds. All contain mini-bars; satellite television; private terrace; marble bathrooms.

Meals: The Juice Bar offers a light spa luncheon buffet and freshly pressed juices. Mediterranean dining is offered in L'Olivier; Li Bai serves Chinese cuisine. All dining is a la carte.

Facilities: 37,650 square-foot spa with German hydrotherapy equipment; six massage rooms; four jet showers; two affusion showers; two facial rooms; four rooms for body wraps; steam; sauna; Turkish hammam; gym and fitness room; pool with aquatic circuit.

Services & Special Programs: A personal program is created for each guest after consulting with a spa doctor. Treatments range from those dealing with getting in shape to back care to a special anti-stress marine cure for men.

Rates: $$

Best Spa Package: The six-night Thalassotherapy Cure starts at $1,280 per person, based on double occupancy in the low season (November–March). This includes four thalassotherapy treatments daily, a superior category of room, and breakfast and lunch or dinner daily.

Credit Cards: Most major

Getting There: Flights from London, Paris, Amsterdam, and Zurich to Tunis. British Airways flies four times a week from Gatwick; Tunisair has four flights a week from London's Heathrow. The hotel concierge can arrange airport transfers or you can use a taxi.

What's Nearby: Bardo Museum (famous mosaics); the Tunis medina (twenty minutes away); archeological tours to Thuburbo Majus.

MIDDLE EAST

THE RITZ-CARLTON SHARM EL SHEIKH

Om El-Seed, Sharm El Sheikh, Egypt

here was a time when the principal glories of Sharm El Sheikh—or simply Sharm, as its aficionados call it—were all underwater. For when it comes to scuba diving, no place on earth, not even the Great Barrier Reef, can match the richness and color of the Red Sea's aquatic kingdom. But the 1999 arrival of the five-star Ritz-Carlton made this desert outpost a prime resort destination.

The hotel spa, considered one of the finest in Egypt, offers an exceptional range of treatments, worthy of Cleopatra. A particularly exotic one is called Sweet Blessings. In an Arabian beach tent overlooking the Red Sea, you are given a foot massage, a hand and foot scrub with a warm aromatic oil mask, and a body massage. Even the bottles containing the pure Egyptian essential oils and natural herbs are beautiful to behold. Another, called Red Sea Ecstasy, is said to be the ultimate stress reliever. A foot scrub and massage to soothe tired feet is followed by a warm, aromatic flower bath to calm and relax the nervous system and enliven your spirits. And where else could you find an Egyptian Coffee Scrub or delve into Cleopatra's Secret (a milk bath with lavender)?

Enhancing the spa experience are the guest rooms, where no expense has been spared on finishing

touches. Every room has an expansive view of the Red Sea, and robes, slippers, and premium bath essentials are found in the bathrooms. You may request that a spa therapist prepare a Cleopatra milk bath or an aromatic flower bath for you in your own room.

The sensuous pleasures of the spa are enhanced by the starkness of the Sinai landscape. You may have seen the Nevada desert. You may have been to Morocco, but you've never seen a place like this before. It's a beauty so barren that it is almost surreal, framed by magnificent waters of the clearest neon blue. Scuba in the morning and shiatsu in the afternoon—this is revitalization to the max.

Spa treatments not given in the tent are given in the air-conditioned health and fitness center. The fitness center also offers sessions with a private trainer, a 2-mile power walk, stretch and tone classes, aerobics, water exercise classes, boxing, and one-on-one body contouring consultations. The gym is fully equipped and staffed. There is no progressive fitness program here, but the diving opportunities more than compensate.

Diving in the Red Sea and spa treatments at the Ritz—the combination makes for a mesmerizing experience.

Ancient Formulas for Lasting Beauty

The natural ingredients used at Sharm El Sheikh's spa—fresh organic herbs and essential oils and aromas—are similar to those used in ancient Egypt. The specially trained staff offers international expertise and personalized treatments. A popular one is the boreh scrub, used to ease muscle pain and improve circulation. While your body is wrapped in thermal blankets to keep the penetrating heat in, your head and back are massaged with an herbal blend made from fresh clove, nutmeg, cardamom, black pepper, and ginger. You won't need aspirin afterward!

The Wonder of the Waters

The Ritz-Carlton Sharm El Sheikh
Om El-Seed, Sharm El Sheikh
PO Box 72
South Sinai, Egypt
Phone: 20–62–661–919
Fax: 20–69–661–920
E-mail: ritzcarltonssh@sinainet.com.eg
Web site: www.ritzcarlton.com

Season: Year-round

General Manager: Eric Swanson

Spa Director: Lee Sutton

Reservations: 800–241–3333 (Ritz-Carlton Worldwide Reservation Center)

Spa Appointments: 800–241–3333

Accommodations: 307 guest rooms, including forty-eight suites and twenty-five Ritz-Carlton Club rooms. Contemporary Middle Eastern decor with classical touches; remote control television; minibars.

Meals: The Cafe for all-day dining inside and outside; La Luna, Italian cuisine; Asian-influenced Blue Ginger; lobby lounge and library for afternoon English tea; the Waves, for light fare and cocktails, in a huge tent beside the Red Sea; the Pyramid Bar.

Facilities: Spa and fitness center; full-service beauty salon; three lighted tennis courts; diving center, two swimming pools; volleyball; meeting facilities; five exclusive beaches with coves; swim-up bar; outdoor amphitheater; gift and sundry shops.

Services & Special Programs: Ritz-Carlton Kids Club; Ritz-Carlton Club (special concierge and room service offerings); baby-sitting; executive business services; diving and fishing tours; camel safaris.

Rates: $$$

Best Spa Package: The Ramses Reign includes a hand and foot scrub, a body glow, an aromatic steam bath, a breeze wrap, and full-body massage. The three-and-one-half-hour treatment is added to the accommodation rate, which ranges from $260 to $420 per night double occupancy.

Credit Cards: Most major

Getting There: A forty-five minute flight from Cairo's International Airport, or a five hour drive from Cairo. The hotel concierge can arrange transfers from the Sharm El Sheik Airport.

What's Nearby: The Red Sea, one of the best dive sites in the world; snorkeling; desert safari tours; Mount Sinai (three hours away); St. Catherine Monastery (three hours away); the tourist villages of Sharm El Sheikh and Dahab; Na'ama Bay with restaurants, casino, and nightclubs.

CARMEL FOREST SPA RESORT

Haifa, Israel

The Carmel Forest Spa Resort is set into a hillside in the forests of the Carmel Mountains. The hotel is hardly visible until you round the driveway. Dedicated to renewal and relaxation, this is Israel's top destination spa. With views stretching to the Mediterranean and acres of manicured lawns, the resort draws inspiration from nature and the Bible. According to the ancient sage Maimonides, "The wholeness of the body preceded the wholeness of the soul." Today's mantra is relaxation and pampering.

An extensive menu of facials, skin care, and bodywork distinguishes the spa. Treatments feature mud from the Dead Sea, seaweed, and aromatic oils made for the resort from flowers and herbs used in biblical times. Ayurvedic massage appears here for the first time in Israel, as do Parisian facials by Decleor.

Surrounded by a nature preserve, the spa offers unique peace and quiet. Signs posted on the grounds call for quiet, and, astonishingly, the guests generally comply. Guests range from Tel Aviv fashion models and stressed-out software executives to television news presenters and immaculately coifed forty-something women wearing lots of jewelry. Children under sixteen are not welcome. There is no bar, but you can order wine with dinner. The restaurant gets noisy, but most of the talk is about politics. As one woman explained, Israeli parents worry about their kids doing military service. Men and women on duty actually get special rates to come here for a few days of R&R, adding a young element not often found at Israeli spas.

Lavishly decorated, inside and out, the building belies its origin as a sanatorium constructed with German reparation money for Holocaust survivors. Converted as a world-class resort by Ben Yakar's Isrotel Hotel Group, the hotel rooms and spa facilities are top-notch. Among unique features: indoor swimming pool with view down the mountain, adjoining reading and music rooms with fireplaces, an imported Turkish steam room (hammam) for body scrubs. Interiors have lots of glass, tile, and polished wood floors. Native stone walkways lead to trails through the forest.

Borrow a mountain bike or join the daily guided fitness walk. Activities are scheduled every hour, from body shaping in the morning to a predinner stretch. Choices include yoga, chi gong, tai chi, aquaerobics, and FitBall sessions. Resort guests have free access to all scheduled programs, including lifestyle lectures in

English and guided meditation. At night there are movies, concerts, and guest speakers (in Hebrew) on subjects like sexuality and women's health. The all-inclusive tariff covers three meals daily, even barbecue nights. The menu may be low-fat, but the buffets are extensive, with cooked-to-order steak and seafood, and there's no limit on seconds.

Staffed by experts from Israel and abroad, the resort offers spa services a la carte or in packages. Day spa arrangements without room can be prescheduled, and you may want to take advantage of discounts offered on Saturdays, when scheduled activities are limited.

Controlling Stress Naturally

In a country where stress is daily news, Carmel Forest Spa Resort is an island of peace and tranquillity. Revitalizing programs include weight loss and meditation, guided hikes and tai chi. Being in the forest adds to serenity, and spa treatments are designed with natural products derived from local plants and herbs. Anti-stress workshops focus on tools to prioritize your daily life. At day's end, relax on the terrace and drink in the view of forest and sea, a natural tranquilizer.

Biblical Resources for Rejuvenation

Carmel Forest Spa Resort
PO Box 9000
Haifa 31900
Israel
Phone: 972–4–8307888
Fax: 972–4–8323988
E-mail: carmelf@isrotel.co.il
Web site: www.isrotel.co.il

Season: Year-round

General Manager: Stephen W. Ayers

Spa Director: Guy Nadler

Accommodations: Destination spa with 126 rooms, including sixteen suites, facing the Mediterranean. All with private bath, balcony, or wooden terrace. Amenities include robes, slippers, air-conditioning.

Meals: Buffet breakfast and lunch, dinner menu served. Salad bar and extensive selections of yogurt, grains, vegetables, and fruits complement cooked-to-order eggs, fish, and steak. No strict kosher rules, just fresh, low-fat meals. Herbal teas, coffee available.

Facilities: Comprehensive physiotherapy and pampering in a focused environment. Aerobics studio, indoor and outdoor swimming pools, gymnasium. Turkish hammam, private hydrotherapy baths.

Services & Special Programs: Massages range from Swedish to Hawaiian lomi lomi, Thai, shiatsu, four-hand ayurveda, and sports. Reiki, reflexology, craniosacral balancing, mud and seaweed wraps, facials, aromatherapy. Guided walks, exercise classes. Nutrition counseling and structured weight-loss program. Stress-management program.

Rates: $$$

Best Spa Package: Five-day anti-stress program (Sunday to Thursday) teaches positive, practical steps for managing stress. On arrival, the resort nurse checks your medical record and gets a body composition report. Individually tailored exercise and meal plan, plus daily selection of treatments, are included in this $779 package, per person, double room.

Credit Cards: MasterCard, Visa

Getting There: From the Haifa-Tel Aviv Old Road outside of Haifa, follow signs for Carmel Forest on Beit Oren Road, Route 70 (twenty minutes).

What's Nearby: Vered Hagalil dude ranch, Hammat Gader hot springs, Safed artist colony, Biblical sites of the Galilee and Nazareth, Druze village, Tiberias hot springs, Caesarea beaches, golf.

THE DEAD SEA: SPA TOWN

Dead Sea, Israel

ife-enhancing waters and mud are the main attractions at Dead Sea resorts. Lying an astonishing 400 meters (1,312 feet) below sea level, the Dead Sea has a unique, healing environment, one that has been documented since biblical times. It attracts vacationers as well as persons seeking relief from rheumatism and skin problems, and taking a cure here today is a combination of age-old natural elements and high-tech therapy.

The drive from Jerusalem to the Dead Sea takes less than an hour and passes through 2,000 years of civilization. Arid desert suddenly gives way to a silver-colored sea, as the road turns toward a flowering oasis at Ein Gedi, the massive fortress of Masada, and the Ein Bokek hotel area. Set against the bleached hills of the Judean Desert, the region is a vast nature reserve, where wildlife like the Nubian ibex can be spotted among ruins of ancient cultures.

Strung along the shore, the modest kibbutz and glamorous high-rise hotels all boast in-house spas. Standard facilities include two pools, one with Dead Sea water, the other with thermo-mineral sulfur water. Treatments range from mud wraps and massage to facials and hydrotherapy tubs.

Staffed by skilled professionals, some Dead Sea spas specialize in medical treatments for which the seaside microclimate, mineral-laden water, and mud have achieved recognition, although not universal acceptance. But for vacationers, there are state-of-the-art oases at the **Hyatt Regency Hotel, Golden Tulip Resort, Crowne Plaza,** and other members of the Dead Sea Hotel Association.

Along with water sports, these destinations offer freshwater swimming pools and a variety of restaurants, from kosher to Oriental, steak house to Italian.

Exploring the region starts at Masada, a mountaintop fortress that King Herod transformed in 35 B.C. as his winter palace. Hikers brave the heat and dust to follow a serpentine Roman path to the summit, but a quick cable car ride allows you to enjoy panoramic views of the sea and desert. The ruins tell a story of heroism by Jews who defied the might of the Roman empire.

Plan a day trip, or stay a week; packages are offered at all the resorts. Hiking trails at **Kibbutz Ein Gedi** take you past bird sanctuaries, waterfalls, springs, caves, canyons, and an early Bronze Age temple. A thriving health resort where modest accommodations come with access to hot springs and mud treatments, this hillside kibbutz also operates a day spa on the shore road. Here you can purchase cosmetics and bath products made with Dead Sea minerals, water, and mud.

At the top-rated **Hyatt Regency Dead Sea** in bustling Ein Bokek, the Mineralia Spa rests on a hill commanding views of the Judean Mountains. Palm trees and lush gardens shelter the glass-walled Roman pool, providing a respite from the sun. There are six mud therapy rooms and seventeen private rooms for skin care, massage, and beauty treatments. Aerobics and group exercise are scheduled in a well-equipped fitness center where workouts come with a view of the water. A private medical clinic provides dermatology care and postsurgery recovery, plus natural health and complementary medicine programs.

Awesome as the Dead Sea looks, there is a calming effect in the pristine air. Sunlight's harmful rays are filtered by this oxygen-heavy, salt-laden atmosphere. Floating effortlessly in the warm, oily water is better than a water bed, and it gives your skin a tingling, healthy glow.

Balneotherapy

Balneotherapy is a European term for therapeutic bathing. The role of balneotherapy in the treatment of rheumatism is a subject of much debate in medical circles. Although the therapeutic value of bathing in the Dead Sea has been reported for at least 2000 years, systematic study of the effects of balneotherapy have started here only recently. The sea's concentration of minerals (about 30 percent) and chemical composition (large amounts of magnesium and bromide, rather than sodium chloride, which is the predominant salt in most European spa waters) are said to account for its healing properties. According to recent research, while bathing in the sea, your relative weight is practically nil, so moving sore joints and muscles becomes easier. Definitive studies are still lacking, but bathers who coat themselves in mud and frolic in the Dead Sea waters emerge with a healthy glow.

Taking Natural Healing to a Higher Dimension

Dead Sea Regional Tourist Organization
Dead Sea Post 86910
Israel
Phone: 972–7–668–8808
Fax: 972–7–658–4150
E-mail: info@deadsea.co.il
Web site: www.deadsea.co.il

Season: Year-round

Rates: $–$$$

Credit Cards: Most major

Accommodations: Ein Bokek on the southwestern shore has 2,800 hotel rooms, mostly in high-rise resorts close to a shopping mall. Kibbutz Ein Gedi offers motel-style rooms for 200 guests, a freshwater swimming pool, and central dining hall.

Getting There: From Jerusalem and Tel Aviv, scheduled motor coach service operates daily, except Saturday. Rental car or taxi available at Tel Aviv Ben-Gurion International Airport (150 kilometers).

HERODS VITALIS

Eilat, Israel

nspired by legendary kingdoms, Herods Shera-ton Resort Eilat rises on the shore of the Red Sea like a vertical village. This complex consists of the family-oriented Palace, where Middle Eastern traditions meet high-tech fun and games, and the Vitalis tower, which shelters a self-contained spa with lifestyle programs.

The magnificent Vitalis spa is a total experience. Everything is geared toward your physical, emotional, and spiritual well-being. From the time you awaken in your luxury spa guest room or suite, there is a sense of timelessness. Set against a panorama of sea and mountains, the desert climate engulfs you in a relax-ing, tension-free experience.

Getting away from it all doesn't mean you can't have fun. The namesake of this vast resort, King Herod, was a Roman ruler of Judaea who enjoyed tak-ing the waters and having nightly orgies. Managed by Sheraton, this is a family resort for Israelis who can burst into a hora at the drop of a matzo ball. Activities range from water sports to theme restaurants. So you can enjoy the Vitalis spa, then dip into the action at the Palace pool.

Herods Vitalis is an adults-only stand-alone tower with sixty-four rooms and three floors of spa facilities devoted to making you look and feel your best. Indoor and outdoor treatment rooms take advantage of the seafront location, offer-ing the most extensive selection of bodywork, skin care, and hydrotherapy in the Middle East. Waterview weight training in an air-conditioned gym, and both indoor and outdoor exercise pools and aerobics stu-dios, keep fitness buffs busy. Special emphasis on exer-cise in the pools includes body toning and aqua stretch classes. Relax in a thermal mineral salt pool, hydro-massage pool, or under cascading waterfalls.

Dining on the outdoor terraces at Vitalis is another perk for spa guests. There is a special daily menu for your personal nutrition program, as well as gourmet spa cuisine. Many activities are held in small groups, enabling single persons and couples to make new friends. Structured programs, (three, five, or seven days) called Lifemasters are all about learning to stay well. Participants share the excitement and fun of exer-cise and recreation. A personal focus can be included, such as weight reduction, body toning, sports training,

or relaxation. Each program includes face and body treatments, fitness classes, workshops, lectures, and meditation. Eastern philosophies mix with the latest in stress management techniques to help you manage a personal program of well-being.

Located on the shores of the Red Sea, the southernmost point of Israel, Vitalis offers guided walks and excursions for a variety of fitness levels. Borrow a mountain bike to enjoy cycling trails through the wild desert landscape or sunrise in the mountain nature reserve. Kayaking in the sea strengthens muscles of the upper body as you explore this fabled part of the ancient world.

Beauty from the Sea Comes Naturally

Ancient springs on the site of the Herods Resort were thought to bring youth and rejuvenation. Much visited by spice caravans, the Vitalis springs' mineral-rich water is combined with modern technology in treatments designed for relaxation. Combinations of seawater, sea algae, and bath products by Repechage and Yon-ka are featured. An innovative hydrotherapy experience combines underwater massage with color and light, aromatic oils, and therapeutic minerals. Your body and soul experience a unique sensation of floating in a sea of color selected to lift your spirits.

Red Sea Rejuvenation at Vitalis Spa

Herods Vitalis
North Beach, Eilat 88000
Israel
Phone: 972–7–638–0000
Fax: 972–7–638–0060
E-mail: dana_alter@sheraton.com
Web site: www.herods.co.il
Season: Year-round
General Manager: Micky Schneider
Spa Director: Moti Zingboim
Fitness Director: Zur Sofer
Reservations: 800–945–2008
Accommodations: Herods Vitalis has sixty-four nonsmoking rooms, including four suites, fourteen single rooms, and forty-six double rooms, all with balcony and sea view. Bathroom has Jacuzzi, hair dryer, robe and slippers. Herods Palace offers 300 rooms, themed to historical periods of the region, with kitchenette and minibar. All the rooms are air-conditioned, have color TV, radio, and personal safe.
Meals: Herods Vitalis has gourmet spa cuisine in the 7 Spices Spa Restaurant, which features seafood and Middle Eastern specialties. There is a special daily menu of low-calorie selections.
Facilities: Twenty-seven body treatment rooms, ten massage rooms, seven skin care rooms, three hydrojet massage rooms, exercise pools, soaking pool, dry and wet saunas, gym with full line of exercise equipment, roof garden with mud treatments, jet showers and cascades, beauty salon with cosmetic treatments.
Services & Special Programs: Bodywork and skin care a la carte; Lifemasters all-inclusive programs designed to effect a positive change in lifestyle.
Rates: $$$
Best Spa Package: Three-Day Lifemasters, per person. Double $675–$975, including accommodations, meals, treatments.
Credit Cards: Most major
Getting There: By car from Jerusalem, four hours. Road #1 south to Road #90 via Dead Sea, Aravaa Valley. Scheduled flights to Eilat from Tel Aviv airports on Arkia Airline or Israir, one hour. Free shuttle bus to Herods.
What's Nearby: Eilat Mountain Nature Reserve, bird-watching sanctuary, King Solomon's Pillars, underwater observatory.

MÖVENPICK RESORT & SPA—
SANCTUARY ZARA SPA
Amman, Jordan

ince biblical times the Dead Sea has been famous for mud and salts. Today these natural resources are still much sought after. Sanctuary Zara Spa, which opened on the shores of the Dead Sea in 1999, offers relaxation, rejuvenation, and pampering to those seeking the luxury of Dead Sea treatments in a nonmedical setting. Here you can wash away your stress and jet lag under the mosaic domes of Eastern-inspired thermariums, or enjoy a fitness workout on state-of-the-art equipment.

The location, the lowest on earth, translates to year-round sunshine, dry nonpolluted air, high oxygen pressure (due to the low altitude), and filtered ultraviolet radiation that allows increased exposure to the sun without burning. Guests stay at the Mövenpick resort, a two-story village complex built of traditional stone and plaster to conform to the environment.

Sanctuary Zara Spa harnesses the power of the Dead Sea by using its water in many of the pools and by using the mud and water in a majority of the sixty treatments on the spa menu. The approach is holistic, and treatments such as dry flotation are exclusive to Sanctuary Zara. Guests lie on a warm-water water bed while therapeutic oils and lotions are worked into the skin and relaxing aromas sweeten the air. And you can enjoy the experience in different ways, such as with a mud wrap facial, with the addition of herbal essences, with anticellulite oils, or in an aroma cream wrap. Five kinds of facials use the Zara healing mud; other series use Thalgo products from France and Murad products from the United States.

An exclusive antiaging clinic is staffed by consultants who guide you into a treatment program based on your needs; you can select from ultrasonic cleansing skin peels to a nonsurgical face-lift.

Hydro treatments include the salt revitalizer and the affusion shower for back and leg massage. There are also aromatherapy massage treatments, as well as classic Swedish massage. Since you are in a part of the world where the hamman, or public bath, is part of the culture, you should try the traditional hamman soap massage, an invigorating experience that will leave you squeaky clean.

The aquamarine mosaics of the Sanctuary Zara Spa harmonize with the earthy hues of the Mövenpick village setting, and the outdoor pools are especially captivating at sunset when silhouetted by the spa domes. Here, at the lowest point on earth, spa-goers discover a higher form of well-being.

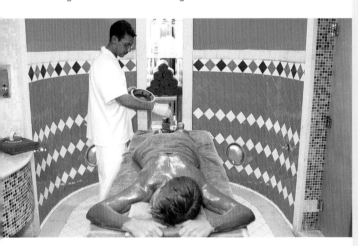

Mövenpick Resort & Spa—Sanctuary Zara Spa
Sweimeh, Dead Sea Road
PO Box 815538
Amman 11180
Jordan
Phone: 962–5–356–11–11
Fax: 962–5–356–11–22
E-mail: dseamp@globalone.com.jo
Web site: www.movenpick-deadsea.com

Season: Year-round

Spa General Manager: Sanctuary Spa Group of Covent Garden, London, England

Reservations: 800–344–6835

Accommodations: 230 guest rooms in the Mövenpick resort. All rooms have a balcony.

Meals: The Koi Carp Lounge at the spa serves nutritious cuisine indoors and in the shaded courtyards.

Facilities: Heated hydro pool; Kneipp foot massage pool; indoor Dead Sea pool; state-of-art fitness suite; ladies-only fitness suite; activity studio; men's and women's Turkish hamman; mud therapy suite; hydrotherapy treatment suite; health and beauty therapy suite with nine therapy rooms; manicure and pedicure room; spa boutique; terrace with sundeck.

Services & Special Programs: Complimentary tote bag, robe, and locker; facial and skin-care treatments; rejuvenating and antiaging treatment programs; hydro experiences; body, slimming and firming programs; aromatherapy massages.

Rates: $$

Best Spa Package: The 7 Day Deluxe Package is $532 and includes a long list of treatments: spa consultation, hydropool, dead Sea pools, Kneipp Massage Pool, Thermariums, lifestyle evaluation, exercise program, Sanctury Zara Dead Sea Salt Scrub, Express Facial, three aromatherapy massages, Sanctury Zara Spa manicure and pedicure, three Dead Sea Mud Wraps with Herbal Essences, and two personal training classes. Accommodations are additional.

Credit Cards: Most major

Getting There: Fly British Airways to Amman, Jordan. The hotel can arrange transfers from the airport. The hotel is 42 miles from Queen Alia International Airport.

What's Nearby: Petra, an ancient rose-red Nabatean city carved in stone, two hours away. The Red Sea Resort of Aquaba is three hours by car. Roman ruins of Jerash are 1½ hours by car.

BURJ AL ARAB—ASSAWAN SPA
Dubai, United Arab Emirates

oaring above the Arabian Gulf, the billowing sail-shaped structure of Burj Al Arab dominates the skyline as you approach Jumeirah Beach. This architectural and engineering marvel stands on a man-made island like a beacon to seafarers. Inside at the Assawan Spa the pleasures of the Middle East mingle with European beauty therapies.

The atrium elevator of the Burj Al Arab hotel transports you to a world of exotic luxury at the lavishly decorated spa on the eighteenth floor. Its window walls face the sea. Two indoor swimming pools and Jacuzzi baths are surrounded by majestic mosaic columns. Separate areas for men and women—richly tiled and built of white marble and granite—are complimentary for hotel guests.

Therapists here specialize in shiatsu, reflexology on pressure points of the feet, Thai massage, and deep-tissue Swedish massage. Finishing touches come in a secluded beauty salon offering hair and nail care for men and women.

Opened in 1999, and taller than the Eiffel Tower, the all-suite Burj Al Arab hotel is on a man-made island that is linked by a causeway to the airport road. There is a helipad on the twenty-eighth floor if you want to make the trip in fifteen minutes. Or the hotel will send its Rolls-Royce Silver Seraph to meet you at the airport.

The interior atrium could be a space ship. Services, however, are old-fashioned: butler service is provided for every one of the 202 duplex suites. A concierge on every floor sets up your restaurant and spa reservations and completes registration in your suite.

The themed suites are split-level visions of splendor equipped with high-tech gadgetry (like a wide-screen 42-inch wall-mounted TV set in the lounge). Embellished with Carrara marble on the floors and walls, with

accents of Azul Bahaia granite imported from Brazil, the style is Cleopatra meets Louis XVI.

Seafood done with Arabian spices or simply grilled tops choices in the hotel's sumptuous restaurants. The view from top-floor or deep-sea theme restaurants almost makes the food seem unimportant. New spa cuisine is served in the atrium and can be delivered to the spa if you want to relax in a robe.

An oasis dedicated to feeding the senses in every way, Burj Al Arab is a taste of Arabian hospitality that embraces the best of the new alongside traditions of the past.

Taking the Waters, Arabian-style

A fusion of civilizations, where traditions of Arabic hospitality combine with western technology, the Assawan Spa maintains separate but equal facilities for men and women. Named after a stone known for its purity and healing properties since ancient times, the spa offers the latest in European facials and body wraps. Notable are the Swiss La Prairie skin care products and its exclusive Caviar collection. From France, Thalgo micronized seaweed brings marine minerals into body treatments. Ladies bathe in a pool named for dewdrops, *katr enada*, retreat to private treatment rooms named after perfumes such as *yasmyna*, *meska*, and *allaylac*. Masculine fragrances of sandalwood (*assandal*), aloe (*aludah*), and saffron (*zaeferan*) provide names for treatment rooms at the men's pool, named *ma'sama'* or "water of the sky." Suspended over the sea, the pools lap at the window walls, creating the feeling of infinity.

Burj Al Arab—Assawan Spa
Jumeirah Beach
PO Box 74147
Dubai
United Arab Emirates
Phone: 971–4–301–7777
Fax: 971–4–301–7000
Web site: www.burj-al-arab.com

Season: Year-round

General Manager: Wolfgang Nitschke

Accommodations: An all-suite hotel, with 202 one- to three-bedroom duplex units on twenty-eight double-height floors. Marble bathrooms, Irish bed linens, Internet hook-ups, and wraparound sound systems are in every suite.

Meals: Mediterranean, seafood, and spa restaurants.

Facilities: The Assawan Spa has separate facilities for men and women, each with nine treatment rooms. Indoor swimming pools, hydrotherapy baths, two gyms. Beauty salon with separate sections for men and women. Library has books in English and Arabic, billiards table, light meals. Outdoor swimming pool and ocean beach adjoin the hotel.

Services & Special Programs: Facials, Swedish massage, reflexology, shiatsu, Thai massage, seaweed body wrap; salon for hairstyling, nail care, makeup consultation. Personalized program for each guest is planned prior to any treatment. Special programs for mothers-to-be; prewedding package.

Rates: $$$

Best Spa Package: The Assawan Executive Day package ($165) includes full-body aromatherapy massage, manicure, women's shampoo and blow dry, or men's hair cut. Gratuity of 10 percent and 10 percent tax are added to cost of services.

Credit Cards: Most major

Getting There: From Dubai International Airport, by car or taxi on the Al Dhyafa Road (twenty-five minutes). Served by British Airways and ninety international carriers. Visitor visa and passport are required for entry.

What's Nearby: Dubai Museum in Al Fahidi Fort, Emirates Hills Golf Club, bird-watching at Khor Dubai wildlife sanctuary, old city markets (souks), and tax-free shopping. Sports include camel racing (Thursday and Friday during winter months), Thoroughbred races, polo, golf, sailing.

PACIFIC RIM

BEGAWAN GIRI ESTATE

Ubud, Bali, Indonesia

egawan Giri, a twenty-two-suite luxury retreat set on twenty undulating acres of lush jungle, is something between a hotel and a private garden estate. Its five residences, called Sound of Fire, House of the Earth, Forest in the Mist, Wind Song, and Clear Water, are named after the elements. The resort property contains over 2,500 rare trees. *Architectural Digest* discovered Begawan Giri and devoted nine pages to its design in the July 1999 issue. Building materials range from drums from Timur to beams of recycled ironwood telephone poles.

Begawan Giri's unconventional spa program has no structured daily plan, and you can forget about anything remotely linked to aerobics or a StairMaster. Nor will you find Swedish massage, four-layer facials, or body wraps. This is more of a mind spa, where self-awareness and growth are the mantras. The Buddha kecapi treatment ("Express yourself from the heart")

sets the stage for the therapy here. Treatments are one-on-one sessions, personalized and slow-paced.

At Begawan Giri you can experience confidential sessions with a visiting master who urges you to connect intuitively with your body through Balinese herbal remedies, meditation, and massage. Or you can experience yogaia wave-medicine, which includes "guidelight trance journey sessions," a combination of yoga, meditation, emotional release and clearing, and movement.

Dining at Begawan Giri is an exotic journey. At the Biji Restaurant Chef David King creates simple dishes using fresh, authentic ingredients obtained from the on-site farms (poultry, fish, and prawn), vegetable gardens, fruit trees, and flower nurseries. Guests may dine anywhere on the estate, and meals may be ordered any time of the day or night. Nothing is rushed here—

you'll have to search to find a clock. Time is measured by the singing of the birds, the glow of the setting sun, and the crescent of a silvery moon.

Ubud is Bali's cultural center. The main street is lined with a surprising number of art galleries, craft boutiques, wood-carving studios, and souvenir shops. The creative energy is palpable—everyone seems to be an artist at heart. Begawan Giri is an extension of this positive force, and just being there is a mystifying experience. While sipping a ginger, lime, and honey tea, anticipating a massage with a dash of Balinese herbs, you may wonder just what reality is.

Aqua-Bouquets for Your Bath

The Javanese *mandi lulur*, better known on Bali as the "royal wedding treatment," is thought to both smooth and sweeten the skin. It calls for a body mask of rice flour, turmeric, sandalwood, and jasmine. After the mask dries, the skin is rinsed with honey and yogurt. The next step, a flower bath, is easy to duplicate in your own bathtub. Gently float rosebuds in your bathtub in warm water. Soak for fifteen minutes and inhale the fragrant aqua-bouquet! Follow your floral bath with an application of floral-based lotion.

An Idyllic Mind-Focused Paradise

Begawan Giri
PO Box 54
Ubud 80571
Bali, Indonesia
Phone: 62–361–978888
Fax: 62–361–978889
E-mail: begawans@indo.net.id
Web Site: www.begawan.com
Season: Year-round
General Managers: Bradley and Debbie Gardner
Reservations: 62–361–978888 or 800–225–4255 (Resorts Management)

Accommodations: The resort has five residences containing either four or five suites each. Accommodations may be custom-designed as an individual-suite rental or entire-residence rental. Each residence has air-conditioning, separate dining and living pavilion, a private pool, a library/study room, twenty-four-hour room service, a kitchen and pantry area, and master bedroom suites with private deck with Jacuzzi and pavilion.

Meals: The Biji Restaurant provides foods from the resort's own gardens and farms. Guests may dine anywhere on the estate, twenty-four hours a day. There is also an amphitheater bar.

Facilities: Library with books, CDs, and movies; satellite and cable TV; natural spring pools and waterfalls; water gardens; a lush outdoor space where treatments can take place (guests can also choose to have them in the estate); the Source Spa outdoor amphitheater.

Services & Special Programs: Each residence has its own butler and laundry facilities; personal tours; trekking tours.

Rates: $$$

Best Spa Package: The best value is the suite for $475 per night, which includes breakfast for two. Spa treatments are additional.

Credit Cards: Most major

Getting There: Many international airlines offer routes to Denpasar's Nigurah Rai International Airport. The estate can arrange for your transfer, which is included in the cost of your accommodations.

What's Nearby: Ubud, cultural activities; white-water rafting; golf; scuba diving; bicycling; trekking tours.

FOUR SEASONS RESORT BALI AT JIMBARAN BAY

Jimbaran, Bali, Indonesia

f you have ever harbored thoughts of a spa hideaway with tempting treatments, flower-filled bathtubs, and moonlit massages, this is the place to hang your straw hat. Celebrities such as Cindy Crawford, Whitney Houston, and Sylvester Stallone flock to the Four Seasons Resort Bali at Jimbaran Bay, enticed by the privacy and treatments so captivating that *USA Today* named it one of the "Ten Great Spas for Him and Her." The innovative treatments differ from traditional American treatments in technique, ingredients, and orientation.

This low-rise resort on thirty-five lush acres has 147 airy, spacious one- and two-bedroom villas that are intimately arranged, with twenty villas clustered around seven village squares.

The 10,000-square-foot spa with nine treatment rooms features treatments and products—potions as well as lotions—indigenous to the island. In any language, they are an exotic experience, designed for those who seek the unconventional. Try the lulur Jimbaran,

using ginger root, spices, ground turmeric and a fresh yogurt splash. Soaking in a warm bath filled with flower petals is an ancient Indonesian tradition. You'll also find body wraps, body elixirs, healing waters, facials, and massages.

One unique approach to body beautification is called the "coconilla." A body scrub that combines fresh shreds of young coconut, vanilla beans, and coconut milk polishes the skin while naturally adding moisture and luster. The process is completed with a rub of coconut lotion. Graceful and gentle Balinese therapists guide you through the treatments. You may have to be awakened when the procedure ends.

The spa bar serves healthy cuisine and can revitalize you with refreshing tonics and elixirs. Other dining choices range from gourmet cuisine to casual munching. Warung Mie, the newest dining spot, presents exotic and traditional noodle dishes from Japan, China, Vietnam, Thailand, and Indonesia. Guests dine at large, antique communal dining tables while the chefs cook

right before their eyes. The resort also offers a cooking class that celebrates the island's culinary traditions and preparations.

Various honeymoon packages are offered at the Four Seasons Bali, where idyllic weddings take place daily thanks to the resort's wedding consultants who shepherd couples through the process from permits to reception.

The Jimbaran experience is definitely a "Bali high."

Four Seasons Resort Bali at Jimbaran Bay
Jimbaran, Denpasar 80361
Bali, Indonesia
Phone: 62–361–701010
Fax: 62–361–701020
E-mail: fsjimbarau@bali=paradise.com
Web site: www.bali=paradise.com/four-seasons/jimbarau

Season: Year-round (less rainfall April through October)

General Manager: Christopher Norton

Spa Director: Belinda Shepard

Reservations: 62–361–70–10–10 or 800–332–3442

Accommodations: 139 one-bedroom villas; 6 two-bedroom villas; and 2 royal villas; compact disc and cassette sound system; television and VCR (video and CD library in lounge); telephone; deluxe bathrooms; robes and slippers; in-room safe; air-conditioning and fans.

Meals: Five main restaurants: the Warung Mie (exotic and traditional noodle dishes); the Pool Terrance Cafe; the Taman Wantilan Restaurant (bayview dining with contemporary and spa cuisine); the Terrace Bar and Lounge; and the Pantai Jimaran (alfresco beachside cafe).

Facilities: 10,000-square-foot spa with nine treatment rooms, fitness facility, salon; 112-foot swimming pool with waterfall into free-form soaking pool; two tennis courts; library and lounge; art gallery; meeting facilities.

Services & Special Programs: Beach activities center with complimentary windsurfing, sailing, and snorkeling equipment and instruction; twenty-four-hour villa meal service; private tennis lessons; wedding coordination and receptions; cooking classes; arranged tours to arts and crafts centers and cultural events.

Rates: $$$

Best Spa Package: The four-night Romance in Bali includes round-trip transfers, fruit and flowers, breakfast daily, candlelight dinner in your villa, and a lulur Jimbaran spa treatment for each partner. The cost is $2,198 plus tax and service charge.

Credit Cards: Most major

Getting There: Many international airlines offer routes to Denpasar's Ngurah Rai International Airport. The resort is only a fifteen-minute limousine ride from the airport.

What's Nearby: The Bali Golf and Country Club's 18-hole course; scuba diving; white-water rafting; bicycling and trekking tours; art galleries; cultural events.

LE MERIDIEN NIRWANA GOLF & SPA RESORT
Tanah Lot, Bali, Indonesia

reathtaking vistas accentuated by volcanic mountain backdrops, rice terraces, and views of the Indian Ocean greet guests as they enter the five-star Le Meridien Nirwana Golf & Spa Resort. Opened in 1997, this sprawling, 278-room resort is a world unto itself with lush gardens and deep-blue pools enhanced by views of the crashing surf. It is no wonder that the Pacific Asia Travel Agents Association awarded Le Meridien "The Best New Resort Hotel in Asia" in 1998.

The resort complex is made up of low-lying buildings and laid out in an ecofriendly way. Rice terraces alternate with belts of forest, broad fairways, streams, and tropical flora. At least 70 percent of the resort is dedicated to landscaping and open green spaces.

Guests choose from a variety of accommodations, including twelve Balinese-style bungalows, all with private plunge pools and marble bathrooms. The two-bedroom bungalows are ideal for families. There are also twenty executive suites with separate bedroom and living areas. All guest rooms are furnished in the Balinese style and have spacious balconies, perfect for watching the orange-hued sky at dusk.

Three Balinese-designed bungalows are devoted to the spa, which features a variety of Balinese treatments. A recently added treatment, *nyuh gading sreed,* is wonderfully exotic. A body scrub made from the pulp of a young yellow coconut and turmeric seeds is used to cleanse and exfoliate the skin. The treatment, used historically for religious ceremonies, is followed by a traditional Balinese massage. Also new to the spa is *singgul beraban,* or beraban scrub, which uses a mixture of ground coffee beans, volcanic rock, pumice stone, and red rice flour to form a paste that cleanses the pores and exfoliates dead skin. This is also followed by a Balinese massage using soothing moisturizers. The Balinese mud treatment is highlighted by cool jasmine-scented water poured all over the body. The spa menu also includes a variety of massages such as Swedish, French, lomi lomi, and Balinese, in addition to facials. Treatments may also be taken in the privacy of your room or in one of the outdoor huts with their spectacular ocean views.

The hotel has three Balinese swimming pools, a waterslide, and a swimming lagoon with a man-made, white-sand beach and waterfall. A Greg Norman–designed 18-hole, par-71 golf course is uniquely land-

scaped with rice fields serving as roughs and hazards. The Indian Ocean backdrop makes this course one of the most beautiful in the world.

This traditional Balinese spa set in paradise promises a memorable stay.

A Spa Treatment Good Enough to Eat

The young yellow coconut and turmeric seed scrub, once reserved for religious ceremonies, has been adapted for use in the spa here. All of the ingredients used for the exfoliation and cleansing process are natural and free from commercial processing. Because the ingredients used in the scrub are all edible foods with vitamins and minerals, the body does not need to reprocess them, according to the spa therapist. As a result the beneficial effects of the forty-five minute treatment are felt sooner. The full-body treatment at Nirwana has three phases: The body scrub ensures that the skin is exfoliated; the body mask allows the newly opened pores to absorb the vitamins and minerals; and the full-body massage relaxes the body and improves circulation. The total 120-minute process, known as *nyuh gading sreed*, simply stated is a coconut/turmeric scrub, a carrot/seaweed/lime body mask, and a Balinese massage. Yum!

Le Meridien Nirwana Golf & Spa Resort
PO Box 158
Kediri, Tanah Lot, Bali
Indonesia
Phone: 62–361–815–900
Fax: 62–361–815–901
E-mail: meridien@denpasar.wasantara.net.id
Web site: www.lemeridien-bali.com

Season: Year-round

General Manager: Gerard Hotelier

Spa Director: Made Suartajaya

Reservations: 62–361–815–900 or 800–225–5843

Accommodations: 228 rooms, including one- and two-bedroom villas and executive suites. Rooms offer marble bathrooms with separate showers, in-room safes, and fully stocked minibars.

Meals: Nirwana Restaurant is the signature restaurant of the resort serving gourmet Balinese specialties. The resort also hosts a pool grill, the Cendana Restaurant for all-day dining, and the Nautilus Pub. The lobby lounge, overlooking pools, gardens, and ocean, serves an elaborate high tea. There is no spa menu, but the French culinary staff can accommodate special requests.

Facilities: Full-service spa with authentic Balinese body treatments; beauty salon; three swimming pools; waterslide; swimming lagoon; 18-hole golf course; conference facilities; fitness center; two tennis courts; gift shops.

Services & Special Programs: The Pirates Club for children, with supervised games, pool, and playhouse; guest services center arranges daily activities; daily complimentary shuttle alternate days to Ubud, an arts colony.

Rates: $$

Best Spa Package: The three-night Spa and Life Style Package offers deluxe accommodations in a one-bedroom villa with its own private plunge pool, an open-air and indoor shower, daily breakfasts for two; airport transfers; complimentary spa consultation; six health and beauty treatments per person; unlimited squash, tennis, gym use; and complimentary shuttles to shopping and Ubud. The package costs $1,181 for two, double occupancy.

Credit Cards: Most major

Getting There: The Ngurah Rai Airport in Denpasar is thirty minutes away by car. Airport transfers can be arranged by the hotel.

What's Nearby: Tanah Lot Sea Temple; Ubud, a flourishing art colony; art colonies of Mas and Celuk; Sangeh Monkey Forest; Mengwi Temple.

INN SEIRYUSO

Shimoda, Japan

implicity and silence so luxurious that all you want to do is sit for hours, watching the light, listening to rippling water. This silence is the first thing you notice at a ryokan, or traditional Japanese inn, like Seiryuso. Stepping into the reception area, you enter a realm of shadows and screens, tatami mats and polished stone.

Always a country where tradition melds with First World living, Japan has raised the ritual of bathing to an art form in the onsen. These hot-spring bathhouses are everywhere, in isolated forests, on beaches, and at mountain resorts. Staying at a ryokan is a different way of seeing the world, where space, time, and self are in harmony. Seiryuso has all the classic amenities, plus outside and inside baths fed by hot springs.

The bath ritual is observed in exquisite detail, but there is no health club, no swimming pool, no dining room. Don a light cotton robe provided in the room, slip into wooden clogs, and follow the maid to a private soaking pool. First you wash your body by dipping water from a pail. Then you climb into the tub. By the time you have soaked to a lobster-pink shade, the table has been set in your room for dinner. Prepare for a two-hour ceremony of culinary art. Each of the courses (usually ten) is served like a miniature artwork. Maids shuffle in and out amid a flurry of bows and smiles, bringing in one course after another. This traditional tasting dinner may account for half the price of your room.

Massage and body treatment services distinguish

Seiryuso from older inns. Spa services are separate from the baths, performed in your room, and should be requested in advance of your arrival. Guest rooms, in six pavilions set in beautiful gardens, capture the enchanting Pacific light and air.

One step beyond the onsen, literally, are the outdoor garden baths, beloved by both visitors and Japanese alike. From the indoor enclosure, where one washes up with modern bathing apparatus, a door leads to the heightened pleasure of bathing in the garden. These baths are sculptural masterpieces in green slate rock, basic angles, and curves. Protected from the wind, and opening onto scenic views and cooling fresh air misted by steam from the water, they are favorite places for after-dinner soaks.

Seiryuso, built about one hundred years ago, resolutely clings to tradition. Aesthetically pleasing, the interior garden has stone-paved walkways amid century-old trees. Ryoken etiquette is followed precisely, but you'll see many people strolling around town in their robes. Following a bath, it's considered beneficial to your skin not to shower, as thermal water leaves a natural moisturizer on your body.

Spa Haiku

The Japanese speak of *wabi* and *sabi*, terms that connote loneliness, simplicity, and rustic purity; think of a haiku (or poem), in which the spaces between words convey as much as the words themselves. The overall effect is to screen you from the world, making you free to meditate. Time stops. A deep sense of relaxation, a cedar tub in your bathroom, and the sweet smell of the garden are your reward.

The Zen of Hot Springs at a Traditional Ryokan

Inn Seiryuso
2-2 Kochi
Shimoda-shi
Shizuoka-ken 415-0011
Japan
Phone: 81–0558–22–1361
Fax: 81–0558–23–2066
E-mail: ubpi@seiryuso.co.jp
Web site: www.seiryuso.co.jp

Season: Year-round

General Managers: Kenichi and Hideo Tanaka

Accommodations: Thirty spacious traditional rooms equipped with modern amenities are in six pavilions. All have private bathroom with cedar tub.

Meals: Kaiseki menu of small plates featuring seafood, vegetables, miso soup, steak filet wrapped in bacon, tofu with caviar, sashimi, lobster or large shrimp, fruit, green tea, sake, and beer. Dinner and breakfast, afternoon tea, included in room rate. Gratuity not expected; 8 percent tax added to bill. Snacks are available in Casa Vino, but there is no dining room.

Facilities: Hot baths (rotenburo) in garden, tubs inside, in-room massage and body treatments.

Services & Special Programs: Massage, shiatsu, reflexology.

Rates: $$$

Credit Cards: MasterCard, Visa

Getting There: From Tokyo by train, take the shinkansen (bullet train) to Shimoda, taxi 3.5 kilometers from station. By car, Tomei Highway to Route 135 (250 kilometers from Narita Airport).

What's Nearby: Gulf of Japan, Naoshima Cultural Village, Mount Fuji.

THE DATAI—MANDARA SPA
Kedah Darul Aman, Malaysia

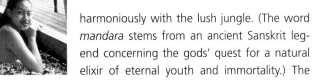

n a faraway island surrounded by deep-blue water, almost at the Earth's edge, is The Datai. This 108-room, five-star retreat is a piece of paradise where the stars shine so brightly at night you can almost reach out and touch them. Surrounded by an unspoiled rain forest, this tropical resort resonates with the sounds of birds. The air is tempered by soft breezes from the Andaman Sea. This startlingly beautiful resort on the northwestern top of Langkawi has one of the most private and hard-to-find spas in the world.

You'll find the Mandara Spa along a wooded stream in four free-standing villas designed to blend harmoniously with the lush jungle. (The word *mandara* stems from an ancient Sanskrit legend concerning the gods' quest for a natural elixir of eternal youth and immortality.) The treatments at Mandara, which have such exotic names as Andaman Ecstasy and Langkawi Luxury, have been inspired and influenced by Bali. One two-and-one-half-hour specialty is called the Ultimate Indulgence. It uses two therapists per guest, starts with a refreshing foot-bath (using salt from the Andaman Sea), and includes a natural pumice, peppermint conditioners, a natural body scrub, and a warm aromatherapy flower bath, while you overlook the rain forest. Follow this with the

Mandara massage and conclude with a soothing facial and reflexology treatment for your feet. More traditional treatments at the spa include lulur, boreh, coconut scrub, a Bali coffee scrub, and a rain forest herbal scrub.

The fifty-four deluxe guest rooms and suites are housed in forty free-standing villas scattered throughout the rain forest and connected by a series of pathways. All have steam showers, outside bathtubs, and private balconies that jut out over a stream. The decor and furnishings are stunning in their straightforward, natural style.

The Pavilion, an authentic Thai restaurant, provides open-air dining among the treetops, while the Dining Room serves Malaysian and Western cuisine.

Adjacent to the resort is the 18-hole Datai Bay Golf Course, carefully landscaped to blend with the surrounding natural beauty. The Datai, submerged within this mystical island of jungle-covered mountains, lakes, caves, and waterfalls, is a perfect oasis from which to explore all there is to uncover in the realm of self-discovery.

Jet Lag Antidote

Jet lag does not have to ruin the start of your holiday. With a bit of forethought and on-arrival care, you can avoid feeling tired and stressed and begin to enjoy your holiday refreshed and relaxed. While on the plane, wipe your face and neck regularly throughout the flight with a warm, damp washcloth sprinkled with two drops of lavender and one drop of ylang-ylang essential oil. After eating, rub the washcloth over pulse points to soothe, calm, and promote sleep. Always drink plenty of water during a flight, and avoid alcohol. Once you arrive at The Datai, use the spa's tranquillity massage oil blend for a prebath massage, then from the spa's new bath menu, choose the special bath aimed at relieving jet lag. You will feel as if your holiday has truly begun.

*Where Nature and Spa
Treatments Harmonize*

Mandara Spa at The Datai
Jalan Teluk Datai
07000 Pulau Langkawi
Kedah Darul Aman
Malaysia
Phone: 60–4–959–2500
Fax: 60–4–959–2600
E-mail: datai@ghmhotels.com
Web site: www.ghmhotels.com
Season: Year-round
General Manager: Jamie Case
Spa Director: Ayu Mudiasih
Reservations: 60–4–959–2500 or 800–223–6800 (U.S.)
Spa Appointments: 60–4–959–2500 or 800–223–6800
Accommodations: Fifty-four deluxe rooms and four suites. All villas and suites have private terrace, elevated dining area, and CD player. All accommodations have veranda views of jungle or Andaman Sea. Suites feature a bedroom with separate living area and dining table.
Meals: Authentic Thai cuisine at the Pavilion, in an open-air, treetop setting; Malaysian and Western dishes at the Dining Room; alfresco dining at the Beach Club.
Facilities: The Mandara Spa located in four individual villas; the 18-hole Datai Bay Golf Course; gymnasium; boutique; library; two tennis courts; beauty salon.
Services & Special Programs: Concierge; car hire and chauffeur-driven island tours; nature walks led by resident naturalist; shopping tours, including one to the night market; complimentary nonmotorized water sports.
Rates: $$$
Best Spa Package: Rates for a deluxe room are $318 per night double occupancy. Tax and service charges are included.
Credit Cards: Most major
Getting There: Guests fly into Kuala Lumpur and then take a fifty-five-minute connecting flight to Langkawi on Malaysian Airlines.
What's Nearby: Temurun Waterfall; Kok Beach; Datai Bay; Tengkorak Beach; Cenang Beach; the Budaya Craft Centre; the Langkawi Crystal Factory.

MALAYSIA 195

BANYAN TREE PHUKET RESORT

Amphur Phuket, Thailand

anyan Tree Phuket is one of Asia's most luxurious spas, voted "World's Best Spa Resort" in 1999 by *Condé Nast Traveler*. But you won't find sophisticated equipment or cutting-edge technology here. The drive to rev up in the gym is not part of the picture. Nor are doctors. You decide what is best for you.

The theory behind the treatments is not technology but touch. The absence of gimmicks and gadgets is evident in the treatment areas, many of which are outdoors, surrounded by lush gardens and a panoply of gorgeous flowers. The ambitious and comprehensive spa menu includes several exclusive treatments, such as one called the "honey release massage," which uses fresh orange juice mixed with pure honey to release muscle tension, increase blood circulation, and moisturize the skin.

Then there is the one called "oasis of enlightenment"—fifty minutes of sheer joy that begins with a choice of wet steam or dry sauna, a cold shower to stimulate the skin, and a cleansing loofah scrub to remove dead skin cells. The treatment continues with a relaxing, warm Jacuzzi enhanced with freshly picked herbs and essential oils; after this revitalizing ritual, you are "anointed" with a body moisturizer. Spa guests emerge from these rarefied treatments with a blissful smile.

The gardens of the resort flow into and around the guest villas, which are among the most spacious in Asia, each with its own garden, raised king-size bed, and sunken open-air bath. For ultimate luxury, choose one of the villas with its own private swimming pool.

Banyan Tree Phuket Resort
33 Moo 4 Srisoonthorn Road
Cherngtalay, Amphur Phuket 83110
Thailand
Phone: 66–76324374
Fax: 66–76–32375
E-mail: phuket@banyantree.com
Web site: www.banyantree.com

Season: Year-round

General Manager: Abid Butt

Reservations: 66–76–324374 or 800–525–4800 (Small Luxury Hotels)

Spa Appointments: 66–76–324374

Accommodations: 108 spa pool villas and two-bedroom pool villas, plus fifty-eight two-bedroom villas with private swimming pools. All have king-size beds and open-air baths.

Meals: Tamarind Restaurant offers light fusion cuisine with a range of culinary styles that includes Thai, Mediterranean, Indian and Japanese. The cuisine is high in fiber and vitamins, low in fat and cholesterol, and has no added sugar and salt. The juice bar offers a large selection of fresh vegetables and health juices, smoothies, assorted teas, and wines.

Facilities: Full-service spa; golf club; outdoor swimming pool; two tennis courts (one flood-lit); gallery of indigenous arts and crafts; a free-form pool with bubble mats and a rapid-water canal.

Services & Special Programs: Horseback riding; fishing; daily tours; bungee jumping.

Rates: $$$

Best Spa Package: The two-day program includes four hours of treatment the first day and three hours on the second day. You select a focus, such as inner wisdom or enlightenment; each focus offers a different combination of treatments, which might include, among others, a steam or sauna, seaweed body mask, Indonesian massage, aromatic elixir, and pedicure. The cost of accommodations and dining is added to the package price. Villa accommodations start at $350 per night, double occupancy, plus tax.

Credit Cards: Most major

Getting There: Take British Airways to Bangkok. There is a one-and-one-half-hour flight to Phuket Airport. The resort is twenty minutes by car from the airport. Transfers can be arranged in advance.

What's Nearby: Phang Na Bay for sea canoeing and scuba diving.

The spa's setting is spectacular, from the lap pool set in a fragrant garden to the outdoor treatment areas. Once your senses have been awakened here, you will understand why most spas in Asia are compared to the Banyan Tree.

The Joy of Ginger Tea

Kim and Cary Collier, an American couple considered by many to be the pioneer spa consultants in Asia, recommend ginger (*jahe*) tea as an antidote for jet lag. They lived in Indonesia for seven years, devoting their energy toward the study of traditional spa therapy. The Colliers find this recipe for ginger tea effective in relieving indigestion and in improving systemic blood circulation. Boil a cup of hot water; cut and peel a fresh ginger root. Boil this in the water for two minutes. After it is boiled and before you turn off the stove, crush the ginger root in the water. Add a tablespoon of unrefined sugar (*gulah merah*). Allow the water, crushed ginger, and unrefined sugar to steep for five minutes before serving. Relax and slowly sip the tea. The tea should be sipped during and after your flight. You will find ginger tea at various spas using Jamu treatments. It is often served iced.

CHIVA-SOM INTERNATIONAL HEALTH RESORT

Hua Hin, Thailand

his destination health resort, set on seven acres of beachside gardens near the king's summer palace, accommodates those seeking a rare blend of fitness, spa cuisine, skin care, and rejuvenating treatments. The resort, which offers fifty-seven private units in Thai-style pavilions, was the brainchild of Boonchu Rojanastien, Thailand's former deputy prime minister. With the help of private investors, his dream has become a reality. Together they set high standards, so expect a serious wellness program and a well-qualified staff. Chiva-Som was named "Second Best Overseas Spa" by *Condé Nast Traveler* magazine in 1998 and 1999. In 2000, the resort was named number one in the Destination spa category by *Conde Nast Traveler*'s readers.

The fifteen treatment rooms have separate heat treatment suites for men and women. Treatments range from aromatherapy and face and body massages to body reshaping. There are also a music therapy room, a flotation chamber for de-stressing, and outdoor massage pavilions for special pampering. The spa program was developed by an international staff and is managed by an international team. As a result, you will meet an international clientele in your classes and at meals.

The belief at Chiva-Som ("haven of life") is that mind, body, and spirit should work in unison and that putting them in balance will prevent or help cure many age-related illnesses. All guests receive a private medical consultation. Physicians, nurses, and dietitians are on staff. Recommended programs may include such alternative methods as equilibropathy, a combination of acupuncture techniques, exercises, and spinal correction. Iridology, an analysis of markings in the iris, is used to reveal information about the digestion, circulation, and other body systems.

A typical spa day could start with a power walk along the beach or an exercise class in the air-conditioned gym. Yoga is presented in pavilions designed especially for the purpose. The bathing pavilion features an indoor

pool for aqua aerobics, a plunge pool, a Kneipp bath with pebbles for massaging the feet, and a large hydropool.

The spa cuisine is a harmonious blend of Asian and Western specialties. It is gourmet in preparation and presentation while being both low-calorie and highly nutritious. Herbs, vegetables, and fruit are grown in the resort's private organic garden. Wine and champagne are the only alcoholic beverages served. For those seeking weight loss, a dietitian will provide a  sensible program. Meals are served in an emerald-green dining room with air-conditioning or on an outdoor terrace. Those on an unrestricted diet may dine at the Waves seafront restaurant, which serves healthy snacks and beverages. The Orchid Lounge serves coffee and tea throughout the day.

Exotic Chiva-Som meets its goal of integrating mind, body, and spirit in its personalized training, enlightenment exercises, luxurious body treatments, and healthy cuisine. This realistic wellness program, carried out with a staff to guest ratio of four to one, on a beautiful twenty-five-acre natural setting by the sea, is fit for a king or queen.

Chiva-Som International Health Resort
73/4 Petchkasem Road
Hua Hin, Prachuab Khiri Khan 77110
Thailand
Phone: 66–32–536–536
Fax: 66–32–511–154
E-mail: bkkoff@chivasom.co.th
Web site: www.chivasom.net

Season: Year-round
General Manager: Ana Maria Taveras
Spa Director: Maria Keen
Reservations: 032–536–536 or 800–525–4800 (Small Luxury Hotels of the World)
Accommodations: Fifty-seven guest accommodations are located along the beachfront in either private Thai-style pavilions or oceanview rooms or suites. Guest room interiors were designed by international and Thai designers.
Meals: Rates include three spa cuisine meals a day in the dining room with Asian and western specialties. During the day, the Waves Restaurant serves healthy snacks and beverages. The Orchid Lounge offers fruit juices, coffee, and tea.
Facilities: Conference room; spa with fifteen treatment rooms, beauty bar with hairdressing and manicure and pedicure services, outdoor massage pavilions; air-conditioned gym; bathing pavilion with indoor pool, multilevel unisex steam room, plunge pool, Kneipp bath, and large hydropool; outdoor seaside pool.
Services & Special Programs: Lectures; board games in library; arts and crafts at boutique; water sports, from windsurfing to sailing; private medical consultations and nutritional counseling.
Rates: $$$
Best Spa Package: The seven-night package (ranging from $2,734 to $5,859 plus taxes) includes accommodations, three Chiva-Som spa cuisine meals daily, individual health and beauty consultations, and choice of a daily massage, fitness class, and leisure activity. Add to this a spa bath, loofah scrub, and Oriental foot massage.
Credit Cards: Most major
Getting There: Guests can fly on British Airways to Bangkok and then on to Hua Hin Airport. The resort is fifteen minutes from the airport. The resort can also arrange ground transportation from Bangkok International Airport or Bangkok City; a three hour's drive.
What's Nearby: The Summer Palace; Floating Market; Sam Roi National Park; Pala'u Waterfall.

THE ORIENTAL HOTEL BANGKOK—
THE ORIENTAL SPA

Bangkok, Thailand

his is a city spa, a Thai-style house sublime in its simplicity and grace that has been recognized as "Best Spa in the World" by *Travel and Leisure* magazine. Appropriately referring to itself as a "temple of well-being," the spa is housed in a 120-year-old residence across the Chao Phraya River from the Oriental Hotel Bangkok.

The hotel is another story. It's legendary as a favored haunt of Graham Greene, Somerset Maugham, and Joseph Conrad. And it's been rated as the "Number One Business Hotel Worldwide" by the British publication *Business Traveler*.

The 1,000-meter Oriental Spa is a haven of tranquillity. The Thai-style house is made from beautifully carved golden teak wood; and soothing aromas fill the air. The myriad of beauty and relaxation treatments are performed in the privacy of your own luxurious suite—many of suites have been frequented by such VIPs as Elizabeth Taylor, Goldie Hawn, and former President George Bush.

Spa services are for a full day or half day. The six full-day programs include such offerings as the Oriental spa day: an Oriental herbal wrap, a marine balneotherm treatment, an Oriental massage, a European

The Oriental Hotel Bangkok—The Oriental Spa
48 Oriental Avenue
Bangkok 10500
Thailand
Phone: 66–2–659–9000
Fax: 66–2–659–0000
E-mail: reserve-orbkk@mohg.com
Web site: www.mandarinoriental.com/bangkok

Season: Year-round

General Manager: Kurt Wachtveitl

Spa Director: Orawan Choeysawat

Reservations: 800–223–6800 (Leading Hotels of the World); or 662–236–0400; or 800–526–6566 (Mandarin Oriental Hotel Group).

Spa Appointments: 662–439–7613

Accommodations: 361 guest rooms and thirty-five suites; rooms in garden wing rooms are split-level; all rooms offer color satellite television, refrigerators, minibars, dual phone lines, and river views.

Meals: Ciao (Bangkok's only outdoor Italian restaurant); the Normandie (French cuisine); the Sala Rim Naam restaurant (spicy Thai fare).

Facilities: Oriental Spa; two swimming pools; sports center with high-tech gym, tennis courts, squash courts and sauna; barbershop and beauty shop; flower shop; shopping arcade; fully equipped business center.

Services & Special Programs: Thai cooking school; Thai cultural program; Oriental river cruises to the old capital and the summer palace; boat rides to River City shopping mall; butler service on each floor; golf arrangements and transportation; helicopter service to airport; medical service; twenty-four-hour room service; laundry and valet service.

Rates: $$$

Best Spa Package: The Perfect Day gives you the ideal way to experience the spa. This five hour program is $155 per person. To this add the cost of accommodations at the Oriental Hotel, which range from $250 to $320 for River Wing rooms, and from $380 and up for the Suite, per night, double occupancy. Add 10% service charge and taxes.

Credit Cards: Most major

Getting There: The hotel is close to Bangkok's new sky-train station and within easy access to Bangkok International Airport by expressway.

What's Nearby: River City (antiques shopping); New Rod (arts, crafts and silverware); championship golf courses; Ayudhaya, the ancient capital.

stress recovery treatment, a manicure or pedicure, a spa cuisine lunch or dinner, and a variety of herbal teas, fruit juices, or mineral water throughout the day. The spa also offers a special ninety-minute jet-lag recovery treatment.

THE REGENT RESORT CHIANG MAI— LANNA SPA

Chiang Mai, Thailand

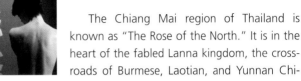

his handsome, seventy-two-suite resort, with its twenty acres of gardens studded with lakes, streams, waterfalls, and countless varieties of plants and trees, is sure to put you in the mood for some of the most luxurious spa treatments in Asia.

You'll find them in the three-level, 9,000-square-foot Lanna Spa, nestled amid tropical gardens, with views of the surrounding rice fields. Inspired by a northern Thai temple and graced with sculpture and artwork, the spa has seven stunning and spacious suites. The Laan Chiang penthouse treatment suite occupies the entire third floor. Here you can experience a rice and spice skin rub (an aromatic massage) along with an aloe and lavender hydrating body wrap. The lavish suite also has Thai and Western massage beds, an outdoor soaking tub in a private *sala* (outdoor terrace), an herbal steam room, and a double semi-outdoor shower—not to mention a breathtaking view of the Doi Suthep Di Pui mountain range.

You may choose from Thai-inspired treatments, such as a honey seed rub or a lemon grass body wrap, or indulge in garden baths, massages, and facials—all presented in spa suites with individual soaking tubs on semienclosed private terrace. Five suites are equipped with private herbal aromatherapy steam rooms, and two spa treatment suites have double rainshower massage beds. The relaxation lounge is the perfect sanctuary for repose between treatments. There is also a full-service beauty salon on the premises.

Guest pavilion suites are designed with rich gold teak timber, handmade local ceramic tiles, and bright accent colors. Teak also predominates in the Sala Mae Rim Restaurant; the natural upholstery is accented by Lanna-style tapestries. The restaurant features fine Thai cuisine, including both northern and vegetarian specialties.

The Chiang Mai region of Thailand is known as "The Rose of the North." It is in the heart of the fabled Lanna kingdom, the crossroads of Burmese, Laotian, and Yunnan Chinese cultures. Combining your spa experience with this fascinating region of the world will make for an unforgettable spa journey.

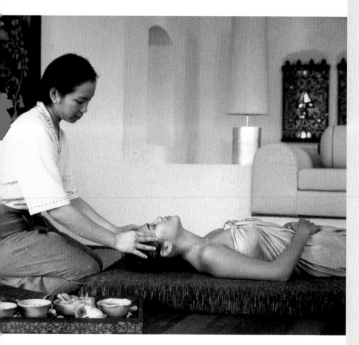

The Regent Resort Chiang Mai—Lanna Spa
Samoeng Old Road
Mae Rim Valley
Chiang Mai 50180
Thailand
Phone: 66–53–298–181
Fax: 66–53–298–190
E-mail: rcm.reservations@fourseasons.com
Web site: www.regenthotels.com

Season: Year-round

General Manager: Michael J. Kemp

Spa Director: Runjratee Kon Jkwanjeun

Fitness Director: Joel Johnson

Reservations: 800–545–4000 or 66–3–98–81

Accommodations: Seventy-two suites with in-room safes, sound system, CD player, satellite television.

Meals: The Sala Mae Rim restaurant serves Thai cuisine; the Elephant Bar is an open pavilion lounge with afternoon tea, cocktails, and after-dinner drinks; the Pool Terrace and Bar offers poolside dining and weekly barbecues.

Facilities: Lanna Spa with seven treatment rooms, outdoor showers, private herbal steam rooms, outdoor soaking tubs, and tropical rainshower massage tables; hair salon; conference and banquet facilities; library; tennis and health club, with two courts and fitness/exercise studio.

Services & Special Programs: Activities for children; personalized sightseeing packages and arrangements; twenty-four-hour room service; overnight laundry.

Rates: $$$

Best Spa Package: Lanna Spa Indulgence (four days/five nights) includes private airport transfers, welcome drink and jasmine garland on arrival, daily American breakfast, daily fresh fruit bowl and newspaper, daily dinner for two, ten hours of spa treatments (five two-hour sessions for two people in a double treatment suite). The cost is $2,030 double occupancy, plus tax and service. Rates change seasonally.

Credit Cards: Most major

Getting There: Take British Airways to Bangkok. Thai Airways operates daily flights between Bangkok and Chiang Mai (ten in summer, fourteen in winter). Limousines are available for airport transfers and local transportation.

What's Nearby: Chiang Mai's temples; Chiang Dao Elephant Training Camp; Wat Phra That Suthep, a holy fourteenth-century shrine on a 5,000-foot mountain; Wat Suan Dok, home to a 500-year-old Buddha.

The Cold-Water Cure for Jet Lag

Just getting to one of these tropical but remote spa resorts can take up to twenty hours—even more if you meet up with unscheduled delays. So when you finally arrive after so many hours cooped up in a plane, you're probably pretty uncomfortable, and your biological clock is pretty out of whack. But there is an unusual way to bounce back. Try cold-water bathing! A cold-water bath can revive your sluggish senses, and some people swear by it. It is said to improve circulation, increase muscle tone, assist in preventing premature aging, build up resistance against colds and infections, and enhance glandular functioning, particularly the adrenals and hormonal production. Spraying the soles of the feet with cold water draws excess blood from the brain and helps relieve cranial congestion, so say believers. After a spray of cold water, massage your neck and shoulders. Then rest in bed for twenty minutes.

CARIBBEAN ISLANDS &
THE BAHAMAS

CUISINART RESORT & SPA
Anguilla, British West Indies

he elongated island of Anguilla in the British West Indies measures merely 16 miles long by 3 miles wide. But within its limited borders is a destination that for spa-lovers that is well worth seeking: CuisinArt, a stylish ninety-three-room resort tucked away on the white-sand beach of Rendezvous Bay. The startling blue-green water of the bay meets with the white-washed villas, designed to resemble the Greek island of Mykonos. This sets the idyllic stage for the intimate, three-level, 5,000-square-foot spa. The gardens surrounding the resort are lush with 37,000 plants, representing 150 species, such as tamarind, guava, citrus, and banana.

The resort's goal is to "bring life the best in healthful living, gourmet cuisine, fitness, relaxation, and pampering." This delicate balance can be experienced by spa guests if they choose to participate in scheduled exercise classes, beach walks, or workouts in the gym, which is located on the first level of the spa. The second level of the spa is reached by a winding staircase that leads to three treatment rooms and a full-service beauty salon. Hair and skin-care products from the Rusk line are left in your room daily, along with a generous selection of seashell soaps and bath salts.

The spa program is unstructured, but the spa director will happily help you schedule classes and treatments. Repecharge skin-care products, a French line, are used exclusively for body treatments, facials, and body scrubs. A schedule of activities is posted daily;

one such might be a half-hour informal talk by the fitness director on the quick route to fitness success.

Those who enjoy healthful dining also usually enjoy the tour of the resort's hydroponic farm, a huge air-conditioned greenhouse that is totally free of soil. Hydroponic farming cultivates plants in nutrient-enriched water without soil. The resulting pesticide-free vegetables—bright red tomatoes, yellow and red peppers, and butter lettuce—are served in the resort restaurants (Santorini for gourmet dining; the Mediterrano poolside). You can also have a lunch that is both healthful and educational at the Hydroponics cafe, tucked away in the greenhouse, where a colorful buffet of salads are served daily and irresistible tropical fruit smoothies are made to order.

One of the best places to sunbathe (or stargaze) during your free moments is on your own guest room patio with its views of neighboring Saint Martin and Rendezvous Bay. Bathrooms are outfitted with Italian marble, and you'll find monogrammed robes there too.

The beach, one of the most perfect in the Caribbean (if not the world), offers plenty to do, but you can just plain relax if that's your pleasure. Comfortable lounges for beach-lovers dot the sand. During the day, guests are treated to homemade sorbet and cool towels. Paradise is sunning and spa-going at CuisinArt.

Sea Salt for Smooth Skin

CuisinArt Resort & Spa uses the island's natural resources in its roster of treatments, from sea salts to stones to the soothing sounds of the sea. One skin treatment uses salt harvested from local salt ponds and combined with pure essential oils to clean, detoxify and exfoliate the skin, while at the same time stimulating and smoothing it. After the skin is renewed, an application of self-tanning lotion is applied to prepare the guest for their holiday in the sun.

A Spa with Gourmet Cuisine on a Caribbean Beach

CuisinArt Resort & Spa
PO Box 2000
Rendezvous Bay, Anguilla
British West Indies
Phone: 264–498–2000
Fax: 264–498–2010
E-mail: reservations@cuisinart.com
Web site: www.cuisinartresort.com

Season: Year-round
General Manager: Marston J. Winkles
Spa Director: Jill Walker
Fitness Director: Peter Vasilis
Reservations: 800–937–9356 (Unique Hotels and Resorts); 877–847–4444
Spa Appointments: 800–937–9356
Accommodations: Ninety-three rooms and suites, surrounded by lush, tropical foliage. Accommodations range from superior rooms to luxury, to junior suites to one- and two-bedroom suites with solariums. Guest rooms include such features as private patios, marble bathrooms, some oceanfront views, and Mediterranean furnishings.
Meals: Gourmet dining in Santorini; poolside dining in the Mediterrano; lunch in the Hydroponics Cafe, tucked away in the greenhouse.
Facilities: Two-level spa; gym; billiards room; tennis courts; hair salon; boutique; tennis pro shop; children's playground; library; swimming pool; croquet field; bocce court.
Services & Special Programs: Daily continental breakfast on guest room patio; satellite television and VCRs on request; equipment for snorkeling, windsurfing, and water-skiing; horticultural tours; boat charters; beach beverage service; laundry services; baby-sitting; day trips.
Rates: $$$
Best Spa Package: Seven-Night Indulgence (available May 1–September 15): accommodations in luxury room, continental breakfast, one massage and one facial (each for one person) one dinner for two, complimentary water sports, use of fitness facilities. Cost is $2,355.
Credit Cards: American Express, MasterCard, Visa
Getting There: Flights are available to Wallblake Airport from neighboring islands served by international carriers. Nearest international airports are on Saint Maarten, Puerto Rico, and Antigua. Ferry service is available from Marigot Bay, Saint Martin, to Blowing Point, Anguilla.
What's Nearby: The islands of Saint Barthélemy (St. Barts), Nevis, and Saint Martin are all day-trip destinations.

SANDALS ROYAL BAHAMIAN RESORT & SPA

Cable Beach, Nassau, The Bahamas

opless thalassotherapy? Mais oui! The French created thalassotherapy, borrowing the Greek word for the sea *(thalas)*, but the Bahamians take it to a new level at Sandals's lavish couples-only resort.

Greeted by a huge, rather fearsome statue of Neptune, the first thing you notice at Sandals Royal Bahamian Resort & Spa is an excess of opulence and grandeur. Roman columns seem to float in the huge swimming pool, and tons of marble, chandeliers, and frescoed ceilings send a message: "If you're looking for luxury, this is the place."

Beneath all the opulence is a gem of a spa. The entrance, only steps from the beach, is marked by fountains and whirlpools. Although almost everything at this all-inclusive resort is covered by the daily tariff, spa treatments are not. The selection of skin care, facials, and massages includes European therapies. Equipped with a Vichy shower, hydrotherapy tub, hot and cold plunge pools, and a salon for hair-styling and nail care, the spa provides welcome shelter from the sun and storms. Guests have complimentary use of eucalyptus steam bath, sauna, showers, and locker rooms. Among special treatments you can charge to the room account are a marine algae masque, seaweed body wrap, and seaweed bath. The featured bath products are Kerstin Florian's Kur, with skin care by Pevonia.

Going au naturel on the resort's private island, Sandals Cay, you can have an alfresco massage by the sea. The powder-pink sandy beach, turquoise sea, and freshwater pool with swim-up bar will satisfy even the most jaded sybarite. Back at the main pool complex, there are waterfalls to sit under for a refreshing massage, cooling mists from fountains, and warm whirlpools. Escape the sun by working out at the fitness center, an air-conditioned penthouse atop the Manor House, with a full circuit of Cybex equipment, free weights, and a personal trainer.

The recent addition of 200 hotel suites stretched the resort along a narrow strip of beach. Accommodations range from spacious beachfront rooms in the original Manor House, to honeymoon villas and suites in the gardens. For a romantic treat, schedule a four-handed couples massage on your balcony or terrace.

Meal choices are varied and extensive in the resort's eight restaurants. But don't expect heart-healthy options among Asian-Pacific, Italian, British

pub, and Continental fare. If you enjoy spicy Bahamian specialties like jerk chicken or beans and rice, head for Cafe Goombay on an offshore island. More formal, dinner in the Crystal Room offers lobster and steak cooked to order, but you need reservations. And the list goes on: burgers at the beach grill, conch chowder and fish-and-chips at the pub.

Scuba diving, tennis, and water sports are freely available. Or you can hide out and do nothing. That's the true luxury of Sandals spa. Service in the spa is highly personalized, as the staff have been trained to anticipate special needs of guests unfamiliar with treatments, or suffering from too much exposure to the sun.

Beyond the Beach, a Couples-only Hideaway

Sandals Royal Bahamian Resort & Spa
Cable Beach, Nassau
Bahamas
Phone: 242–327–6400
Fax: 242–327–6961
E-mail: sandals@grouper.batelnet/bs
Web site: www.sandals.com

Season: Year-round

General Manager: Stephen Ziadie

Spa Director: Karen Sprung

Reservations: 800–726–3257

Accommodations: 405 rooms, including new all-suites tower, garden villas. All air-conditioned, with king-size bed. Contemporary furnishings with antique reproductions, TV, clock/radio, telephones; full bathroom amenities, hair dryer, robes; wet bar, ironing board and iron.

Meals: Unlimited dining at eight restaurants, and open bar (wine, beer, and mixed drinks), included in resort package. Special diets accommodated by advance request. Avoiding salt, fat, and sugar is difficult with so many temptations, but there are healthy salads, grilled fish, and plenty of fresh fruit on the buffet.

Facilities: Penthouse fitness center with Cybex equipment, free weights. Spa has hydrotherapy tub, herbal steam bath, sauna, private massage and skin care rooms, open-air cabanas, locker room with showers, hot and cold plunge pools. Seven swimming pools, tennis, lawn chess, shuffleboard; ballroom and English pub; water sports.

Services & Special Programs: Massage therapies including shiatsu, reflexology, aromatherapy, sports massage, body scrub and seaweed wrap, hydrotherapy bath, moor mud facial, hydrating and deep cleansing facials, men's facial, paraffin manicure/pedicure, hairstyling, makeup.

Rates: $$

Credit Cards: Most major

Best Spa Package: First-time spa-goers can sample treatments in a day spa package ($175, plus tax). To arrive in style, book a suite that includes airport transfers in a chauffeur-driven Rolls-Royce.

Getting There: Complimentary transfers to/from Nassau International Airport. Direct flights from Miami (one hour) on American, Continental, and other airlines.

What's Nearby: Casinos, Sivananda yoga ashram.

GRAND LIDO SANS SOUCI RESORT— CHARLIE'S SPA

Ocho Rios, Jamaica

egend has it that the natural mineral springs cascading into the spa pool at Grand Lido Sans Souci will fill the hearts of couples with the power of passionate lovers who secretly bathed here in colonial times. Today, aquacize in the pool and massage on a coral reef at Charlie's Spa enchant hardcore fitness buffs as well as honeymooners.

The Grand Lido Sans Souci enjoys a private beachfront setting that's light-years away from the busy scene in Ocho Rios, yet close to north shore attractions like Dunn's River Falls. Locally owned and managed, the resort is part of the all-inclusive SuperClubs group, which provides lodging, meals and drinks, golf fees, and scuba-diving instruction in a one-price package. Here spa treatments are included too, on a limited basis.

Spa treatment rooms are housed in colorful wooden kiosks set into hillside gardens overlooking the sea. Ultimate stress relief comes in two gazebos set on coral cliffs, waves crashing below, where couples enjoy a secluded massage. Amid flowering hibiscus, bougainvillea, red tulip trees, palms, and exotic shrubs, a hot tub beckons. Look for spa mascot Charlie, a giant sea turtle, in his rocky grotto at check-in. A bar offers smoothies (or something stronger) while you wait for appointments on a tree-shaded terrace. Despite limited space, the well-trained Jamaican therapists provide a choice of twenty-five-minute back massage, body scrub, reflexology, or facial. And you can get a free pedicure and manicure in the salon. Anything else costs extra (if time slots are open).

Sybaritic escapes in the sea grotto start with a healthy sweat. From a sauna built into

the rock, you relax on a table with the sea lapping below as your body is scrubbed with sea salts, then soothed with peppermint oil. For a secluded soak on the beach, climb into a tiny pool where mineral water seeps through the sand. As you swim in the shallow bay, cool mineral water flows beneath warm salt water, creating a unique experience.

In French, *sans souci* means "carefree," so don't expect a structured program. Join a group doing aerobics to a reggae beat in the open-air beach pavilion, set out on one of the morning walks, or engage in yoga with a sea view. There is an air-conditioned cardiovascular and strength-training room with a few pieces of Cybex, Lifestep, and Schwinn equipment, but no trainers. A clothing-optional beach has its own bar and swimming pool. Even weddings are free, if you meet criteria.

Unlimited food comes with the daily tariff. You will

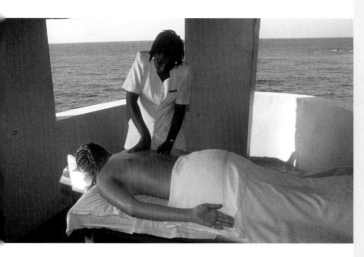

Grand Lido Sans Souci—Charlie's Spa
PO Box 103, Ocho Rios
Jamaica, West Indies
Phone: 876–994–1353
Fax: 876–994–1544
E-mail: reservations@superclub.com
Web site: www.superclubs.com

Season: Year-round

General Manager: Pierre Battaglia

Spa Director: Margaret Spencer

Reservations: 800–GO–SUPER

Accommodations: 146 suites, including eight penthouses, all air-conditioned. Amenities: whirlpool bath in most suites, hair dryer, robes, direct-dial telephone, TV, minibar.

Meals: Japanese and Jamaican specialties mix with Continental cuisine in four restaurants. Unlimited selections, and twenty-four-hour room service.

Facilities: Open-air treatments, natural mineral spring pool, two beaches, four tennis courts (lighted for night play), four swimming pools, three whirlpools, water sports equipment, kayaks, sailboards, bocce, croquet, bicycling.

Services & Special Programs: Complimentary airport transfers, scuba diving with resort certification, waterskiing, golf course fee complimentary.

Rates: $$$

Credit Cards: Most major

Getting There: Air Jamaica, Delta, or American Airlines to From Sangster International Airport in Montego Bay; by car or van, the coastal road to Ocho Rios can be driven in about two hours. Airport transfers are complimentary; rental cars are available at the airport.

What's Nearby: Dunn's River Falls, rafting.

be tempted to taste Jamaican specialties like jerk chicken, callalou soup brimming with local spinach and shrimp, or smoked marlin. Four restaurants and a twenty-four-hour beach grill offer lots of choices.

Grand Lido Sans Souci lives up to its name in the spacious suites. Some are terraced above the beach, others steps from tennis and water sports. For seclusion, eight penthouses offer sunbathing at treetop level. The resort's pink-beige plantation-style buildings are cheerfully accented with white gingerbread trim and balconies.

Entering the gates of Grand Lido Sans Souci is like returning to a tropical Eden where cares are left behind.

No-Worry (Sans Soucis) Skin Care

The signature skin-care line is Sans Soucis, made in Baden-Baden, Germany, by Biodroga. Known in Europe for antiaging treatments, Sans Soucis products are ideal for the Caribbean, according to spa director Margaret Spencer, because their base of Baden-Baden mineral water gives them a light, nongreasy texture. Sun protection is particularly important here, and Sans Soucis uses new technology to screen out harmful ultraviolet rays.

THE RITZ-CARLTON SAN JUAN HOTEL & SPA

San Juan, Puerto Rico

verything about this hotel reflects Puerto Rico's Caribbean flair and Hispanic culture. Opened in 1999 on eight acres of prime beachfront property, the Ritz-Carlton San Juan was voted "Best Hotel in the Caribbean, Bermuda, and the Bahamas" in *Condé Nast Traveler*'s Readers Choice Awards that same year. Spa-lovers have already discovered the wonders of its bi-level, 12,000-square-foot, world-class spa. A dramatic statement in decor and facilities, the spa is yet another jewel in the crown of the Ritz-Carlton hotels.

What makes this luxurious spa unique to Puerto Rico are the treatments that utilize indigenous island products. Its refreshing and revitalizing signature rainforest facial was Inspired by the rains and mist of El Yunque rain forest. A passion fruit massage uses both a tropical fruit elixir and river stones from the rain forest. Taking the concept of local elements and regional products to an even higher level is an hour-long body polish that combines bath gel with extracts of mango and papaya, leaving a tantalizing fragrance in its wake. The spa's therapy features actual sea nutrients designed to hydrate and mineralize the skin. The Vichy shower therapy provides a triple benefit, incorporating water therapy, thermal therapy, and massage with the classic Vichy massage, the Vichy à Deux (with two therapists as it is practiced in the Celestin Spa in Vichy, France), and a "sea glow" massage, which includes an exfoliation of built-up dead skin cells—all followed by a warm shower. Making the spa menu global are the Balinese massage and the Javanese lulur, treatments currently available at only ten U.S. spas.

The Cybex-equipped ground-floor fitness center features weight-training and cardiovascular activities with treadmills, hikers, spinning bikes, and a separate aerobics studio. The locker rooms, separate but equal for men and women, have their respective steam rooms. A coed whirlpool and sauna are available as well. The spa's full-service beauty salon offers manicures and pedicures and includes a spa boutique.

A healthful spa menu is featured in the Caribbean Grill, with specialties such as black bean soup, exotic fruit soup, terrine of grilled eggplant with roasted tomatoes, buffalo mozzarella and tomato coulis, and a papaya tart—all calibrated for calorie and fat gram content.

But the hotel hosts more than a golden-sand shoreline and world-class spa. It is also home to a Puerto Rico's largest casino. The 18,500-square-foot, two-level gaming area features blackjack, craps, roulette, and mini-baccarat. The deluxe guest accommodations offer either ocean or mountain views. Guests will find this location five minutes from the airport an ideal stopover for connecting to other flights, but they may never want to leave.

The Ritz-Carlton San Juan Hotel & Spa
6961 Avenue of the Governors
Isla Verde, Carolina
Puerto Rico 00979
Phone: 787–253–1700
Fax: 787–253–1777
Web site: www.ritzcarlton.com

Season: Year-round

General Manager: Tony Franziti

Spa Director: Catherine Calzada

Reservations: 787–253–1700 or 800–241–3333

Spa Appointments: 787–253–8096

Accommodations: 414 guest rooms, including thirty-four with deluxe king-size beds, four suites with garden views; dual-line telephones, data port, minibar, marble baths, terry robes.

Meals: Caribbean Grill (regional and spa menu); Vineyard Room (California/Mediterranean fare); Ocean Bar and Grill (casual); afternoon tea, cocktails, and light hors d'oeuvres in the lobby lounge.

Facilities: 12,000-square-foot spa with four wet rooms, including one for hydrotherapy, one with a Vichy shower, and one accommodating two people; five massage rooms; two facial rooms. Beachfront 72,000-square-foot swimming pool, two lighted tennis courts, casino, meeting facilities.

Services & Special Programs: Supervised activities for children four to fourteen. Also special spa treatments for children, such as manicures, pedicures, and facials. Twenty-four-hour room service; laundry service; baby-sitting; multilingual staff.

Rates: $$$

Best Spa Package: The nine-hour Day at the Spa includes body polish, body wrap or massage, champagne facial, hairstyling and conditioning, manicure, pedicure, and spa lunch. Cost is $630 plus accommodations. Guest rooms begin at $329 per night. Also worth considering if you have to overnight near the airport is the Buena Salud, which includes a Swedish massage and room amenity, such as a fruit basket or a bottle of wine, with your accommodations ($450 per night double occupancy).

Credit Cards: Most major

Getting There: The resort is just five minutes from the Luis Munoz Marin International Airport in San Juan.

What's Nearby: El Yunque rain forest; historic Old San Juan; Plaza Las Americas (shopping mall). Also, nine championship golf courses, snorkeling, scuba diving, deep-sea fishing, sailing, and windsurfing.

Smoothies Fight Sun Damage

Body-care experts at Essential Elements, known for its line of products for body and skin care, recommend this citrus smoothie as a healthy way to protect the skin from sun damage. Smoothies can be adapted to fit any nutritional need, they say. This one is revved up with vitamins and is as good as it sounds.

CITRUS SMOOTHIE

½ cup milk
1 cup cubed mango
1 banana
½ cup orange juice
1 cup crushed ice
1 tsp. honey
2 slices orange, for garnish

Combine all ingredients, except orange slices, in blender. Blend until smooth. Garnish with orange slices. Serves two.

LE SPORT—THE OASIS

Castries, Saint Lucia

ll-inclusive resorts have proliferated on the sunny Windward Islands, but few include spa treatments in the one-price-covers-everything package. At this laissez-faire spa, you are offered two daily treatments, plus a wide range of fitness and recreational activities, from tai chi to yoga, exercise classes, and meditation sessions. Superior guest rooms on a powder-soft beach and the peaceful spa pavilion, add to a holistic holiday at Le Sport.

Tucked into a secluded cove, ten minutes from the Saint Lucia's bustling capital and cruise port in Castries, Le Sport is a tropical adventure with plenty of pampering. Designed like a plantation, colonial-style buildings spread out along the beach. The Oasis, a $3.5 million temple of well-being, sits atop a hill, isolated from beach sports and group games in the swimming pool. Here you can schedule workouts with a personal trainer, try the latest French skin care by Clarins, or simply do nothing. The lap pool is rarely crowded, and shaded lounges are perfect for reading and snoozing.

Built around an open-air courtyard, the Oasis resembles a colonnaded cloister, the hushed ambience broken only by bubbling fountains. Surrounded by palm trees and clay-tiled roofs, the vista of the sea has a tranquilizing effect. Complimentary services include a bubbling bath with herbs and sea algae, seaweed body wrap, and a circulation-boosting shower administered by high-pressure hose. There is a seawater pool for group exercise, in the style of French thalassotherapy.

Planning a spa program starts with the resident nurse (called "sister" in the formal, British tradition still used by islanders) for a medical checkup. Once complimentary treatments have been scheduled, you're on your own to join aerobics classes and the daily program listed on a bulletin board in the open-air pavilion where breakfast and lunch buffets are served. Sign up for instruction in archery, golf, fencing, and scuba. Outings include jungle walks, guided bike tours, and a visit to the hot springs at Mount Soufrière. You can play tennis day or night, go golfing, or use the putting green at no charge.

Since the resort is all-inclusive, reaching for your wallet is an exercise you can forget. Some extras, however, show up on your account when you depart on the resort's van for the airport. Treatments at the Insti-

Le Sport—The Oasis
Cariblue Beach
PO Box 437 Castries
Saint Lucia, West Indies
Phone: 758–450–8551
Fax: 758–450–0368
E-mail: tropichol@aol.com
Web site: www.lesport.com.lc

Season: Year-round

General Manager: Michael Bryant

Spa Director: Martha Willie

Reservations: 800–544–2883

Accommodations: 102 rooms and suites in four-story buildings facing the sea. Luxury suites come with peaked-ceiling, four-poster bed draped in pink-stripped sailcloth. All rooms have private terrace or patio, bathrobes, hair dryer, telephone, TV, ceiling fans, air-conditioning.

Meals: Three meals daily, plus snacks. Breakfast buffet of fresh tropical fruit, juices, omelette to order, or continental tray delivered to room. Lunch buffet includes fried fish, stuffed chicken leg, rice, assorted vegetables, pizza. Dinner menu offers choice of light fare such as steamed kingfish, veal scallop in champagne sauce, sea scallops with snow peas. Selected wines complimentary with lunch and dinner.

Facilities: The Oasis has hydrotherapy tubs, saunas, hot and cold plunge pools, Swiss needle shower, jet stream pool, whirlpool, fully equipped gymnasium, Clarins salon. Equipment for windsurfing, waterskiing, snorkeling, scuba diving, fencing, archery, golf, tennis; three swimming pools; putting green.

Services & Special Programs: Swedish, Thai, and shiatsu massages, marine baths and wraps, group exercise. Clarins salon for hair and nail care, skin treatments. Couples massage instruction; golf and tennis training.

Rates: $$

Best Spa Package: Clarins anti-jet lag combination of massage, body wrap, and facial. (Le Sport is an all-inclusive resort; all spa services are complimentary; except for a few that come with a minimal charge.)

Credit Cards: American Express, Diners Club, MasterCard, Visa

Getting There: Complimentary transfers from Hewanora International Airport (ninety minutes). Bring proof of citizenship; passport is best.

What's Nearby: Mount Soufrière (mud bath), the Pitons (rock climbing), Diamond Falls (hot springs), Castries craft market.

tut Clarins salon are optional and not included in the body holiday package. Parisian facials, hair and nail care, and stress-reducing massage and mud wraps are on offer at prices that are a bargain if you're paying with dollars.

Beach Balm for Body and Soul

The sea is the origin of life. The plasma in our blood contains elements that match the composition of seawater. French scientists have shown that body fluids are naturally similar to seawater. Algae are rich in vitamins, mineral salts, and trace elements, which are vital for human health. Clarins incorporates seaweed and algae in skin-care products that nurture and protect. After exposure to sun, try an algae body wrap.

CENTRAL & SOUTH AMERICA

KUROTEL

Gramado, Brazil

igh in the mountains of southern Brazil, an Alpine wonderland reminiscent of European resorts surrounds the Kurotel complex in the town of Gramado. Strolling the clean and flowery streets is like being in Bavaria. And in winter (the northern hemisphere's summer), the snow-covered slopes of Rio Grande do Sul could be in the Swiss Alps. Staying at the Kurotel is the best of both worlds.

Established in 1982, the Kurotel grew from the vision of a place devoted to well-being, where modern medical technology and natural medicine's secular wisdom can be experienced. The Kur Gramado (Gramado cure) is based on preventive medicine, a concept that links lifestyle with prevention of illness. Created by an orthodox medical doctor, the program identifies existing problems as well as contributing environmental factors such as stress.

When you arrive at the hotel complex, your first impression is of a mountain chalet; with red-tile roofs and long verandas overlooking a flowering garden. Every Sunday afternoon, guests arrive to start the weeklong kur program. Greeted by Dr. Luis Carlos Silveira and his wife Neusa, you learn that a high priority is placed on physical activity—walks in the woods and a Kneipp hydrotherapy course, gymnastics in the covered swimming pool, and one-on-one training in the gym. Hikes guided by staff members are scheduled daily—the region's dazzling landscapes are a major attraction here.

Monitoring your progress, the team of psychologists, physiotherapists, and doctors use biofeedback equipment to help with control of emotions and stress level. A session on posture, which works on balance and breathing, helps you get to know your body.

Natural therapies and scientific knowledge come together in the Kurotel clinic. The spacious waiting room has a beamed ceiling, an open fireplace, and a juice bar offering herbal teas and fresh fruit. After a personal

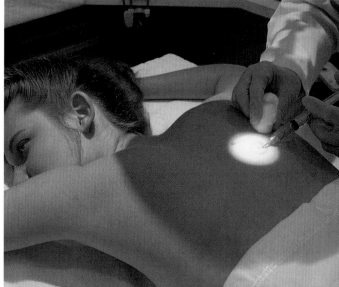

evaluation, a course of treatments is prescribed by the doctors. Facilities are comparable to those at European kur centers, with extensive use of baths, mud applications, and oxygen inhalation. For an advanced diagnostic checkup, there is a half-week program.

Comfort also comes with the kur. Bedrooms are suite-size, and decorated with antiques, country-style furniture, and luxurious draperies. Guests are a sophisticated mix of business, political, and social types from all parts of Latin America who speak several languages. If you feel the need to keep in touch with the office, you can stay in one of the business center suites fully equipped and staffed for international travelers. Meeting fellow guests in the lounge prior to a seated dinner, or in the Finnish sauna and on hikes, helps build a spirit of camaraderie.

Call it a recycling of life, says Dr. Silveira. Getting to know yourself, he believes, provides the courage to defeat old habits and adopt a healthy lifestyle.

From Kneipp to Cosmetics, Updating the Kur

Kur Gramado bases its philosophy of natural medicine on the healing water techniques developed in Bavaria by Father Sebastian Kneipp. For the first time in Brazil, the Kneipp water walk provides a natural exercise. Walking in water up to your calves strengthens body functions, according to the staff. The alternating warm and cold water, combined with the smooth stones underfoot, influences the kidneys and promotes excretion of residues. Kneipp treatments also call for the use of herbs and teas, which can be found at the pharmacy in downtown Gramado. Completing the spa collection are all-natural kur cologne, skin moisturizers, and hair-care products developed and produced in Brazil.

Brazilian Longevity Center's European Alpine Kur

Kurotel
Rua Nacoes Unidas, 533
PO Box 65
CEP 95670-000 Gramado
Rio do Sul, Brazil
Phone: 55–54–286–2133
Fax: 55–54–286–1203
E-mail: reservas@kur-gramado.com.br
Web site: www.kur-gramado.com.br

Season: Year-round

General Manager: Luis Carlos Silveira, M.D.

Spa Director: Neusa Silveira, M.D.

Reservations: 054–800–2196

Accommodations: Suites and apartments with single or double beds, decorated in colonial or baroque style. All have private bathroom with marble-top basins, hair dryer, magnifying mirror, robes. Air-conditioning, TV, and fax are standard, and there is a CD/radio sound system. Apartments come with desk and easy chairs, comfortable sofa; four executive suites have office equipment.

Meals: Based on Swiss techniques, three high-energy meals are served daily. The resident nutritionist adapted recipes with fresh ingredients from local farms, using herbs and spices from the hotel's own vegetable garden. Choices include soups, salads, seafood, chicken, rabbit, and beef, as well as shakes, juices, fruit, breads, and pies.

Facilities: Hydrotherapy baths and Kneipp water walk, galvanic baths, footbaths, respiratory inhalations, mud packs, indoor and outdoor swimming pools, gymnasium, exercise equipment, beauty salon. Medical clinic for diagnostic services.

Services & Special Programs: Massage, underwater massage, fango with sea algae, reflexology, skin care, acupressure. Programs for stress management, antiaging, health evaluation.

Rates: $$$

Best Spa Package: Week-long Kur program includes medical evaluation, meals, lodging, and treatments. Prices vary with the season and start at $1,475 single occupancy, $1,285 double occupancy.

Credit Cards: MasterCard, Visa

Getting There: From Rio de Janeiro, Sao Paulo, or Montevideo, by air to Porto Alegre (one hour). Rental car at airport.

What's Nearby: Atlantic Ocean resorts.

TARA RESORT HOTEL—SCARLETT'S FOUNTAIN OF YOUTH SPA

San Jose, Costa Rica

osta Rica offers nature lovers lots of alternatives, from bathing at volcanic hot springs to touring coffee plantations. Hikers and birdwatchers are enchanted by nature preserves on both Pacific and Caribbean coasts. And now there is a serious spa.

Close to a gleaming new airport, Tara Resort Hotel is a vision of the old south. A popular meeting place for members of Costa Rica's large American colony of retired couples, the three-story hotel looks like a southern mansion, complete with white-columned verandas and shamrock-shaped swimming pool. Tara was built as a private residence by a Dutch movie fan inspired by *Gone With the Wind*. Climbing an impressive wooden staircase framed by vaulted ceiling, you have a choice of suites with names like Scarlett O'Hara, Rhett Butler,

and Robert Lee's Retreat. The Atlanta Dining Gallery, draped in red velvet, has a menu that ranges from New York strip steak to Pacific lobster. Coffee and refreshments are served on the terrace overlooking the city far below.

Nights are cool up here, causing smog in the valley, and afternoon showers from May through November. Scarlett's Fountain of Youth Spa has remedies: Try the body wrap with volcanic mud or the rain forest aromatherapy bath with essential oils made from Costa Rican flowers and plants. Prices for treatments are about half what you pay in the United States, and the staff speak English. Spa hours are Tuesday through Sunday 9:00 A.M. to 6:00 P.M. Spa facilities include saunas, steam room, swimming pool, Jacuzzi. The *Gone With the Wind* theme is carried over to the

names of several treatments—e.g., Ms. Melanie's Mellow Massage, Rhett's Deep Tissue Massage, Scarlett's Seaweed Cocoon.

American owned and managed, Tara is an excellent base for exploring the country's natural attractions. Bicycle tours are a recent addition to Tara's exercise program, and a great way to learn about the beauty of surrounding areas. Guides check out mountain bikes, helmets, gloves, and bottled water at the morning briefing. Although bike rentals are available if you want to go off on your own, group tours are escorted and include refreshments. Weaving past old farmhouses and the residence of the U.S. ambassador, bikers have a choice of challenging trails, 9 miles or a 17-mile plunge that descends 4,000 feet, ending at a butterfly farm. Along the way, stops are made to visit a church and a pottery. A support van follows the group, returning to the hotel in time for a muscle-soothing massage.

Searching for wildlife doesn't mean a rigorous mountain trek. Take a taxi or bike to the zoo in suburban La Garita. Paved paths through gardens of towering tropical trees and stands of bamboo provide a colorful setting. Created by a private organization for reproduction of endangered species, the zoo introduces colorful examples of flora and fauna from all parts of the country.

Southern Charm in Central America

Tara Resort Spa—Scarlett's Fountain of Youth Spa
San Antonio de Escazo
Escazu 1250
Costa Rica
or U.S. office (also for reservations):
Interlink 345
PO Box 02-5635
Miami, FL 33102
Phone: 506–228–6992
Fax: 506–228–9651
E-mail: taraspa@racsa.co.cr
Web site: www.tararesort.com

Season: Year-round

General Manager: Richard Shambley

Accommodations: Fourteen suites with large bedrooms and private bath. Furnished in a mix of antique reproductions locally made; bedroom has balcony, ceiling fan. Fully air-conditioned.

Meals: Complimentary continental breakfast. Lunch on terrace can be salad of seasonal greens, grilled chicken. Dinner features grilled sea bass or tilapia, apple strudel.

Facilities: Spa building with private treatment rooms, sauna, hydrotherapy tub, exercise equipment. Outdoor swimming pool.

Services & Special Programs: Massage, reflexology, body wrap, facials, men's skin care, salon for hair and nail care.

Rates: $

Best Spa Package: Six-night Spa Experience includes deluxe suite, two meals daily ($30 credit per day), and a one-hour daily spa treatment. Try rain forest aromatherapy with essences of flowers, fruits, and herbs grown in the Costa Rican forest. Single is $1,112–$1,235; double is $944–$1,049 per person; includes taxes and services.

Credit Cards: Master Card, Visa

Getting There: American and Continental are among airlines with connecting service to San Jose. Tara Resort Hotel is twenty-five minutes from the airport. Airport transfer $20.

What's Nearby: San Jose Plaza de Cultura, Mercado Central, Coffee Plantation tour.

SPAS AT SEA

JUDITH JACKSON'S SEASPA—RADISSON
SEVEN SEAS NAVIGATOR

Radisson Seven Seas Cruises

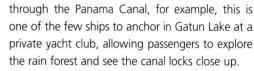

cents of mountain flowers, pine trees, fruit, and plants perfume Judith Jackson's SeaSpa aboard Radisson's *Seven Seas Navigator*. Personalized aromatherapy massages, facials, and baths are signature services designed to enhance your sense of well-being by reducing stress levels. In the hands of skilled therapists trained by Jackson, the experience reaches a higher level of relaxation, awakening the soul to a spirit of discovery.

Combining luxury and adventure, the *Navigator* cruises Asia, Australia, the South Pacific, the Caribbean, and South America. Accommodations for 490 passengers are all suites, ranging from 301 square feet to an enormous 1,173 square-foot-master suite, almost all with private balcony. Ideal for long cruises, *Navigator's* big-ship amenities, attentive personal service, and no-tipping policy add up to a unique experience. On cruises through the Panama Canal, for example, this is one of the few ships to anchor in Gatun Lake at a private yacht club, allowing passengers to explore the rain forest and see the canal locks close up.

Judith Jackson's SeaSpa complements the *Navigator's* intimate design. With just six treatment rooms, it may be the smallest spa at sea. Located on the uppermost deck of the ship, brightened by natural light, the spa adjoins an aerobics studio and cardio-fitness studio with sea views. Unlimited access to the exercise equipment and scheduled classes lets you set your own schedule. Personal trainers are available to plan your exercise regimen.

Outpacing ships of similar size for comfort and spaciousness, and with its exclusive SeaSpa and stress-buster treatments, the *Navigator* charts exceptional cruise vacations.

Stress-Buster Aromatherapy

**Judith Jackson's SeaSpa—
Radisson *Seven Seas Navigator***
Radisson Seven Seas Cruises
600 Corporate Drive
Fort Lauderdale, FL 33334
Phone: (954) 776–6123 or (800) 285–1835
Fax: (954) 722–6763
Web site: www.rssc.com

SPA DU SOLEIL—*SEABOURN SUN*

Seabourn Cruise Line

ith more ships cruising the world than ever, marine designers are competing to build the biggest and best spa at sea. Responding to passenger demand for enhanced spa services aboard their upscale ships, the Seabourn Cruise Line teamed up with Steiner Leisure Ltd. in 1999 to create the Spa du Soleil aboard the ten-year-old *Seabourn Sun*.

With a 30-foot lap pool, ten treatment rooms, and separate sauna/steam rooms for men and women, the two-level Spa du Soleil sets new standards in comfort and elegance. In addition to the latest amenities and exercise equipment, the Roman-style decor of pillars, murals, and sculptures of goddesses is complemented by a soft color scheme, terra-cotta and mosaic tiling, and lots of natural light. What's special here are Steiner's personalized programs: Ionithermie, a cellulite reduction system that employs electrodes attached to targeted areas of the body; the Aphrodite suite, where you sink into a dry-float bed while getting a seaweed wrap ($170); the Cleopatra bath suite; and the Rasul mud chamber.

Spa du Soleil packs extraordinary elegance into compact spaces. Thanks to window walls, there is a feeling of being at sea that is energizing and relaxing. While on a treadmill, stepper, or bike, you have an expansive view of the sea as well as the lap pool and whirlpools. Awaiting a treatment in the quiet lounge, you can have herbal tea, Evian water, and fresh fruit.

Seabourn Sun updates its Scandinavian heritage in both services and accommodations. Suites on the penthouse deck, closest to the spa, are among the most spacious afloat, and have a private balcony. With built-in cabinetry, curvaceous sofas, original art, soft lighting, and crystal vases filled with fresh flowers, the feeling of peace and tranquillity perfectly complements the spa experience. You can have room service any hour of the day or night, at no charge, and the minibar is restocked daily with bottles of Evian.

Designed for a maximum of 758 passengers, the *Seabourn Sun* is the epitome of well-being afloat.

Unregimented, your days at sea provide the freedom to sample spa services and maintain a healthy regimen. Compared to the behemoths being built today for Caribbean cruising, *Seabourn Sun* turns back to an era of stylish informality and formal dining. If you want lots of action, bingo, and deck games, this is not your ship. *Seabourn* passengers are sophisticated (about half European and half American) and demanding. Really top cabin.

Classic Ocean Liner Elegance Creates Total Relaxation

Spa du Soleil—*Seabourn Sun*
Seabourn Cruise Line
6100 Blue Lagoon Drive
Miami, FL 33126
Phone: (305) 463–3000 or 800– 929–9391
Fax: (305) 463–3010
Web site: www.seabourn.com

STEINER SPA—CUNARD *QUEEN ELIZABETH 2*

Cunard Line

urprisingly modern, this grand dame of the seas sailed into the new millennium in great shape. Thanks to the Steiner Spa, you can enjoy the latest in thalassotherapy treatments with fresh seawater as well as micronized marine algae. Featuring some of the most elaborate hydrotherapy facilities afloat, as well as exercise equipment and personal trainers, the *QE2* lets you ship out in style.

Crossing to Europe or America aboard this great liner is like a six-day resort vacation. All the elements of a spa program are at your disposal, as well as temptations like nonstop food, tons of caviar, and Champagne. If that's not your cup of tea, then consider the *QE2*'s six-night New England–Canada cruise from New York in late September.

Launched in 1969, *Queen Elizabeth 2* (usually called *QE2*) seems to get better with age. She underwent a major refit in 1999, after the company became part of the Carnival Cruise Corporation, and retains her high standards in first-class staterooms and suites, as well as the Queen's Grill dining room. On cruises as well as crossings, you get the virtual run of the ship, but your stateroom or cabin category determines the restaurant in which you dine. There are twenty-one types of accommodations and five restaurant categories.

The indoor seawater pool is open 7:00 A.M. to 7:00 P.M. Adjoining the pool are Cybex, StairMaster, and LifeFitness exercise equipment, plus classes, at no charge. The boat deck is for running or walking laps, but the open-air swimming pool on upper deck can be crowded when the ship is at full capacity of 1,740 passengers. A better bet is deep down in the hull, on deck six: The Steiner Spa boasts a room-size pool with bubbling jets for underwater massage. Sauna and steam room (coed) adjoin the pool and locker rooms; a $10 facility charge goes on your shipboard account. The receptionists schedule massage and other treatments. Seaweed body masques and facials are among services in ten private rooms. Try a multijet hydrotherapy bath, where you soak in freeze-dried algae, or clear you sinuses with seawater mist at inhalation stations.

Traditions Updated With Thalassotherapy

Steiner Spa—Cunard *Queen Elizabeth 2*
Cunard Line
6100 Blue Lagoon Drive
Miami, FL 33126
Phone: (800) 728–6273
Fax: (305) 463–3010
Web site: www.cunardline.com

WINDSPA—WINDSTAR'S *WIND SURF*
Windstar Cruises

ombining the adventure of yachting with the amenities of a luxury cruise ship, the 312-passenger *Wind Surf* is in a class by itself. Soothing and tastefully decorated staterooms, healthy gourmet dining, and the full-service WindSpa enhance cruises to romantic ports on the French and Italian rivieras, as well as in the Caribbean.

Framed by five tall sails, *Wind Surf* can dock in ports not accessible to big cruise ships. Distinctive itineraries on the Nice-to-Rome cruise during summer months include calls at Monte Carlo, Saint-Tropez, and Portofino. Caribbean cruises January through March start in Barbados. Standard cruises are seven days; year-end eleven-day sailings add ports.

Recreation ranges from aerobics to scuba. The ship's built-in marina lets you enjoy water sports right from the deck. Equipment for snorkeling, waterskiing, kayaking, and windsurfing is available on a first-come basis, at no charge. Scuba divers are charged $65 per tank. Excursions by Zodiac boat add to your sightseeing and shopping in ports. Or simply stake out a spot on deck and swim in the heated saltwater pool.

Wind Surf is for people who hate big cruise ships. With no formal evenings and a relaxed dress code consisting mainly of chic resort wear, the unregimented experience of the ship plus its extraordinary service adds up to a cruise adventure to cherish.

Ready for serious pampering? Head for the WindSpa on marina deck. Caring and courteous aestheticians provide stress-busting treatments and sun protection. This is one of the few ships to have a hydrotherapy tub for aromatherapy soaks. And there are eight rooms with oceanview portholes. So relax with a seaweed wrap or sports massage. Staffed and operated by Steiner, spa services are charged to your account aboard ship. Booking a package prior to sailing gets you priority on appointment times.

At sea the *Wind Surf* sails with all the stability of an America's Cup contender. This ship is built for comfort, and its length ensures smooth sailing. One of the most spectacular sights is her tall sails rising at sunset as she glides effortlessly toward the next port. It's instant karma.

Sailing a Small Ship with a Big Spa

WindSpa on *Wind Surf*
Windstar Cruises
300 Elliott Avenue West
Seattle, WA 98119
Phone: (206) 281–3535
Fax: (206) 286–3229
E-mail: information@windstarcruises.com
Web site: www.windstarcruises.com

GLOSSARY

Abhyanga-rhythmic: An herbal oil massage performed by two therapists, followed by a hot towel treatment.

Acupressure: A finger massage intended to release muscle tension by applying pressure to the nerves.

Aromatherapy: A massage with oils from plant and flower essences intended to relax the skin's connective tissue and stimulate the natural flow of lymph.

Ayurvedic treatments: Four-thousand-year-old treatments from India based on teachings from the Vedic scriptures, using oils, massages, and herbs.

Balneology: The traditional study and practice of water-based treatments using geothermal hot springs, mineral water, or seawater.

Bindi: Bodywork combining exfoliation, herbal treatment, and light massage.

Body polish: The use of large sea sponges to gently cleanse, exfoliate, and hydrate the body.

Chi gong: A Chinese energy exercise that uses breathing and body movements recharge energy.

Complementary medicine: Complements to traditional Western medicine incorporating the ancient arts of acupuncture and Chinese herbal medicine.

Crystal healing: Healing energy believed to be generated by quartz and other minerals.

Drinking cure: A medically prescribed regimen of mineral water consumption.

Fango: A mud pack or body coating intended to promote the release of toxins and relieve muscular and arthritic pain.

Glycolic exfoliation: A process that uses a natural enzyme (found in citrus fruit) to break down the glue bond that holds dry skin on the face, soften lines, and smooth skin.

G5: A percussive hand massage to relax tense muscles.

Gommage: A cleansing and moisturizing treatment that makes use of creams applied with movements similar to those of an extensive massage.

Hatha yoga: A system of yoga that focuses on bodily control through the use of *anasas* (postures).

Herbal wrap: A treatment in which moisture, heat, and herbal essences penetrate the skin while the body is wrapped in hot linens, plastic sheets, and blankets. It is intended to promote muscle relaxation and the elimination of toxins.

Hot plunge: A deep pool for the rapid dilation of the capillaries.

Hydrotherapy: Underwater massage; alternating hot and cold showers, and other water-oriented treatments.

Hydrotub: An underwater massage in deep tubs equipped with high-pressure jets and hand-manipulated hoses.

Inhalations: Hot vapors or steam mixed with eucalyptus oil inhaled through inhalation equipment or in a special steam room to decongest the respiratory system.

Kneipp kur: Treatments combining hydrotherapy, herbology, and a diet of natural foods, developed in Germany in the mid-1800s by Father Sebastian Kneipp.

Lomi lomi: A Hawaiian rhythmical rocking massage.

Mud wrap: A body treatment using warm mud to cleanse pores and lift impurities.

Naturopathy: Natural healing prescriptions that use plants and flowers.

Panchakarma: A type of massage therapy that uses warm, herbalized oils, and aims to restore balance to the body.

Paraffin wrap: The process of removing dead skin cells with hot oil and Japanese dry-brushing techniques, then applying melted wax infused with emollients.

Pilates method: Strength and flexibility training movements developed by Joseph H. Pilates during the 1920s.

Pizichilli: A purifying experience in which a continuous stream of warm, herbalized oil is poured over the body as two therapists perform a gentle massage.

Pressotherapy: Pressure cuffs used to improve circulation in the feet.

Pressure point massage: Massage and bodywork that use pressure on designated body parts connected to major nerves to relieve stress.

Reflexology: Massage of the pressure points on the feet, hands, and ears, intended to relax parts of the body.

Reiki: An ancient healing method that imports universal life energy through the laying on of hands and mental and spiritual balancing. It's intended to relieve acute emotional and physical conditions.

Roman pool: A step-down whirlpool bath for one or two people.

Russian bath: A steam bath designed to flush toxins from the body.

Salt glow: A cleansing treatment that uses coarse salt to exfoliate the skin.

Scotch douche: A showerlike treatment with high-pressure hoses that alternate hot and cold water; intended to improve circulation through rapid contraction and dilation of the capillaries.

Seaweed wrap: A wrap using concentrated seawater and nutrient-packed seaweed. Minerals, proteins, rare trace elements, and vitamins are absorbed into the bloodstream to revitalize the skin and body.

Shirodhara: An Ayurvedic massage in which warm herbal oil is dropped on the forehead ("the third eye") and rubbed gently into the hair and scalp.

Sitz bath: Immersion of the hips and lower body into hot water then into cold water to stimulate the immune system. Also a Kneipp treatment for digestive upset.

Spa cuisine: Fresh natural foods low in saturated fats and cholesterol, with an emphasis on whole grains, low-fat dairy products, lean protein, fresh fruits, fish, and vegetables and an avoidance of added salt and products containing sodium or artificial colorings, flavorings, or preservatives.

Spinning: A group exercise class on stationary bicycles intended to provide aerobic conditioning by pedaling quickly at varied resistance levels.

Stress management: A program of meditation and deep relaxation intended to reduce the ill effects of stress on the system.

Sweat lodge: A Native American–inspired purifying ritual that takes place in a natural sauna made of rocks.

Swedish massage: A treatment that duplicates gymnastics movements, using stroking, kneading, friction, vibration, and tapping to relax muscles gently. It was devised at the University of Stockholm in the early 19th century by Per Heinrik Ling.

Swiss shower: A multijet bath that alternates hot and cold water, often used after mud wraps and other body treatments.

Tai chi: An ancient Oriental discipline of exercise and meditation based on movements intended to unite body and mind.

Target heart rate: The number of heartbeats per minute that an individual tries to attain during exercise, ideally 60 to 90 percent of the maximal heart rate. The American College of Sports Medicine recommends maintaining the target rate during exercise for 20 to 30 minutes three to five days per week.

Thalassotherapy: An ancient Greek system of water-based treatments using seawater, seaweed, algae and sea air.

Vichy shower: A hydrotherapy treatment that involves lying on a cushioned waterproof mat and being showered by jets.

Watsu: An underwater treatment blending the techniques of deep tissue massage, acupressure, shiatsu, and yoga.

Yoga: A discipline of stretching and toning the body through movements or postures, controlled deep breathing, relaxation techniques, and diet. A school of Hindu philosophy advocating physical and mental discipline for the unity of mind, body, and spirit.

Zen shiatsu: A Japanese acupressure art intended to relieve tension and balance the body.

ABOUT THE AUTHORS

BERNARD BURT is an internationally recognized authority on the spa industry and a writer and leader in the field of spa vacations and fitness travel. His column "People & Places" appears in *Spa Management Journal* and *Pulse*, the magazine of the International Spa Association (ISPA). He has also written articles for such leading magazines as *National Geographic Traveler*, *Travel & Leisure*, and *Spa Magazine*. The Board of Directors of the International Spa Association recently named Burt recipient of its Dedicated Contributor Award. The award honors his commitment to industry standards and his professional values.

PAMELA LECHTMAN is a writer, editor, and radio personality who has visited more than 500 spas worldwide. For the past thirty years she has been writing about spas, and her articles have appeared in more than 100 newspapers and magazines. She spent eight years at *Shape* magazine developing spa travel and cuisine features. She produced spa videos for the tourism boards of Switzerland and Italy and has produced and hosted several travel and health radio talk shows. In 1999 she served as an advisor for the *National Geographic Traveler* survey of American spas.